# THE BATTLE THAT
# SHOOK EUROPE

# *The* BATTLE THAT SHOOK EUROPE

### POLTAVA AND THE BIRTH OF THE RUSSIAN EMPIRE

## PETER ENGLUND

I.B.TAURIS

LONDON · NEW YORK

Reprinted in 2013 by I.B.Tauris & Co. Ltd
6 Salem Road, London W2 4BU
175 Fifth Avenue, New York NY 10010
www.ibtauris.com

Distributed in the United States and Canada
Exclusively by Palgrave Macmillan
175 Fifth Avenue, New York NY 10010

First published in Swedish as *Poltava* © Peter Englund/Bokförlaget Atlantis,
  Stockholm 1997
First published in the United Kingdom in 1992 by Victor Gollancz
First published by I.B.Tauris & Co. Ltd in 2003

ISBN: 978 1 78076 476 4

A full CIP record for this book is available from the British Library
A full CIP record is available from the Library of Congress

Library of Congress Catalog Card Number: available

Printed and bound by CPI Group (UK) Ltd, Croydon, CR0 4YY

This book is dedicated to Private Erich Måne, of the Fifth Section, Hundra Parish Company, the Uppland Regiment of Foot. His wife's name was Karin Matsdotter. A cannonball struck Erich in the chest, early on the morning of 28 June 1709, and killed him. His body was buried at the place he died, in a field some four kilometres north-west of the town of Poltava, in the Ukraine, where it still rests.

# Contents

# Maps

# Introduction

dread Pultowa's day
When fortune left the royal Swede
Around a slaughter'd army lay
No more to combat and to bleed.
The power and glory of the war,
Faithless as their vain votaries, men,
Had pass'd to the triumphant Czar . . .

BYRON

Some knowledge of the Great Northern War of 1700–1721 is essential for an understanding of the evolution of modern Sweden: the conflict is as formative an episode in Swedish history as civil wars and revolutions have been in the histories of other western nations. The politics, foreign policies and social conscience of the present Swedish state are rooted in the convulsions of this struggle, which only ended when the country's resources had been totally exhausted.

The causes, course and long-term effects of the war have been examined by Swedish historians with unflagging interest ever since. Much of the phenomenal success of Peter Englund's account of its pivotal phase, the Russian campaign of the Swedish army and its culmination at the battle of Poltava, must be attributed to his presentation of familiar history, the common property of most educated Swedes, from an original and very modern point of view.

For the duration of the war, and throughout the eighteenth century, the fortunes of Sweden under Charles XII were almost as fascinating to the rest of Europe as they were to native Swedes. In England James Thomson, in *Liberty (IV)*, 1736, and Alexander Pope, in *An Essay on Man (IV)*, 1734, commented briefly in conflicting terms on the people and the king. Thomson, a Whig patriot, thought of the Swedes as 'the manly race' who 'wise and dauntless, still sustain' the cause of freedom; Pope links Charles XII with 'the Macedonian madman', Alexander the Great. Daniel Defoe had produced a contemporary report, *The History of the Wars of Charles XII*, in 1715; but it was Voltaire's *Histoire de Charles XII*, 1731, one of the most frequently retranslated and reissued books in publishing history, which kept European interest alive. In 1740 Henry Fielding translated a French version of the eye-witness campaign account of the Swedish chronicler, Adlerfelt, who was killed at Poltava. (Fielding also makes a glancing critical reference to Charles in *Jonathan Wild*, 1743). According to Boswell, Dr Johnson's magisterial summing up of 'the warrior, Charles of Sweden' in *The Vanity of Human Wishes*, 1749, provides 'as highly finished a picture as can possibly be conceived'.

In Russia, this victory over the Swedes in 1709 is still seen as of far greater historical importance than the defeat of Napoleon a century later. The father of Russian literature, Alexander Pushkin, remarked in 1834 that 'the wars waged by Peter the Great were beneficent and fruitful. The successful transformation of the whole nation resulted from the battle of Poltava'. Six years earlier Pushkin had produced what Nabokov has called 'his marvellous narrative poem' *Poltava*, which presents Peter the Great as a kind of demi-god and ends with a vivid description of the battle:

> Swede, Russian – stabbing, hacking, slashing,
> The beat of drums, the cries, the gnashing,
> the roar of cannons, stamping, neighing, groans
> and death and hell on every side.

Outside Sweden and Russia, however, general knowledge of this decisive upheaval at the interface of East and West has faded. Although translations of Voltaire's classic and other treatments in English have appeared at fairly regular intervals – two excellent contemporary studies are Professor Ragnhild Hatton's *Charles XII of Sweden*, and *The Swedish Imperial Experience 1560–1718* by Professor Michael Roberts – their appeal has perhaps been limited to the specialist in European history. The modern English-speaking reader may well never have heard of Charles XII or the Great Northern War. Some outline of the wider historical context, as traditionally perceived, may therefore help towards an understanding of the viewpoint adopted by Peter Englund, as well as partially explain the powerful impact of his account on Swedish readers.

At the outbreak of the war in 1700 Sweden had been at peace with her neighbours for more than 20 years, since the battle of Lund against Denmark in 1676. For most of this period, until his death in 1697, Sweden had been governed by Charles XI, one of the most unpretentious kings ever to rule a European country. He instituted several reforms, most notable of which was the *reduktion*, whereby the land holdings, wealth and power of the upper aristocracy were drastically reduced. In a non-egalitarian age Sweden became a meritocratic society unique in Europe. This society had been created at the price of monarchical absolutism, however, and the resultant constitution was the virtual divine right of the king, combined (rather oddly, to English minds) with the Protestant faith and values which had animated Sweden since before the time of Gustavus Adolphus, and which in England had been at their most fervent under Cromwell.

Two other features of Charles XI's reign were of almost equal importance for Sweden's performance under his son, Charles XII. First, his thrift, which placed the nation on a sound financial base in the initial stages of the war; and second, his reorganization of the Swedish army and introduction of a unique form of military conscription known as the *indelningsverk*, or allotment system. The provinces of the country were subdivided into small areas called *rota* (for infantry) or *rusthåll* (for cavalry), each of which had to supply one soldier, maintain him in peacetime and replace him if lost in war. All the provincial Swedish regiments of foot named in Englund's account of the battle were raised in this manner. Officers had to start their service in the ranks, and were promoted almost exclusively on merit. The result was a highly cohesive and apparently invincible army. The conscripted regiments were supplemented by other units (mainly cavalry) raised by normal 18th century enlistment methods, mostly from the native populations of Sweden, Finland and the Baltic states, but also, by the time of Poltava, from Saxon volunteers or ex-prisoners of war.

When Russia, Denmark and Poland-Saxony combined to attack Sweden at the turn of the 17th century and the 18-year-old Charles XII embarked on his headstrong career to astonish the world, he had therefore inherited both the authority and the wherewithal. The Sweden of 1700 was almost certainly the most efficient, best organized and administered, probably the most technically advanced and, *pro rata*, the strongest state in Europe. However, the combined population of the hostile coalition confronting it was roughly 30 million: the population of Sweden and Finland (then part of Sweden) was probably less than 1.5 million. Sweden had never been a rich country, and although covering a large area, was very sparsely populated.

For the army in the field the odds were more favourable, and the Swedes were not often outnumbered by more than about four to one. On several occasions the forces opposing them, of varying nationalities, were less than double their own strength. The rapid capitulation of Denmark in 1700 was followed by a victory over a Russian army at Narva, on the Baltic in Estonia, which astounded Europe. By winning the battles of the Dvina in 1701, Klissow in 1702, Pultusk in 1703, Punitz in 1704, Gemäuerthof in 1705 and Fraustadt in 1706, as well as innumerable lesser engagements, Sweden attained a remarkable political and military supremacy. Augustus II, Elector of Saxony and King of Poland, was deposed and replaced. For eighteen months, at a time when the War of the Spanish Succession was simultaneously turning western Europe into one unending battlefield, Charles XII was its acknowledged arbiter, to whom the Duke of Marlborough, three years after the battle of Blenheim, paid respectful court, and to whose demands for religious freedom of worship in Silesia the Holy Roman Emperor, Joseph I, felt obliged to accede.

Few could have foreseen this course of events in 1700; but by the end of 1707, when the Swedish army, then generally considered the finest in Europe, left Saxony to carry the conflict into the heart of Russia, equally few would have predicted the disasters so graphically described in Englund's pages. The precise effects of the eclipse of Swedish influence by Russia at this time are obviously incalculable, but the outcome of the battle must have profoundly altered the subsequent course of European history. For Sweden, the next century saw the demise of monarchical absolutism, the emergence of a two-party political system, and an ever more resolutely neutral and pacific attitude to all conflicts outside the country's borders. The last shot fired in anger by a Swedish army (against Napoleon) took place as long ago as 1813.

Nevertheless, in Professor Roberts' words: 'Charles XII . . . still remains a matter of fierce controversy and bitter partisanship' within Sweden; and Peter Englund's narrative can be seen as one of the latest and most eloquent blows in this debate. While Swedish sentiment cannot remain unmoved by the steadfast resistance of the youthful Charles and his small armies to the impossible odds pitted against them throughout the war, it also has to be critical of his wilful hubris, the ultimately futile sacrifice of the nation's manhood and the rapid and permanent loss of an international standing built up over the preceding one and a half centuries. Charles has been the object of extremes of chauvinistic hero-worship as well as unbridled vituperation. Literary interest, since about 1850, has tended to dwell on the ambivalence of the relationship between the king and his long-suffering subjects: this aspect has been treated by numerous writers, notably August Strindberg, and the Nobel Prize winner, Verner von Heidenstam.

Peter Englund has brought a novel and dramatic insight to the theme by centralizing interest on the complex, tortuous character of General Lewenhaupt, and extending the detailed narrative beyond the battle to the army's humiliating retreat and capitulation. The reader's attention is directed to the acute dilemma of the individual (and by implication the nation) faced with superior hostile forces, and the critical choice between resistance and surrender. In the book's final section the descriptive narrative rises above the more overtly partisan presentation of the background to the conflict in the earlier chapters. The transition towards a genuinely tragic vision of the culmination of the Russian campaign for the ill-fated army gives the account a compelling fascination, and produces a strong sense of identification with the hapless Swedish soldiers.

Apart from the innately epic nature of the story, *The Battle of Poltava* would not have become the most successful book by a Swedish author for the last decade had it not also been for his skilful selection from the wide range of memoirs, diaries and eye-witness accounts of the battle, and his ability to marshal them into a satisfyingly coherent narrative. The style of Peter Englund's Swedish is spontaneous, colloquial and at times almost oral, and although it has been felt necessary to adapt this style slightly for the English-speaking reader, some effort has been made to preserve its vivid immediacy, and to retain the spirit and tone of the original work.

A few of the points that defy translation, or are lost to the reader ignorant of Swedish history, merit comment. The resonance of many of the Swedish names cannot be reproduced. The king's famously laconic (but probably apocryphal): 'Hierta, your horse', encapsulates the relationship between king and subject, but gains extra poignancy from 'hierta' meaning 'heart'. The name is also spelt 'Gierta' and occurs as 'Gieta' in *Mazeppa*, a narrative poem published in 1819 by Lord Byron, who assumed that the self-sacrificing officer – 'wounded and bleeding to death', according to Voltaire – had 'died the Russians' slave'. In fact, he died in Stockholm in 1740, aged 74.

Lieutenant Hierta was one of the Drabants, the king's élite bodyguard so frequently mentioned. The entire corps consisted of men of officer rank: a Drabant Lieutenant ranked as a Colonel to the rest of the army, and a Drabant Corporal was the equivalent of a Major. Of the 147 Drabants who left Sweden with the king in 1700, only 14 remained in 1716. The corps was eventually disbanded after the king's death in 1718.

The term 'tremänning', applied to the Uppland cavalry regiment present at the battle, arises from the Swedish conscription system already mentioned. As the war progressed, and Swedish ranks became more and more depleted, more men were needed and the demands on the Swedish populace became increasingly severe. New regiments were raised by requiring two or more *rusthåll* or *rota* to combine in providing an additional conscript. The men forming a 'tremänning' cavalry regiment had each been supplied by three *rusthåll* combined.

It would be particularly emotive for a Swedish reader to be reminded of the virtual extermination of the conscripted foot regiments of Dalecarlians and Upplanders at Poltava. The provinces of Dalecarlia and Uppland are thought of as Sweden's heartland, the core of the ancient, unconquered realm of prehistory, whose men had rallied to the nation's liberator, Gustavus Vasa, in 1520.

The now obsolete Swedish unit of currency, the daler in copper or silver coin, is mentioned several times. The monetary system, already complicated, became almost incomprehensible as the state resorted to increasingly extraordinary financial measures in order to meet the mounting cost of the war. As some indication of the daler's value, in 1705 a clerical bookkeeper's annual salary might be about 400 silver daler. Five silver daler would buy a soldier's greatcoat, or a barrel of wheat grain. Abraham Cederholm's ducats were each worth about four and a half silver daler. There were three copper daler to one silver daler, and the value of the riksdaler was approximately three silver daler. By 1731, when Captain Strokirch received compensation from General Lagercrona for horse theft on the battlefield, a barrel of grain cost seven silver daler.

In the chaos on the banks of the Dnieper Regimental Chaplain Sven Agrell lost his journal, in which he had recorded the 730 Swedish miles he had marched since leaving his home. The Swedish mile was generally reckoned to be the equivalent of six English miles, and the term is still used to denote 10 kilometres.

This adaptation of Peter Englund's gripping and moving account is deeply indebted to the generous comment and advice of Jonathan Backhouse, Pamela Gibson, Peter Grant-Ross, David Burnett, Roger Smith and David Ross; and especially to Simon Shaw for his expertly informed review of the military detail and historical background. The remarks above on Swedish recruitment methods, and the monetary system, are largely drawn from *Swedish Colors and Standards of the Great Northern War*, by Dan Schorr, Editions Brokaw, 1987; *Swedish Weaponry since 1630*, by Holmquist and Gripstad, The Royal Army Museum, Stockholm, 1982; and *Vad kostade det?*, by Lagerqvist and Nathorst-Böös, LTs förlag, Stockholm, 1984. The four lines quoted from Pushkin's *Poltava* were translated by Vladimir Nabokov.

*Peter Hale*
*London, 1992*

# PROLOGUE

Had it been possible, men would have put might
into the hands of right.
But we cannot handle might as we would like,
since it is a palpable quality,
whereas right is a spiritual quality
which we manipulate at will.
Therefore, right has been put into the hands of might,
and that which we are obliged to do,
we give the name of right.

Hence derives the right of the sword,
because the sword confers a genuine right.

BLAISE PASCAL, *Pensées* (1670)

# The Stoat

Until his death in captivity, long after the tragedy had moved to its inexorable end, the Swedish general would still clearly recall the incident of the stoat.

The third day was hot and heavy. It was the height of summer. Grey with fatigue and tormented by diarrhoea, he sought a place where he could sleep briefly in the shade. Someone put up a makeshift screen against the sun. Near a small cart belonging to a *cantinière* a cloak was spread across two poles taken from a stack of battle-standards. He took off his coat and waistcoat. Folding them to lie on, he pillowed his head on his cloak and hat.

He had only been resting a short time when he felt a slight movement. Alarmed, he sat up and examined the cloak at his head. Finding nothing, he decided he must have imagined the disturbance. A few moments passed, and then again he felt something move. He now jumped up and gently raised the cloak. From inside the hat below the cloak, the head of a stoat emerged. He swiftly gripped the two ends of the hatband, and the animal was trapped. He called out, and showed two nearby officers the live stoat he had caught in his hat. One of them pulled on a glove and grasped the squirming creature, to examine it curiously.

A thought struck him. Just like this stoat, an entire army had crept into a trap. He told the officer to release the stoat unharmed, and breathed a prayer: that as this creature had regained its freedom, they also might 'depart this place unscathed'.

This was an eventful year. Coldest winter in living memory. Famine in France. A man called Richard Steele produced the first issue of his periodical, *The Tatler*, in England. In Italy, excavations started on the town of Herculaneum. Off the coast of Chile a ship rescued a marooned sailor, Alexander Selkirk, who had spent four years alone on one of the Juan Fernandez islands. The Afghans in Kandahar rebelled against the Persians. A new and reform-minded Shogun, Tokugawa Tenobu, came to power in Japan. And, in Russia, General Adam Ludvig Lewenhaupt returned a trapped animal to freedom.

# THE MARCH

Some time before a great age dawns, in the year 1700, the East will seize its plunder, aided by the power of the moon, and the corners of the North shrink to within the kingdom.

Far from his realm the King will succumb in battle, his followers flee to the vale of the golden crescent . . .

NOSTRADAMUS, *Prophecies* (1555)

# 1 · *Sunday Morning*

The war had been raging for nine long years. This morning the signs were clear that a decisive encounter was imminent, perhaps only a day or two away. It was Sunday. Round the sun-bleached little town of Poltava two great armies were deployed: one Swedish, one Russian. They stood facing each other like savage beasts, crouched and poised to spring. The town was under siege by the Swedes, and cautiously, step by step, the Russian army had been closing in. Russian troops were now camped before Yakovtsi, barely five kilometres away. Swedish sentries could see them working hard to fortify their new camp. In the Swedish army too, preparations were in hand for the coming battle. Until this summer morning, the troops on both sides had been scattered over the Ukrainian steppe. Now they were bunched together near Poltava, tense and expectant. Their tails were threshing from side to side. They were ready to grapple and fight, and the only question left unanswered was which would strike first.

As the Russians gradually approached, the warm days of May and early June passed in continual skirmishing. There had been countless clashes and minor actions, mostly provoked by roving Russian cavalry. Today, 27 June 1709, was no exception. Sleep-dazed shouts of alarm had already echoed round the Swedish encampments early this morning. A couple of squadrons had swept in over the outermost posts, slaughtered a few soldiers and threatened to ride right into the camp before they were beaten off. Normal routine was fairly quickly restored. Today was the second Sunday after Trinity, and at nine o'clock it would be time for divine service.

Stringent church discipline was the order in the Swedish army, with strictly regulated regimental prayers every morning and evening, and divine service each Sunday and Holy Day. This routine was of great importance and cancelled only in exceptional circumstances. In spite of the bitter cold of the preceding winter, with its legacy of frozen corpses and amputated limbs, prayers had been conducted every day under open skies.

This Sunday the king, Charles XII, attended divine service with the regiment of Life Guards. The text was read by the battalion chaplain, Andreas Westerman, aged 37. It was Westerman's fifth year in the army.

He had been recruited to the colours in 1705, six months after his wedding. During the years he had spent in the field his wife and only son had died. It was a learned man who preached to the kneeling guardsmen this morning. He had once argued a case in a dissertation with the elegant title *De Adiaphoria in Bello, vulgo neutralitate*. But the war had now thrust his hands down into the mire of an ugly reality, a world apart from scholarly disputations, great celebration dinners and other refined academic pursuits. The previous year, at Holowczyn, he had travelled round in a barrow and performed the last rites for screaming men, dying in the mud. During the winter he had only with the greatest difficulty been able to force himself to visit the sick bays, which were filled with amputees and the dying, stinking of pus and dirt.

Westerman and his colleagues were important cogs in the machinery of the Carolinian army. They comforted the crippled and the dying. They kept a close watch on the entire course of the soldiers' lives, and conducted all religious rituals. The people of this era can only be fully understood by realizing they were all believers. Religion was indispensable; atheism virtually impossible. A world without a God could hardly be imagined. The world was dark and cold and man was small and naked, subject to divine omnipotence by his own incapacity. Religion was a vitally important means of influence and control over the populace, enlisted men and peasantry alike.

In the army, efforts were made to increase the soldiers' willingness to fight, and to allay their fears, by instilling in them a variety of religious thought patterns, some purely fatalistic. An assault on a battery of enemy artillery was always a bloody and costly affair. The men were discouraged from trying to evade enemy fire by seeking cover. Instead, they were to advance with heads held high and reflect that 'no musket-ball can hit a man except God will it, whether he walk straight or crooked'.

After the battle the officers were urged to remind the men that everything happened according to the will of God. In this way the troops could be expected to conduct themselves 'with courage and ready zeal' in the next engagement. Field chaplains like Westerman had an important role to play in disciplining the fighting men and in building up their morale. They were the policemen of the spirit and the flesh.

This church parade was a factor in the maintenance of discipline. The soldiers prayed to the Almighty that He should teach them to be faithful to their superiors and 'zealously to carry out whatever may be commanded me by my officers in His name'. The servants of the church also had a role to play in battle. Usually they accompanied their flock out on the battlefield to support and watch over them. There are instances of chaplains who fell in battle when attempting to turn faltering soldiers back into fire.

This strict church discipline is even more understandable when we realize that the entire army were firmly convinced that God had great influence on the fortunes of war. One of the infantry ordinances plainly stated that 'since all blessings derive from God in the Highest then His great and holy Name ought truly to be worshipped'. It was a matter of keeping in with the Almighty.

The majority of the soldiers were probably firmly convinced that God was really on their side. This could be taken as proven by the long string of victories the Swedes had enjoyed from the time war had broken out some nine years earlier. Those with the correct mental attitude could tell that God's blessing on Swedish arms was not just a half-hearted cheer from some celestial vantage point: quite the reverse. A great number of battlefield victories in past years were considered directly due to divine intervention. At the landing on Sjælland the stormy sea had been quelled by the king's glance; at Narva a heavy fall of sleet had been sent by God to conceal the assault at precisely the right moment: the whole of the daring crossing of the Dvina had been favoured by providential good fortune; at the battle of Saladen higher powers had totally misdirected the Russian cannon fire; at Fraustadt it was again snow which drove most opportunely into the eyes of the enemy and which disappeared, as if by magic, when the Swedish battalions made their breakthrough. Even at the battles of Pyhäjoggi and Warta, the Almighty was seen as having had a hand in the action.

To think along these lines, and conjure divine providence from events which were random or hard to account for, was completely natural for pre-industrial man. And these ideas were positively underscored by the highest command. From pulpits and at church services in the field men like Westerman intoned that the Swedes were favoured by God: they were his chosen people and instrument. Nor was this mere playing to the gallery; even the king was firmly convinced of its truth. Like the Children of Israel the Swedish soldier had been placed on earth to punish heretics and sinners. Those ripe for a flogging were the evil, ungodly princes who had started the war without just cause.

Proof of elect status could be demonstrated by cabbalistic legerdemain with words. One chaplain proved to his squadron that the Swedes were the Israelites of their age by reversing the name Assur (Assyria, the enemy of Israel) to obtain – Russa!

The Swedish private was thus clad in a Christian armour which would not only make him fight with greater resolve and confidence, but also turn him into a more ruthless soldier. The Lutheran orthodoxy which had drawn its Old Testament strait-jacket over Sweden promoted thoughts and ideas which authority was not slow to drum into the rank and file. Punishment and revenge were powerful elements in the message and in the proclamation which blared out over the kneeling battalions was the certitude that no mercy could be shown when God demanded retribution. The men were induced to slaughter and burn in the name of the Almighty. The grisly massacres inflicted by the Old Testament Israelites were used to justify the army's savagery.

This theory that God favoured Sweden was based on a circular argument, whose simplicity was both its greatest strength and its greatest weakness. The evidence was overwhelming. The victories on the battlefield proved that God was on the Swedish side. But if a great battle were to be lost one fine day, then everything would fall apart. The Swedes would be hoist on the petard of their own propaganda. God would apparently have shown that he had allowed his mandate to be transferred to the enemy, a frightening concept. There were those who fancied, on this hot summer day, that they could perceive signs that all was not exactly as it ought to be. Behind phenomena such as the winter's exceptional cold and untimely thaw there were some who were inclined to discern more than just a few meteorological quirks. There were intimations of a punishment from God on Sweden and the Swedes. Could it be possible that God now, in June 1709, had removed his protecting hand from his chosen people?

Westerman was not allowed to conduct his service in peace this morning. A band of Russian Cossacks appeared in the middle of the sermon. They rode in, shouting and shooting, and finally arrived a few hundred metres from the Swedish bivouacs. Some of the Zaporozhians allied to the Swedes rode into an attack on the noisy intruders, who allowed themselves to be driven off without great difficulty.

This incident was not particularly remarkable. It was yet another instance of the petty raiding whereby the Russians tormented the Swedish army. The raids caused little real damage in terms of men killed or equipment lost, but their effect on morale was all the greater. These incessant skirmishes took place night and day. They robbed the Swedish troops of essential rest and led to an almost permanent state of readiness which sapped their strength. To this should be added the effect of the oppressive heatwave which had lain for many days over the Ukraine. Some were heard to say that the heat was positively unnatural. Many in the Swedish army had begun to show signs of profound exhaustion.

Hour by hour the Russian pressure increased. There was no relief from the ferocious nagging round the outposts which continued for the rest of the morning. On the wooded heights which overlooked the river Vorskla there was an advanced detachment of Swedish cavalry, posted there to obstruct the Russian patrols constantly prowling round the army. It clashed with one of them: three troopers were shot. The outpost was rapidly reinforced with 20 musketeers and six horsemen.

The relief provided by prompt countermeasures would have been evident during skirmishing on the Saturday. A section of Life Guards, commanded by a Captain von Poll, had been standing behind a small rise, concealed by bushes. They had come under distant fire from Cossacks. Four men had been shot, one after the other. Then a member of the army supreme command, General Adam Ludvig Lewenhaupt, rode forward. Twenty musketeers were detached under an 18-year-old ensign, Malcolm Sinclair, to try to lure the Cossack snipers into an ambush.

This young ensign – unlike his commander, von Poll – survived the war. He had quite a successful subsequent career, becoming a member of the secret commission of the Swedish Parliament, the Riksdag. In 1738 he was sent to Turkey to solicit the sultan's aid in the new war looming with Russia. On the way home from this mission he was murdered, for his papers, by Russian agents. This deed caused feelings to run high in Sweden. Sinclair's death was vigorously exploited in the vengeance propaganda of the Hat party, in the form of the Sinclair ballad, 90 verses long. His fate was a contributory factor to the outbreak of a new Russian war which began in 1741. Thus he survived this war in order, ironically, to play a part in causing yet another by his death.

Sinclair's troop was placed in ambush, motionless behind cover. The soldiers were given strict orders not to open fire until the Cossacks had been lured within musket-range. Lewenhaupt then took a smaller detachment of dragoons and rode towards the Cossacks. They pulled back at once. The general later discovered that these Cossacks had been detailed to divert the Swedes' attention while a group of senior Russian officers made a reconnaissance. The Swedes tempted them on by riding back a short distance, making a pretence of having suddenly taken fright. Seeing this, the Cossacks quickly regained their courage and spurred on at a gallop with loud shouts and cries, the dust dancing round their horses' hoofs. When the Swedes wheeled about to face them they also immediately halted, and began firing with their detested guns at a distance of over 200 metres. The Cossacks were generally good shots and had long rifled guns known as Turks. With these they could hit their targets at distances far greater than the Swedes with their crude, smooth-bored muskets.

Lewenhaupt and the dragoons then retired again, and were again pursued. The chase immediately gave way to shooting when the Swedes pulled up. The game continued like this for some time. Finally the enemy troop was manoeuvred into the prepared ambush and well within range of the Swedish muskets. At this point the concealed men rose up. A thundering volley rolled over the pursuers. Clearly shaken but strangely unharmed they fled the field. There were no further attacks that day.

During this incident however the general noted something which gave him serious cause for thought. The volley had been completely without effect. He had seen the Swedish musket-balls drop to the ground, kicking up small jets of sand, barely 20 metres from the muzzles. If the rest of the powder was as feeble as this it would be devastating for the army's strike power. This was very disturbing, when everything pointed to the imminence of a major battle. During the course of the Saturday Lewenhaupt reported what he had noted to Charles XII. The king refused to believe him.

But now it was Sunday, and around midday the time was again ripe for renewed Russian attacks. Three more cavalry squadrons rode up the broad, billowing plain outside the small village of Ribtsi. The village gardens marked out the long northern edge of the Swedish cavalry's encampment. The Russian troopers began shooting at the sentries; a number of regiments were ordered to mount.

The counter-attack was headed by a section of the Östgöta cavalry regiment commanded by an 18-year-old troop captain, Axel Wacht-meister. Yet again the over-intrusive visitors were driven off after a minor skirmish. The losses were relatively slight; three Swedish troopers died. Ebbe Ridderschantz, one of the king's gold-laced bodyguard, the Drabants, was another casualty. Someone had noticed a sizeable group of Russian general officers outside Ribtsi, where they had been taking a closer look at the Swedish dispositions. Ebbe, out in the field on a reconnaissance mission, had been caught napping by the Russian attack. He was severely wounded by a sword-thrust straight through the body.

A little later there came another hint that something significant was in the offing. The king had recovered remarkably well from the fever of the preceding days, a side-effect of the musket-ball which had struck his foot on 17 June. A young man of 27 years, with a high forehead, large nose, full lips and imperious mien, a King by the Grace of God, accustomed to command and accustomed to being obeyed, he was well enough, sitting on a litter, to inspect a position on the heights next to the river. This was the same outpost which had seen action earlier in the day, and been reinforced.

Countermanding previous orders, the king decided without more ado to withdraw the whole detachment, clearly judging it no longer necessary. One of the officers assumed – bearing the Russian attack in mind – that this step had been taken because it had now been decided to put an end to 'these, and other insults'. He took it that the king's intention was to launch the army into an attack on the Russian host biding its time a few thousand metres further north. This assumption was entirely correct.

# 2 · *The Road to Poltava*

Deep in the heart of the Ukraine stood a Swedish army, thousands of miles from its homeland. What mysterious forces had brought about this situation? We need some account of the background to the conflict – which later came to be known as the Great Northern War – and the whole of the Swedish imperial experience.

By this time the remarkable Swedish Empire had been in existence for about 150 years. Its foundation can be traced back to the collapse of the Order of Teutonic Knights. A political power vacuum appeared in the Baltic regions, which the Russians were quick to exploit. They made a thrust towards the sea, and captured Narva. Poland and Denmark also took a hand in the action. The Swedish crown was approached with appeals for assistance. These originated in part from discontented merchants in Reval, deprived of fat profits since the lucrative Russian trade had transferred to Narva. Sweden decided to join the scramble for power, and in the early summer of 1561 Swedish troops landed at Reval. The burghers and nobility in three of the Estonian provinces were prevailed upon to acknowledge Swedish sovereignty. The leap across the Baltic had been taken, and a prolonged contest for dominance in north-east Europe had begun.

A long succession of wars now followed, mainly fought out between Sweden, Denmark, Poland and Russia. Periods of peace occasionally intervened, but never lasted. A completely new kind of armed struggle appeared on the war arenas of Europe. The petty wars of the previous age were replaced by wide-ranging, major conflict. An old war would merge with a new: one war led to another. Most of the northern encounters favoured the Swedish crown and one piece of land after another was seized at the expense of less fortunate neighbours. In this way Sweden came to endure almost exactly a century of near-continuous warfare.

During 1660–61 Sweden concluded three important peace treaties: in Oliva with Poland, in Copenhagen with Denmark and in Kardis with Russia. With these treaties the expansionary phase of the Swedish imperium came to an end. The era of grandiose conquest was over. The booty that Sweden had managed to claw in was, to say the least, substantial. Poland had been forced to relinquish Livonia. On the German front the province of West Pomerania, part of East Pomerania, and Wismar, Bremen and Verden had been acquired. Denmark lost Jämtland, Härjedalen, Halland, the islands of Gotland and Ösel, as well as Blekinge, Bohuslän and Skåne. Ingria and the fiefdom of Lexholm had been taken from the Russians, shutting them off from the sea. Now came a phase of consolidation. The Swedish state, like a boa-constrictor, composed itself to digest its swallowed prey in peace and quiet. A period during which the conquered lands were secured and defended lasted for the rest of the 17th century.

Undeniably, this was a very impressive historical phenomenon. From having been an unnoticed, unimportant and undeveloped marginal state, Sweden stepped rapidly forward out of the shadowy wings and secured for herself one of the main roles on the wider political stage of Europe. The country swiftly became a first-class power.

Down the years, numerous historians have been attracted to the problem of accounting for Sweden's improbable expansion, and several schools of thought have evolved, each successively dominating academic thinking on the topic. A widely accepted early theory attributed the country's sudden growth to a series of circumstances which menaced her security and made the conquests more or less obligatory. The theory's main preoccupation was with different major upheavals outside the country's borders. Russia, with her endless hinterland, had begun to expand again; the old power structure in the Baltic was in dissolution because of the collapse of the Hanseatic League and the Teutonic Knights; and the Counter-Reformation also had some political impact which was felt all the way up to the north. Added to this was the ancient struggle with Denmark for regional hegemony. Swedish conquests, according to this view of historical forces, were driven by apprehension for her safety in the face of external threats. Buffer zones were built up against inimical neighbours in an effort to create what are called natural borders: a tenuous concept.

Similar reasoning is employed by those who explain Sweden's rise less by her own impetus than by the weaknesses of her neighbours. External circumstances favouring Swedish expansion are selectively pointed out. Poland became piecemeal more and more weak and divided. Russia was enfeebled after Ivan the Terrible's bloody regime – popular uprisings and confused dynastic civil wars had paralysed the country. A deep and crippling feudal division prevailed in Germany; and even Denmark's situation deteriorated. All this opened an opportunity for Sweden, with her meagre resources, to grow at the expense of these debilitated states.

These opinions have been countered by a quite different interpretation: the driving force behind the policy of conquest was primarily economic.

The Swedish monarchy wanted to establish a monopoly in Russian and north European traffic with the West. Its aim was to control this trade, and impose customs duties. The opportunity arose when the Teutonic Order fell. Sweden and Poland (and Denmark to some extent) began a stubborn tug of war over the very lucrative trade routes, while Russia strove to reach the Baltic in order to establish direct links with the merchants of western Europe. Similar economic aims were on the agenda during the Great Northern War.

A fourth model seeks to explain the expansionary impetus in terms of internal social conditions. The underlying cause was the Swedish aristocracy, a feudal class which, through war, could expand and wax rich at the expense of the peasantry at home and abroad. The peasants in Sweden, however, were strong enough to resist too great an extortion by state and landowner, and foreign conquests gave the nobility the opportunity of looting from outside the country whatever they were unable to obtain within it. Protracted exploitation by means of war became an effective alternative.

With Sweden at war and growing stronger, the ruling classes made substantial gains. A nobleman was offered an accelerated career advanced by rapid coups. The national conquests are presented as actions inspired by feudal interests concerned to secure and increase their estates and possessions around the Baltic. Moreover it has been contended that the innate logic of this warfare, and its financing in particular, had a tendency to create war by its own momentum. With an army well and truly placed on field footing by the state, it would be spurred on to moving as quickly as possible beyond its own borders and out into enemy territory, where it would support itself by greater or lesser sophisticated methods of plunder. To maintain an armed force within the borders would mean economic disaster. Swedish war financing was so conceived that while her army was victorious the system worked perfectly, but any reverse threw all calculations into disarray. Peace would be positively catastrophic.

By ceasing to search for a single prime cause we may come to recognize that these apparently widely differing ways of looking at the problem can be combined. Objections to each viewpoint arise from the absurdity of straining to prove that everything derives from one isolated factor.

The power-vacuum theory probably tells us least. It may perhaps account for the extent of the conquests, but really fails to explain what inspired them. The economic theory, which sees expansion as an attempt to seize control of trade, is supported by a great deal of evidence showing that commercial aims did play a major part. Nevertheless, they were not the motive force behind all important strategic decisions. Trade objectives could even play a clearly subordinate role to the more purely political.

During the hundred years it took to build up the Swedish imperium, those in power were faced by widely varying challenges and shifting situations. Sometimes economic aims were dominant, sometimes considerations of politics and national security, and sometimes they coincided. The sharp distinction between political and commercial motives is in many respects illusory. These threads were woven together. A desire for security led to war. The new type of warfare which first appeared during the 16th century swallowed up enormous resources and forced the increase and safeguarding of national economic reserves.

Without a doubt, however, internal conditions in Sweden played an extremely important, even decisive, role as catalyst for the long succession of wars and the unparalleled expansion.

Nevertheless, it should not be supposed that all these cataclysmic wars were waged by princes and aristocrats because they were stupid or evil or possibly both. These conflicts resulted from the feudal system: war was quite simply the shortest route to swift and sudden profits. The economy was dominated, not to say crippled, by an underdeveloped agriculture which improved so sluggishly that it was often difficult to discern any change at all. Territorial conquest and the spoils of war were the only means of making a swift killing. This principle applied to states as well as individuals.

There is also an important difference between a capitalist and a feudal society. The place for competition in a capitalist system is within the economy, within the marketplace. The normal place for feudal competition was on the battlefield, and the standard means of competing was with the sword. In a capitalist economy competing rivals can prosper side by side. In a feudal economy this does not work, because the central measure of value, land, cannot expand: it merely changes ownership – an exchange effected by the weapon in hand. The numerous long wars were thus an almost inescapable consequence of the feudal social system.

It is easy to infer that it must have been in someone's interest to pursue this blood-stained policy. Vested interests, it is said, never fail to run true. Without shadow of doubt, the Swedish aristocracy grew rich on the Swedish imperium. By upbringing and education from infancy the nobleman was conditioned for the trade of the warrior. For scions of the nobility with ambition there were on the whole only two routes worth considering: public service or the military. Of these alternatives the way of the sword was without question the more attractive. At certain periods more than 80 per cent of the male nobility were engaged in the military sphere.

Their view of war differed greatly from ours. War was not an *a priori* evil, but a prime opportunity for a career and a quickly improved standard of living: the most fitting occupation for a true nobleman. In their eyes, *peace* was an irksome danger, threatening demobilization and straitened circumstances. A high-born aristocrat, Gustaf Bonde, once stated in Council that during the wars endured by Sweden 'many a knight had been employed and made himself useful, so that he was enabled to maintain his living, where otherwise he would have had to starve in misery at home'. Adam Ludvig Lewenhaupt – the general who had taken part in ambushing the Cossacks – remarked that 'I am more gratified by the slightest trifles in war and in foreign lands, than to go squandering my substance on the vanities of the age, in ignominy here at home.' This was probably quite a common sentiment among his peers. This positive attitude to war persisted during the 18th century. The constant elbowing for the all-too-meagre offices of peace caused many a nobleman to look back with longing at past times of turbulence and strife.

Among contemporaries during the nights of iron in the imperial period there were many who condemned war as merely a means of securing the position of the aristocracy and preserving internal peace. Noblemen were deemed to profit from war in several ways. The best estates would be given to them as reward for their services. Out on the battlefield they became rich on plunder and pay. Those nobles who in spite of everything remained at home could, by means of the special system of taxation, receive from their peasants half of what the Riksdag appropriated for armaments. The aristocracy, and the monarchy, were also said to make use of conscription as a method of getting rid of refractory peasants. Some have even asserted that it was not the wars which caused conscription of men into the army, but the need for conscription as a disciplinary measure which caused the wars.

Nevertheless it will not do to simplify to excess and draw a picture of the nobility as a pack of rabid bloodhounds, perpetually thirsting for new strife. They could claim a considerable sense of responsibility for state and community, and some historians have wanted to depict the Swedish aristocracy of this period as the most progressive in Europe. It was possible, besides all the warriors, to find many good statesmen, brilliant scholars, countless competent administrators, skilled poets and outstanding natural scientists among the nobility. The wars were often a burden on them as well, and not every nobleman was a warmonger. There were Council members who opposed expansionary policies, and consistently advocated peace. In spite of this we will unquestionably find both the majority of war architects and the majority of war profiteers in the ranks of the aristocracy.

What made the Great Northern War somewhat singular was that it did not begin, as previously, with a Swedish offensive. This time her neighbours struck the first blow. Nevertheless, it was an out-and-out war of *revanche*. The attackers were primarily concerned to regain lands taken from them during the preceding period, and what the Swedish soldier fought for at Poltava was the retention of this plunder. The stalwart blue-coats of King Charles battled and died on behalf of those who profited by the imperium and wanted to keep it; that is to say, all those Swedish aristocrats who had acquired great and splendid estates in the captured lands, the capitalist trade coteries making profits in the East European trade, and the Swedish state which exacted its customs and excise from this vast commerce. It was these players who first and foremost were threatened when the storm-clouds gathered at the end of the 17th century, and it was clear that another major conflagration lay ahead.

# 3 · The War

This war, which had sent a great Swedish army into the heart of the Ukraine, was a direct consequence of imperial dominion. Those in power stubbornly defended what had been won in the previous epoch. But if security was the aim, the result was a paradox: Swedish security had declined. The imperium had been built at the expense of Denmark, Poland and Russia. There was no indication that these states were going to accept their swingeing losses in passive silence.

In Denmark the ache for a war of *revanche* was like a septic tooth. The Danes aimed to break the Swedish hegemony encircling them, and win back their lost provinces. In Poland, too, plans were nurtured to start a reconquest of lost territories, although they were less well defined than the Danish. Poland had really only one access to the sea: through Danzig. The Polish-Lithuanian and White-Russian areas on the other hand aimed for a passage through Riga, in Swedish Livonia. The new ruler crowned in Poland in 1697, the Elector of Saxony, Frederick Augustus II, known as 'The Strong', had to swear an oath before his coronation, containing a clause requiring him to regain the country's lost possessions.

In Russia, also, savage preparations for *revanche* were being plotted. The main interest of the Russians was to regain Ingria since the loss of this region had excluded them from the Baltic. At the signing of the Peace of Stolbova in 1617, when the province had come into Swedish hands, the Russian emissaries had made themselves plain: sooner or later Ingria was going to revert to Russia. By the middle of the 17th century the Russian state had already resumed its expansion. The accession of the monstrous and remarkable Peter I marked a new phase in the country's history. An enormous undertaking was begun with the aim of turning isolated, backward Russia into a modern European state. Access to ice-free ports was a matter of life and death for Russian trade. Following their failure to secure free maritime passage in the Black Sea by force of arms, Russian eyes turned to the Baltic and the Swedish provinces there. The importance of the Baltic ports had increased substantially, largely thanks to a growing traffic in a variety of Russian products.

The situation was charged and primed. If political events were to unite anti-Swedish powers in taking concerted action, northern Europe could well erupt into a major war. By the end of the century the signs were emerging: the fuse to the gunpowder keg was alight. Charles XI, afflicted with stomach cancer, died on Easter Day, 1697. His illness had prompted renewed Danish diplomatic activity. Danish reports spoke of famine and serious dissension in Sweden. Some observers thought the country was on the brink of revolt: only a war was needed to spark it off. Very few in the anti-Swedish camp had the insight to realize that these hopes were exaggerated and based on propaganda and wishful thinking. Diplomats and strategists felt that an excellent opportunity was at hand for an attack on Sweden.

Secret negotiations were set in motion, at first only between Denmark and Russia, but later involving Poland as well. In the summer of 1698 Tsar Peter – on his way home to take a personal hand in the torture and mass execution of the Streltsi who had just rebelled in Moscow – met Augustus at Rawa, near Lemberg. After three days of stupendous drinking, mingled with secret political fraternizing, the new-found friends exchanged weapons and clothing to mark their blood-brotherhood, and parted company. For both these potentates the idea of a war on Sweden had become an increasingly attractive proposition. Both had recently been at war with Turkey, and both had drawn a blank. Augustus counted on Polish support if he were to annex Livonia. This would also give him an excuse to maintain his Saxon troops in Poland, further reinforcing his position there.

In the summer of 1699 the political temperature rose yet another couple of degrees. A new crisis developed between Denmark and Sweden. The bone of contention was Holstein-Gottorp. This independent duchy south of Denmark was closely allied with Sweden and had great strategic importance. In the event of a war with Denmark it gave the Swedes an opportunity of squeezing the Jutes between two fires. The Danes saw Holstein-Gottorp as a cocked pistol aimed at their back. The Duke of Holstein had great influence on the young Swedish king and Swedish foreign policy was framed to further the duke's cause. In this tense situation the Swedes took a decision which heaped new timber on already smouldering fires. A number of forts razed some years earlier were to be reconstructed with Swedish aid. Troops were sent over to Schleswig and Pomerania. These measures were not enough to trigger off the war, but they accelerated its approach. Anti-Swedish intrigues intensified, propelling the outbreak of the war the forts were intended to prevent – another irony of history. The Danish authorities began to prepare for war and signalled their aggressive intentions at various European courts. In September 1699 a secret treaty was concluded in Dresden. Denmark, Russia and Saxony united in their intention of making a joint attack on Sweden. The time set for this was January or February, 1700.

Any hopes the conspirators may have entertained of gaining swift and overwhelming victories were soon dashed. Sweden was ready for the assault. Never before in her history had she been better armed for war. The draconian reforms of Charles XI had provided her with a large, well-trained and well-equipped army, a fleet to command respect and a new method of financing war which could stand the strain of its enormous initial cost. The shiny new armour the Swedes could strut in nevertheless had a few ugly spots of rust. The defence of the Baltic states was full of holes: many vital border fortifications were in poor condition. Sea defences were not oriented towards meeting a Russian offensive in the Gulf of Finland. These flaws were to have a fatal effect on the outcome of the war.

Hostilities were initiated by the Saxon forces of Augustus. They went wrong from the start. A clumsy attempt to capture Riga by storm failed in February 1700. In March the Danish army marched into Holstein-Gottorp. In July the Swedes responded with a lightning attack which knocked Denmark out of the war. With naval aid from Holland and England a Swedish force landed on the east coast of Sjælland, only a few kilometres from Copenhagen. With the Swedish army stamping at his gate, King Fredrik of Denmark had second thoughts about the war and agreed a hasty peace. The Swedes were enabled to turn their ships, cannon and bayonets towards the East. There, by now, another country had joined the band of aggressors, namely Russia, who had declared war a good week *after* the peace with Denmark.

This points to serious defects in the planning of the attack, which presumably saved Sweden in the first year. The conspirators had failed to draw up a joint military plan of action. Their co-ordination was therefore extremely poor.

The Russians' entry was delayed because they wanted first to conclude their war with Turkey. Mustering the motley army the tsar intended using against the Swedes took rather a long time. Their first objective was Narva. The city was laid under siege somewhat late in the day. When Swedish forces landed on the Baltic coast early in October, the Saxons, unluckily for the Russians, had withdrawn. The Swedes could concentrate single-mindedly on the relief of Narva. On 20 November 1700, 10,500 Swedish soldiers attacked an entrenched Russian siege force estimated at 33,000 men (plus another 35,000 support militia) and won a victory as great as it was unexpected.

In July the following year the main Swedish force crossed the Dvina, defeated a Saxon army and occupied Courland. The direct Saxon threat against Livonia was eliminated. This also meant that it was possible to raise the blockade of the Courland ports, which had been causing Holland and

England considerable annoyance. The occupation of Courland also gave Sweden much better control of the important mouth of the Dvina. Important rye-growing districts came into Swedish hands and a dangerous trade rival to Riga was knocked off the board.

At the outset the war was probably rather popular in Sweden. It was not unusual for people to cross the Baltic and join the army at their own expense. Whereas during the Thirty Years' War it had been common to seek exemption from conscription by entering the mines, now the traffic went in the opposite direction. Men deserted the mining areas and factories in order to enlist. And many discovered, especially the higher ranking officers, that war could be profitable.

Count Magnus Stenbock provides a good example. At the outbreak of war he was 35, with experience in Dutch, Imperial German and Swedish service. He took part in the relief of Narva and was promoted to major-general soon after the battle. Apart from this leap upward in his career, the outbreak of war brought a whole series of benefits for the count. First and foremost were the spoils of plunder: many thousands of daler in ready cash, purses filled with Russian coin and quantities of valuables such as jewels and silver tankards and goblets. Other 'fripperies', including marten-lined bedspreads and beds, salt-cellars, weapons, chasubles and chalices, crucifixes, candle-sticks and braided greatcoats, found their way home to the estate. As the months rolled by, large sums of money were transferred to Sweden, to be used to purchase new lands.

Then there were the more indirect profits which Stenbock raked in by supplying the army with various necessities. He was advised to slaughter his herds and bake rusks from his corn harvest, then sell these products to the military authorities. A fourth incentive for Stenbock was the defence of family estates in the Baltic provinces. In a letter home to his mother after Narva, where he was wounded, he remarks that he had 'risked a black eye for the salvation of her property here in Livonia'. Magnus Stenbock is a good instance of how the men at the top could really benefit from the war.

But it is anachronistic to moralize over war-plunder. For both officers and men booty was an important inducement in combat. It was seen as something legitimate, honourably won by sweat and blood. Looting was a practice used to encourage the men, fully permitted on the battlefield and carefully regulated in the articles of war. The only real circumscription was that no one was allowed to rake in the plunder, or tipple, until the enemy had been defeated. Everything taken on the battlefield belonged, with a few exceptions, to the officers and men, and had to be divided among them. The reward dealt out to a paralysed trooper was a tiny crumb compared with what went to his officers or the highest command. This can be shown by the way the plunder won at Saladen, in 1703, was shared between participants:

A wounded captain received 80 riksdaler
An unwounded captain: 40 riksdaler
A wounded lieutenant or ensign: 40 riksdaler
An unwounded lieutenant or ensign: 20 riksdaler
An unwounded NCO: 2 riksdaler
A wounded private: 2 riksdaler
An unwounded private: 1 riksdaler

An enlisted man would never be rich; he could count himself lucky if he survived. The rank and file had to give their lives to help build up the fortunes of officers of the high aristocracy, family fortunes sticky with blood, some lasting to this day.

In the autumn of 1701 Swedish forces became enmeshed in battles between a number of different Polish factions, and in January of the following year the army entered Poland. The war was now divided into two battle arenas. In Poland the main Swedish army marched back and forth to subdue the unwilling land, with the object of dethroning Augustus. In the Baltic states, small Swedish forces were slowly but surely pushed back by a Russian army which just as slowly and surely became larger and more competent.

The Swedish forces left to defend the Baltic were patently inadequate. Splitting these forces into three autonomous corps without an overall commander was also a major error. Each separately was far too weak, and operations were not co-ordinated. The situation was not improved by the supreme command issuing an embargo against sending any reinforcements to the Baltic; these were required on the Polish front. While Charles XII toured Poland year after year, one strategic point after another fell to the enemy up on the Baltic. The Russians reached the Gulf of Finland, and began building ships there. Work started on the construction of what was to become Russia's new capital, St Petersburg, on Swedish soil.

The Polish and Baltic peoples suffered greatly as the war proceeded. Maintenance of the Swedish army depended on contributions, meaning in plain language that a swarm of steel-armed locusts ate straight through those regions it descended on. A population living on the edge of destitution before the war began was robbed of life's necessities, and to a certain extent, money, with the aid of threats, fire and torture. The only essential was for the army to get what it wanted, and the country could then, in Charles XII's own words 'suffer as much as it liked'. Senior commanders were ordered to 'extract and rapidly thrash and scrape together as much as you can for the good of the army'. A bitter guerrilla war frequently raged around the Swedish army, and the Polish population did not scruple to slaughter isolated Swedish soldiers. This was countered by the Swedes with ruthless severity. Instructions from the Swedish High

Command proclaimed that malefactors should be executed on minimal evidence, 'so fear should be instilled and they should know, if retribution begin, the child in the cradle would not be spared'.

One instance of the many Swedish acts of outrage was the Nieszawa massacre. In August 1703 this town, south-east of Thorn, was burnt to the ground and its innocent citizens hanged, as reprisal for an attack on Swedish troops in its neighbourhood.

Up in the Baltic the Russians plundered and killed at least as uninhibitedly as the Swedes in Poland. Russian strategy was totally to lay waste the Swedish provinces, so they could no longer serve as bases for Swedish operations. In one of his reports to the tsar, General Sheremetev described his latest ravages with satisfaction: 'I have had the men out capturing and plundering in every direction. Nothing has escaped. Everything is destroyed or burnt. The soldiers have carried off several thousand men, women and children, as well as at least 20,000 dray-horses and cattle.' What had already been consumed, slaughtered or destroyed was not included in this figure, and estimated by him at about double what was transported. The Russian army deported large numbers of the population as living plunder; highly placed officers appropriated many of them for use as serf labour on their estates. Others were sold like cattle in dirty market-places in Russia or ended as slaves among Tartars or Turks.

After several long years of harrying and countermarching down in Poland, Charles XII finally achieved a solid result. Peace was concluded between Sweden and Poland at the end of 1705. The treaty reveals what the soldiery had been fighting for. The grand old Swedish skeleton, *Dominium maris Baltici*, dominion over the Baltic Sea, was pulled out of the closet and dusted down. The peace terms required a large portion of Polish trade to be diverted through Swedish Riga. The Poles had to promise to raze their new port of Polangen so that it would not compete with Swedish ports. Swedish merchants were given greatly increased incentives to settle in Poland, and their rights there were substantially improved. The treaty included an embargo on Russian transit trade to Europe. Even though the Poles were not formally compelled to cede any territory, it was an unpalatable peace the Swedes were forcing down their throats.

The long delayed Swedish march into Saxony – postponed because of the involvement of major European powers in the War of the Spanish Succession – took place in the summer of 1706. Invasion of Augustus's native country brought rapid results. In September peace was concluded on the estate of Altranstädt, near Leipzig. Augustus renounced his Polish throne, recognized the Swedish puppet Stanislaus Leszczynski as Poland's legitimate king and undertook to give no further support to Sweden's enemies. After seven years, two of the three conspirators had been beaten hollow. It only remained to settle matters with the third.

During these years the Swedish army had been deeply involved in a long-drawn-out and seemingly pointless war in Poland. Tsar Peter had been handed an extremely welcome respite, and the Russian army had been reorganized. It had gained valuable experience and a new self-confidence thanks to a long series of successes in the Baltic area. The Russians were allowed the opportunity to fight their way through to the sea. The Swedish provinces had been heavily ravaged and were under extreme pressure. Key places like Nöteborg, Narva and Dorpat had been back under control of the tsar's forces for many years.

All this was now going to be straightened out. Now it was Tsar Peter Alexeivich's turn to pay for his intrigues against Sweden. The whole of Europe was convinced that the stubborn despot in the Kremlin was facing the prospect of a massive defeat. Panic spread in Moscow: many of the foreign inhabitants left the city in anticipation of a Swedish onslaught. Rumours of rebellion and bloodbath filled the air.

# 4 · The Campaign

During the last days of 1707 the Swedish army crossed the Vistula river, moving west to east. Water was poured over the thin ice to freeze and strengthen it. Planks and straw were added. The fragile base heaved and swayed beneath the troops' feet and the dark river waters swallowed a number of wagons, horses and men. But, on the whole, things went according to plan. Behind lay a harried West Poland, and a Saxony from which the utmost had been extracted. Somewhere ahead lay the retreating Russian army. The Swedish host was large and powerful, possibly the best in Europe. Local recruitment and fresh troops from home had swollen it to 44,000 men, one of the strongest forces ever put in the field by Sweden, a poor and sparsely populated country. The army was well equipped and well prepared. New weapons, new uniforms, brimming treasure-chests and large stores of powder, ball, medicines and other supplies bore witness to thorough preparation. Tsar Peter had good cause to tremble.

And tremble he did. The Swedes were repeatedly approached with nervous offers of peace as they advanced, but these were waved away by a self-confident King Charles, certain of success.

Russian strategy for countering the approaching menace was straightforward. The Zholkiyevski plan, laid down a good year earlier, was based on total avoidance of any major confrontation in Poland, relying instead on withdrawal before the enemy offensive and simultaneously scorching and starving all regions through which the Swedes might be expected to advance. The march would be delayed by destroying roads and bridges, and by resistance at carefully selected points. The Swedish army was to be worn down by a series of minor battles and skirmishes. Finally, round the Russian borders, a desert zone of fully 200 kilometres was to be created by human hand, void of people and provisions. It was a brutal strategy grandly conceived, devised to save the homeland by laying it waste.

The war prolonged the martyrdom of Poland. This pitiable country was now having to pay for its military and political weakness; again it became the battlefield of two great powers. On the one hand was a large Swedish army determined to eat its way through an already substantially destitute countryside, and on the other a multitude of Russian forces with only one aim: to destroy as much as possible before their enemy arrived. On crossing the Silesian border the Swedish troops were at once confronted with thorough devastation. The Russians had burnt villages and towns, poisoned wells and terrorized the civilian population. For those who had grown used to the sumptuous billets in Saxony it was like being thrown straight out over an abyss. Poland was the grain of corn between two millstones.

After crossing the Vistula the Swedish army continued its eastward march. Unexpectedly the route led through Masovia, a large area of forest and morass adjacent to East Prussia. This inhospitable region had never before been traversed by an army. With this move Charles XII aimed to out-manoeuvre the enemy dispositions and force the Russians out of the Narew line without conflict.

The Swedish army pushed into Masovia in three columns. The march was hard, leading along bad roads and through deep snow. In deciding on this stroke of military genius the local population, who were not particularly interested in letting this hungry horde into their homes, had not been reckoned with. At first the peasantry tried to negotiate; they wanted personally to point out which roads the troops ought to take and what they themselves were willing to contribute, but their spokesmen were summarily killed. A short and exceptionally bitter guerrilla war flared up. The Masovians took to the woods, ripped up the log causeways on roads through the forests and threw up barriers across the army's route. With the courage of despair, large bands of peasants attempted to halt the march through their land. There was an ambush every day.

The Swedish response was savagely ruthless. Troops were despatched into the woods with orders to kill all men over the age of 15, slaughter all animals that could not be herded away, and burn every village. The guerrilla war persisted stubbornly while the army killed and cut a swathe of devastation through the region. The villages of Masovia disappeared, one after another, in a shower of sparks. The greatest problem for the army was to extort sufficient provisions out of the recalcitrant populace. There was no hesitation in taking to old and well-tried methods of torture. One favoured method was to push the peasants' fingers into pistol flint-locks and tighten these crude thumbscrews until the blood spurted. Another was to tie a thong round the victim's head, then tighten it with a stick until the eyes were squeezed out of their sockets. The army's barbarity in Masovia recorded its greatest triumph when it rounded up small children, beat them and pretended to hang them, to induce compliance from their parents. Some units proceeded from threat to reality and killed the children in sight of their parents.

When, after a full ten days, the army emerged from Masovia's snow-clad forests and came out on the Lithuanian plain it left a wasteland in its wake. One of the Swedes taking part was a 39-year-old colonel of dragoons, Nils Gyllenstierna. He summed up what had taken place, not without a certain complacency, with the words: 'Much of the populace was massacred, and everything standing burnt and laid waste, so I believe those who survived will not quickly forget the Swedes.'

On the 28 January 1708 the king and an advance party of 600 men rode over the Niemen and took Grodno. The city had been evacuated by the Russians hours earlier. Their retreat continued and the Swedes pursued. Bad winter roads took their toll of men and horses, and there was not always a roof to be had for the night. Any habitable cottages were occupied in the first place by the officers and their families and servants. Other ranks had to be satisfied for the most part with huddling together on the snow in the lee of farmyard fences and house walls, or else to gather round the flames of huge log fires. The eastward advance went more or less according to plan for the Swedes, but the Russian army had problems. Their cavalry were unable to follow the directives of the Zholkiyevski blueprint to the letter. They made no great effort to delay the Swedes, and merely fell back. Battle contact between the two armies consisted mainly of brief skirmishing.

The Swedes pushed on strongly, and the Russians eventually found only enough time to burn along the verges of the roads, for the Swedish cavalry were hard on their heels. Rows of dead horses, ridden into the ground, bore witness to the precipitate Russian retreat. The Swedish troops came upon burned villages where charred animal carcases still lay reeking in their stalls. In the main, however, the Russians fled more rapidly than their opponents could pursue, through the persistent snowfall and along the pitted roadways. When the Swedish army's supplies ran low, and the cavalry's horses were on the verge of collapse, the pursuit was broken off. At the beginning of February a halt was made at the little town of Smorgoni, haunt of the bear-tamers of Lithuania. The army had to recuperate.

The Swedish army remained at rest for something over a month, camped over an area ten kilometres wide. The time was mainly employed in assiduous practice of new drill regulations. In spite of the bitter cold, the camp broke up in mid-March. Victualling problems were again acute. Two days' march took the army 50 kilometres further east to the region round Radoshkoviche, where local supplies were somewhat less depleted. Almost three months were wasted there, drilling in the mire and rooting out the peasants' last crumbs of food.

The population tried to conceal what provisions they had by burying them in the ground in artfully constructed hiding-places. Over the years the Swedes had developed methods just as ingenious for discovering these holes. They were so successful that the despairing peasants fancied they employed magical means. The troops discovered that an underground cache would often be hidden where the snow melted more rapidly than on surrounding terrain. They also had special probes fitted with barbs. Straw pulled up out of the earth was a major clue: the holes were often lined with it.

Preparations were made for the summer campaign. Food and other supplies were collected. General Lewenhaupt was called from Courland to meet the king. He was ordered to make his corps ready to march with copious supplies. The main army still suffered deficiencies during the halt; many horses died for lack of fodder. As spring approached, sickness began to wear holes in the ranks. The new recruits suffered particularly badly, being unused to hard living in the field. But they had to wait until the rough, waterlogged roads had dried out and the tender spring grass had thickened so that grazing for the innumerable horses improved. On 6 June 1708 the waiting was over. Leaving a detachment in support of the newly enthroned Polish monarch Stanislaus, an army of about 38,000 men resumed its march.

Uncertainty about which route the Swedish army would take, whether it was going to head north to throw the Russians out of the Baltic provinces or press on straight for Moscow, was soon dispelled. The march steered east, towards what is called the river gate. The two great rivers Dvina and Dnieper created an almost unbroken barrier of water along the Russian border of the time, all the way from the Baltic to the Black Sea. The river gate was the narrow corridor on either side of which both waterways rise to the east. Through this opening ran the great highway to Moscow.

Although this land corridor was clear of major rivers it was nevertheless laced through by many tributaries, which the Russians intended using as lines of defence. Their forces split into several corps preparing to block the Swedish advance. The greatest of the tributaries was the Berezina, and the best passage over it at Borizov. Accordingly this point was grey with weapons and Russian troops in waiting. However, the Swedish command manoeuvred very skilfully: a more southerly route was chosen. At the same time a strong detachment of cavalry moved towards Borizov in a diversionary manoeuvre to deceive the Russians into believing the main thrust would come there. Meanwhile, on minor roads, the Swedish army reached another crossing which was virtually undefended. Once again the Swedes had out-manoeuvred their opponents with minimal losses.

But the intended outflanking movement failed, for the march, weighed down by baggage and the retarding effect of abysmal roads and appalling weather, was too slow. The Russians had time to pull back, and they

## Map 2 · *The Swedish Invasion of Russia 1708–1709*

1. The Swedish army crosses the Vistula in December 1707; and marches east through Masovia. A short, embittered guerrilla war breaks out.
2. On 28 January 1708 the Swedes capture Grodno. The Russians lay waste the land and withdraw east. The Swedish army pursues.
3. The pursuit is broken off at Smorgoni in early February. The army moves into winter quarters.
4. In June the march resumes. Russian forces are out-manoeuvred. The Swedes win a victory at Holowczyn, 4 July.
5. Lewenhaupt breaks camp at the end of June to join the main army.
6. The main army halts at Mohilev, awaits Lewenhaupt, but has to resume its march in August. Attempts are made to confront the Russians, but they continue to withdraw.

regrouped round Holowczyn, behind the little river Babitch. A new attempt would be made to delay the relentless forward thrust of the Swedish host.

Through forest roads the army found its way to Holowczyn. On 4 July, before all units had reached the place, an attack was launched. The point of attack was well chosen. In a furious and bloody battle the Russians were thrown out of their entrenchments. But the Swedes were now made conclusively aware that they were no longer facing the same rabble that had been scattered to the winds at Narva. Russian casualties totalled close to 5,000 men compared with Swedish losses of about 1,200.

When the enemy had fled the infantry sat down to rest, while *cantinières* visited them with bread and aquavit. Chaplains went round the battlefield giving communion to the dying men. The Swedes pitched their tents on the battlefield, which presented an appalling sight: piles of dead men and horses, cannon, knapsacks, copper pans, food and smashed carts in one macabre, muddy jumble. The dead Swedes were earthed over in mass graves with military honours, but most of the Russian corpses were left to lie unburied in the summer heat. A heavy, pungent odour of decay soon came to permeate the area and made it well nigh unbearable to remain there. Dogs ran everywhere feeding off the naked, swollen human remains lying sprawled about the field.

The tsar was infuriated by the outcome of the battle and held a court martial. The local commander was reduced to the ranks and sentenced to pay for lost ammunition and cannon out of his own pocket. Soldiers who had been wounded in the back were assumed to have shown cowardice, and were either shot or hanged.

---

7. The army halts again at the beginning of September. Mainly for maintenance reasons it has to continue south.

8. Lewenhaupt's corps proceeds south. On 29 September Russian forces attack them at Lesnaya. The remnants reach the main army in October.

9. At the beginning of November the army crosses the Desna. Rebellious Cossacks throw in their lot with the Swedes.

10. The army goes into winter quarters. The winter grows increasingly severe. There are a number of minor battles.

11. At the end of January 1709 the Swedes resume the offensive, but bad weather brings it to a halt.

12. The Swedish army is concentrated between the Psel and the Vorskla. A four month defensive phase begins. To fill in time the siege of Poltava starts on May 1.

The way to the Dnieper now lay open for the invading Swedish army. Mohilev, a large town on the river, was occupied on 7 July. The Swedish army camped here for almost a month. This further halt was partly, as usual, because the army had to be revictualled, but mainly because Lewenhaupt's corps from Courland was awaited. Lewenhaupt had prepared for the march as best he could, but when he received the royal command it was already 3 June. It was a difficult task to prepare the troops for the campaign and collect the large quantities of supplies he had to bring. Departure was not possible until the end of the month. The corps, consisting of 12,500 men, 16 cannon and a monumental baggage-train of several thousand wagons, advanced extremely slowly.

When the Swedish army broke camp on 5 August, after its month-long wait, Lewenhaupt's corps had still not arrived. The campaign had to continue. The march did not lead towards the enemy's main force, in a fortified position at Gorki, but moved south-east towards the river Soz, yet another of the Dnieper's tributaries. The Swedes were obliged to keep close to the Dnieper in order not to expose Lewenhaupt's little corps. An attempt was made to lure the Russians into open battle. By forced marches efforts were made to reach first one then another of the enemy's divisions, but these merely fell back, leaving a smouldering, ravaged land in their wake.

At times the Swedes were so close that they rode into abandoned camps where everything had been left behind: tents, horses and even camp whores or such exotica as camels. At Cherikov by the Soz a halt was made for a couple of days and shots exchanged with the enemy across the river. The king, elated and trigger-happy, strode about seizing muskets from soldiers and downing several Russians himself. Only a few minor engagements took place, such as at Dobroye on 31 August and Rayowska on 10 September. They had little result except that a lot of soldiers died. The pursuit of the fleeing Russians continued north-east, towards the large town of Smolensk.

For the high-ranking staff and general officers the war was a long succession of village, town and river names, linked by technical military terms: advances, retreats and forced marches. The reality for the man in the ranks was something else. For him, the connecting links and the grandiose plans did not exist, and there was nothing but a blind tramp through muddy forest paths; over fields and wind-whipped meadows, through dank, dripping forests, over swaying causeways and heaving pontoons, enveloped in a persistent rain which never seemed to stop; hunting an enemy who was hardly ever seen but could be sensed by the clouds of smoke drifting along the horizon.

The summer was cold and rainy and the troops suffered greatly. Crops grew slowly. Unripe grain was cut where it stood in the field and ground in small hand-mills. The dough was baked in cooking-pots or hastily constructed earth-ovens, resulting in a black, evil-tasting bread. Sometimes even this was lacking. It was often difficult for the men to find time to prepare their food. Ahead of them the horizon was dotted with smoke-clouds. Around them roved the Russian light horse. In order to maintain their readiness the soldiers usually slept in their clothes, and many mornings would wake to Cossack yells. These swift-footed enemy warriors were always hovering about. They gleefully attacked the baggage-train, slaughtered soldiers, drivers, stable-lads and the sick, slashed the horses and looted whatever they had time for. When the Swedes faced them, and made to attack, the Cossacks would disperse like smoke, leaving the pursuers only winded horses for their pains.

So roaming soldiers might find their way through unfamiliar forest depths, and the dark and dirty weather, drummers were set out to guide the hungry, thirsty and exhausted men with their thrumming beat. After a long day's march there were often no proper quarters, for the Russians would either have burned all the houses, or kept the quartermasters too occupied to organize billets, causing great confusion in the dark summer nights. In the evening there were tedious duties of sentry-go or heavy fatigues. The army depended on its horses and the horses had to be fed. The men would be sent out to forage for fodder. This could mean long dangerous rides through forest and marshland, filled with hostile Cossacks and embittered peasants lurking in ambush. The soldiers cursed their retreating opponents, blamed them for their labours and contemptuously referred to their Russian foe as Bog-Peter. A decisive battle, which would mean rest and perhaps peace, was eagerly desired. The army was war-weary.

On 11 September they halted near Starycze, a border locality straddling the main highway to Moscow, only about 80 kilometres from Smolensk. The army paused there for a few days, as if to catch its breath. The Russians thoroughly scorched the land between Starycze and Smolensk. The entire plain ahead of the Swedes seemed ablaze. The horizon was heavy with black smoke and at night the sky glowed with reflected light from innumerable fires.

The situation was highly problematical. The Swedes were short of food and a drive for Smolensk meant they would be forced even deeper into the wasteland of ash the Russians were creating. To stand and wait for the still distant Lewenhaupt was not an option because of the lack of supplies. Sickness and desertion were on the increase. The campaign was degenerating into a struggle to keep the army alive. The solution was to turn south: to untouched Severia and the Ukraine where fresh supplies and, God willing, new allies in the shape of rebellious Cossacks were waiting. The move began well, but with the failure to occupy a few key sites the whole operation turned into a hunger march through the Severian forests.

The march south meant the main army could no longer protect Lewenhaupt's slowly trundling wagon-train of supplies. The Russians pursued the corps like hunters after game and finally, on St Michael's Day, 29 September, a Sunday, caught them. A protracted battle took place on a field near the village of Lesnaya. The battle lasted all day and when darkness fell on the broad acres, with corpses spread about, the Swedes were still holding out around the village. It was not until Lewenhaupt's men tried to slip away under cover of night that everything collapsed into chaos. In the pitch darkness confusion reigned: large sections of the baggage-train, as well as cannon, had to be abandoned. Many men, a number drunk to the point of incapability after looting abandoned kegs of spirits, lost their way or disappeared without trace in the dark woods. The next day there was nothing for it but to destroy what little remained of the baggage and to share the horses out among the men. Not until October 11 did this sorry remnant make contact with the main army. Of the expected 12,500 men, well-supplied with artillery, ammunition and provisions, only 6,000 arrived. With them they brought little more than their lives and the clothes they stood up in. The Russians celebrated a great victory.

Now began a race for the Ukraine. Russian and Swedish forces marched at top speed southwards: both sides wanted to take control over as much as possible of this fruitful province. The Cossack hetman, Mazeppa, who had seceded from the Russians, offered the Swedes collaboration and good quarters. Treaties were concluded. It was agreed to put an end to Russian rule. Swedish commercial interests in the area would be recognized: the intention was to re-direct some of the commercial traffic to Europe from Turkey and the Middle East so that it went via the Baltic. Even down here the army carried a lance for Swedish trade interests.

In early November the army made its way over the river Desna and pressed on towards Baturin, a town filled with the highly desired supplies Mazeppa had promised to hand over. Before it was reached, the Russians stormed the town, terrorized and massacred, as a dire warning to all. A large quantity of desperately needed provisions was lost. Hopes of a general uprising against the tsar vanished and the only consequence was a civil war among the Ukrainian Cossacks.

This new theatre of war nevertheless had the advantage of not having been laid waste. It was rich in all the provisions the army so badly needed. In search of even better supplies the march continued south. The Swedes captured the two strongholds of Romni and Gadyach, where a halt was made to recuperate in good quarters. The war had become ever more brutal and embittered. The Russians continued to harass the Swedes with their guerrilla tactics, and killed any sick and wounded they came across.

When, as usual, they fell back before the advancing blue and yellow uniforms, the Swedes tried to create their own zone of devastation. Each regiment was given a sector to plunder and burn. Once again, towns and villages were set ablaze.

Residence in the Ukraine was no sinecure. The cold began to harden. An extremely hostile winter soon held everything in a vice of biting wind and ice. The cold weather hit the whole of Europe: the Baltic, the Rhône and even the canals of Venice were layered with ice. Operations continued, despite this bitter freeze. The Swedish command wanted to drive away the Russian army so that it would be possible to remain secure in winter quarters until the spring. Tsar Peter continued nevertheless to maintain the pressure: in the middle of December the Russians made a surprise move to attack Gadyach. In spite of the inhuman cold Charles XII issued orders to break up from the quarters in Romni: by day and night the troops marched through the snow towards the threatened town.

This was a hellish time. The roads filled with rigid bundles of humanity frozen to death, and with swollen horse carcasses. Those most exposed were perhaps the draymen and lads who drove the wagons. Many froze to their boxes while their ponies either bolted and tangled themselves in their harness, or else quite simply also froze to death. Dead horsemen sat erect in their saddles, the reins frozen fast in their hands, impossible to remove except by severing their fingers. At times the men and horses were so rimed in frost it was difficult to distinguish them from the snowbound land.

The Russians fell back as expected. Only a few were caught and cut down: sometimes so paralysed by cold that they allowed themselves to be slaughtered without lifting a finger. Once into Gadyach there was not enough room within doors for everyone. If they failed to find some cranny in the ground the men had to stand outside in the extreme cold, under bare skies. People died in droves on the town streets. The bodies of hundreds of frozen soldiers, servants, wives and children were collected up each morning, and all day sleds loaded with rigid corpses were driven off to be hidden in some hillside cavity. The field-surgeons worked round the clock. Barrels filled with amputated limbs taken from victims of frost-bite.

On 23 December the Swedish army continued its advance. The objective was to take the town of Veprik and thereby force the enemy back a little further. Veprik, defended by a Scottish officer in the Russian service named Ferber, was eventually taken in spite of rather than thanks to an unskilful and bloody assault. Then nearly a month went by, until the end of January 1709, before the offensive began again. There was a short push towards Kharkov, via Oposhnya and Achtyrka. At Krasnokutsk a minor victory was won in a cavalry clash: the town streets and roads were littered with fallen men. The town was set alight. The flames leapt skywards and through the roaring blaze the cries and lamentations of the inhabitants mingled with the lowing of the cattle the Swedes drove before them through the snow. A sudden thaw put a stop to operations after a time. Heavy rainfall infused the river bluffs with life. The soldiers waded through the floodwaters, and often, with no wood-fires to warm them, camped in the field soaked through, under open skies. When the night frost set in, their clothes were transformed into icy armour.

When the February offensive ended the army was concentrated between the Psel and Vorskla rivers, and a full four month long phase of defence began. The army drew breath and collected its strength before the summer ahead. The Russian forces lay to the east, north-east and west, and continued to harass. The main objective of this Swedish redeployment still further south and east was to facilitate contact with the Zaporozhian Cossacks. Mazeppa negotiated with them on behalf of Charles XII. On 30 March they came over to the Swedes. The strategic situation for the Swedish army had, however, deteriorated little by little and heavy losses had been suffered. At least one-fifth of the army had been lost without it having progressed one step nearer decisive action. It was true that Russian losses had been greater than Swedish, but the Russians were on home ground and could easily replenish their ranks with fresh recruits and new weaponry.

Blows continued to be exchanged while spring breathed new life into the Ukrainian woods and pastures. Russian forces made swift, minor strikes at various Swedish positions. The army was under pressure but still held the initiative. The Swedish command worked hard to bring up reinforcements from Poland, Turkey and the Crimea. To gain time, a siege of the small town of Poltava, held by the Russians, began on 1 May.

There were several engagements while the Russians gathered ever closer to the Swedes, and repeatedly attempted to relieve the town. The tsar's men tried to cross the Vorskla at several points but failed. On the night of 16 June they finally succeeded in crossing at Petrovka, north of Poltava, and a bridgehead was established. On 21 June the tsar crossed the river with most of his army. Meeting no resistance they pushed on towards Poltava the following day. On Saturday 26 June they moved a little nearer and established a fortified camp only five kilometres from the besieged town.

The regions round Poltava seethed with troops, horses and cannon. The air was heavy with an impending detonation. The landscape took on the appearance of the scene of a major, decisive battle. If this was so, it was not for the first time. In the year 1399 the forces of Vitovt, the warlike Grand Prince of Lithuania, had clashed in these parts with those of Edigei, commander of the armies of Tamerlane. In that era the armies of Tamerlane had made their rapacious way westward to resurrect the fallen realm of Genghis Khan. At this place, 310 years earlier, the armed hordes from the East had utterly overthrown the warriors of the West.

# 5 · *Anatomy of a Battlefield*

The arena's eastern rim was bordered by the Vorskla. The river picked its way carefully down to the Dnieper in a southerly direction. It meandered, dividing and rejoining itself in countless loops and ox-bows and the tributary streams and brooks flowing into it had created a small, marshy valley, between one and two kilometres broad. At its widest the river itself was perhaps 100 metres from bank to bank. The banks were sometimes shaded by forest, reaching right down to the green-blue waters, sometimes bordered by soggy, open meadows or steep bluffs. From this waterway, tracing its leisurely course through the vale, the Ukrainian steppe rose to the west to form an extensive level plateau.

Poltava, and the ravines and villages around it, marked the arena's southern border. The town lay near the river, up on the plateau, close to high ground sloping down to the banks. It was sited where the ancient route from Kiev to Kharkov crossed the Vorskla. Poltava was a small town, covering a surface area of little more than one square kilometre, including its outlying suburbs. Like most of the places in this region, it was fortified. The fortifications enclosed an area of about 600 by 1,000 metres.

The enclosed area was divided by one of the many ravines which criss-crossed the landscape. The larger northern section contained the town proper and the southern half consisted of the smaller suburban district of Masurovka. The slopes rising towards Masurovka were covered with cherry orchards which had already fruited. On the plain to the immediate north-west lay yet another outlying village, in turn surrounded by a long curving bank of earth. The houses there had been burned during the siege, and were now only rubble.

Poltava was not well fortified. The Russians had worked hard to improve the defences since the preceding December. The front down to the river, which had been almost completely exposed, had been strengthened. They had also added artillery, so there were now 28 cannon in the arsenal. The wall was of the simplest construction: an earth rampart with wooden palisades, fronted by a shallow ditch.

By now the fortifications were somewhat battered; the palisades scarred and splintered by cannon shot and the ramparts tunnelled through at several points. Above one of the town gates was a large wooden tower, and there were smaller bastions round the fort. One or two had block-houses. The garrison numbered about 4,200 men, including 100 gunners. Another 2,600 townspeople had been mobilized for defence. The commander of this motley force was Colonel Alexei Stepanovich Kelen, who had withstood the siege since the end of April – not as great an achievement as might be supposed. Swedish aims from the outset had mainly been to fill in time and the siege had been conducted somewhat half-heartedly.

The siege-works were directed at Masurovka and the southern fortifications. A siege was a complicated undertaking which usually followed a carefully prescribed formula. This was called the Vauban assault, after the French marshal who had developed new types of siege defences, while simultaneously thinking up equally effective ways of countering his creations. To begin with, circumvallations and counter-circumvallations had to be constructed for protection against enemy sorties or troops outside the fortress. The next step was the digging by night, at a distance of about 600 metres, of a trench known as the first parallel. This housed the batteries of heavy artillery. Thereafter, it was a matter of working closer. At around 300 metres the second parallel was dug, with more batteries, and finally the third parallel, abutting the base of the fortress walls. Between these parallels, access trenches were laid out in zigzag. If the fortress still had not surrendered, underground tunnels called saps were dug, leading right up to the wall so that artillery could effect a breach. The besiegers might also undermine the fortress, plant explosives, and blow everything sky high.

The Swedes had largely followed this formula, if on a minor scale. Three parallels with approaches and the rest had been dug, batteries had been sited, and an attempt made to place mines under the palisades. Initially the king had expressly forbidden an assault, but in an effort to increase the pressure an assault was made on 12 May. A hole had been knocked in the defences and a section of the palisades captured, where a small battery was installed. Swedish pressure was steady, not intensive. There was no really devastating bombardment, but digging below the earth-banks continued. New mines were laid, the garrison made minor sorties and Russian troops made unsuccessful efforts to relieve the town from across the river. Everything was exactly as it ought to be in a siege.

As time passed, conditions in the fortress deteriorated. Kelen had no means of paying the soldiers. Food and ammunition were running low: for want of shot the Russians were using small pieces of iron and stone. Because of the shortage of lead for hand-grenades, they had taken to hurling stones, logs, rotting root-vegetables and dead cats down on the Swedes in the siege-works below. The Swedes responded by throwing stones back, so close were the two sides.

On one occasion the king himself had been hit on the shoulder by a dead cat. The Swedes replied to this unheard-of affront by so bombarding the Russians with hand-grenades that their insults ceased for the day. Other missiles were rather less harmless. Prowling Russian snipers constantly took pot shots at the soldiers and workmen in the trenches. Lives were snuffed out daily. At one post well-aimed fire blew out the skulls of five Swedish soldiers in a single day. The work was dangerous and monotonous. The approach trenches filled with water when it rained and the soldiers waded in mire up to their thighs. Their tents would be soaked and the only benefit of the pelting rainfall was that it washed away the stinking horse carcases which lay spread around the fields and on the slopes.

Immediately to the east of the fortress steep tree-clad banks led down to the river and a field which flooded every year. The field was a quagmire well into early summer, when it dried out into a good three-acre stretch of fine grazing for the local cattle. This summer the swampy patches hatched a myriad frogs and toads, disturbing the night's rest with their croaking. During the night the Russian sentries would call out 'dobriy khleb, dobroe pivo', meaning 'good bread, good beer', to tempt and taunt their adversaries.

South of the town, beyond the bushes and fields sliced by the Swedish siege-works, ran one of the many ravines which scored the Poltava plateau. This long, forest-clad fissure cut steeply into the dry ground and branched out in many gullies. At its bottom ran a stream, with houses clustered here and there. The troops manning the trenches this Sunday, the Söderman-land and Kronoberg foot regiments, had their camp here. Their bivouacs flocked down into the ravine among the brushwood huts left by previous units.

Somewhat south of them camped the Zaporozhian Cossacks. During the siege they combined the role of manual labourers with that of fire-targets for the Russian marksmen. They suffered worse losses here than the Swedes. Their revolt had met with great reverses, and their intrepid fight for freedom from Russian despotism had now taken the form of ignominious hewing, digging and carrying. Toil in the trenches was dangerous and unrewarding. Zaporozhian morale had reached rock bottom and it was difficult to get them to obey orders.

North of the town, through the high ground above the river, ran another long, broad ravine in a north-south direction. It soon disappeared into the extensive Yakovetski forest with its gullies, streams and hidden tarns. Trees separated the Swedish positions round the fortress from the large Russian camp a few thousand metres further on. A good kilometre north-west of the town, on the other side of a swampy depression clothed with alders, rose extended high ground which merged with the green billows of the Yakovetski wood. Its slopes were covered with vineyards and cherry orchards. At the furthest southern point of this high ground was a nunnery, founded in 1650.

The Swedish command, the king and his staff, the Drabants, the field chancellery and royal household were located at this cloister. This Sunday the entire Swedish foot, except for the units engaged in the siege, were camped close by the heights, among the cherry trees and vines. One regiment after another lined up at their camp stations: rows of tall pike pyramids, muskets piled under special covers, tents for *cantinières*, fires and latrines – separate ones for officers and men of course. Because of the rather outlandish terrain with its hills and orchards, the camp was permeated by an air of mild disorder. In normal circumstances an almost geometric precision was striven for. The Guard had been there earlier, but the rest had only camped near the cloister for about five days. The soldiers slept in the open, tents serving no useful function in the sticky heat.

A good four kilometres west of the infantry's leafy camp, out on the undulating plain between the deserted villages of Ribtsi and Pushkaryovka, lay the cavalry. Except for three regiments of cavalry and two of dragoons at other sites, the entire Swedish horse were ranged in one long, carefully aligned row of square encampments, near an extensive network of wooded ravines. The camp's lines had been laid down by no less a person than Field Marshal Rehnsköld himself.

Most of the baggage-train, defended by two dragoon regiments, was located south of Pushkaryovka. The thousands of wagons and carts were partially protected by a large ravine deemed 'impassable'. A deep gorge scarred the landscape behind them. The baggage had probably been sited here to provide a rallying-point for the army in the event of a retreat. With the help of the many-branched system of ravines it would be possible to delay any Russian pursuit here while the baggage was driven south down the road to Kobelyaki and the Dnieper. The Swedish army, even when gathered round Poltava, avoided concentrating its entire force in one spot, as this quickly led to increased mortality. Sickness tended to erupt in the stench and excrement of giant camps and dispersing the troops reduced disease.

The effective fighting strength of the army was now about 24,300 men. This was the hard kernel. There was also a large number of non-combatants whose fortune and well-being depended entirely on the capricious shifts of war. Among them were about 2,250 sick and wounded. Then came about 300 non-combatant artillerymen and 1,100 military civilians and administrators. An indispensable but often forgotten group, without which the army could never function, were the multitude of grooms, labourers, draymen, stable-lads and boys attached to the baggage-train, who often shouldered the least honoured fatigues. They numbered about 4,000.

Another often forgotten group were the women and children. Among officers in particular it was common practice to take the entire household out on campaign: wife, children, a large staff with servants and sometimes even a complete set of furniture. Even private soldiers might be accompanied by families. Included in this itinerant town of canvas tenting were about 1,700 wives, children and servant girls. These were women like the two kitchen maids, Maria Bock and Maria Johansdotter, who saw that the king got fed. Their duties included preparing the game the court huntsman Christoffer Bengt brought in for the royal table. There were others, such as Maria Christine Sparre, aged 21 and born in Pomerania, wife of a trumpeter; or Gertrud Linsen, married to a lieutenant in Dücker's Regiment of Dragoons.

Brigitta Scherzenfeldt, born in June 1684 on Bäckaskog crown estate, near Kristianstad in Skåne, was another. Her father, a cavalry lieutenant, and mother had died when she was a child. Brigitta had been brought up by her relatives. Her schooling was unremarkable; she had received the usual instruction in religion and the customary female skills, or as the account of her life puts it: 'crafts appropriate to her sex and station'. In 1699, aged 15, she had married Mats Bernow, a standard-bearer in the Life Guard, with her family's approval. They had a son. Her husband was called to the army in Poland, however, and Brigitta followed him and settled in Riga. Then misfortune struck twice: the boy died and soon afterwards, in 1703, she heard that Mats had been killed at Thorn. Since her connections in Sweden were now all dead, Brigitta decided to stay on in Riga. After a couple of years she remarried another soldier, Jonas Lindström, a sergeant-major. Jonas served in Lewenhaupt's Courland corps and was ordered east. Brigitta had been in two minds what to do. Her weak links home to Sweden and her love for her husband had persuaded her to follow him through the dangers and hardships. In her 25th year she now stood next to her Jonas in a strange foreign country near a small, palisade-encircled town called Poltava.

Not many had wives with them on campaign, however. Since there were few unmarried women, there would have been considerable sexual deprivation in the army. Understandably, there is little touching this matter in the sources. It can be taken for granted there were prostitutes in the army: in any case, they had been a problem earlier. Some men turned to each other, in spite of homosexuality being a capital offence. We know that 'sodomitic sin' was practised, at least within parts of the officer corps. Bestiality, another capital offence, also occurred. This was punished by an absurdity called triple execution. An account of a man convicted of bestiality, and executed on campaign, relates that he 'was first hanged up,

then put on a pyre, and would have been beheaded: but the executioner
found nothing to strike at'.

The fact that officers and even rank and file soldiers took families into
the field shows that their view of war differed substantially from ours. Even
if war was much the same evil scourge then as now, there are certain
distinctions. For most of the officers, and even for many of the men, war
was a meal-ticket and a career. Nor was it unconditional and all-
demanding: to a certain extent they were able to take a detached view and
choose whether or not to be sucked in. For those who looked on war as a
living, it was a more or less normal state of affairs, and within its sorry
framework there was room for family life. This distancing attitude to war
was shared by ordinary people. Battles could be regarded simply as folk
entertainment. Large groups of civilians journeyed out to watch battles as
if they were gigantic theatrical performances. The practice persisted into
the 19th century.

Down in the river basin there were several Swedish field-forts, including
three bastions linked by long trenches and defences. They had been
constructed in mid-May to counter Russian attempts to fight their way
across the Vorskla. Both sides had clustered their troops round the critical
point and begun intensively digging and fortifying their positions. A series
of hard blows were exchanged. For a while the struggle seemed to be
turning into pure trench warfare, with both sides hacking out trenches on
opposite river banks. After about a month the Russians gave up the contest
and stopped trying to relieve the town in this way. They crossed the river
further north. Swedish troops went over to their vacated earthworks, razed
them and brought back this and that as booty: wooden shovels, vats of
spirits and the odd 'Bog-Pete' who had taken one drink too many and been
left behind in slumbrous stupor.

There were another two or three villages and a few scattered little houses
at the northern and western verges of the Yakovetski woods. Then the
empty face of the plain took over, its dry, sandy soil undulating gently in
even lines. It was mainly quite flat, broken here and there by low rises,
ridges or ravines. For Swedish soldiers, born in densely wooded seven-
league forests, these steppes running out to the far horizon and beyond
seemed very strange. Anders Pihlström, an ensign with the Dalecarlia
regiment, described the Ukrainian landscape in his journal, and noted how
easy it was to lose one's way on its 'large and level fields'.

The plain bordering the Vorskla at this point, however, was hardly a
ballroom floor. From the high point by the steep bluffs near the village of
Patlayovka, the terrain dipped slowly to the west and south. Shallow folds
and depressions interrupted its calm contours. The steppe did not afford a
clear view everywhere, a salient factor in the days to come. It was possible
to withdraw completely from sight by occupying a depression; even

modest ridges could obscure the view and limit a scout's field of vision. This tended to create blind spots and unpleasant surprises.

Not far north of the Yakovetski forest, right on the bluffs by the river, lay the Russian encampment, sited on the discernible ruins of a deserted village. It was very large and soundly fortified: a slightly rounded irregular rectangle containing most of the Russian foot and artillery: more than 30,000 men. Added to which were unknown numbers of baggage-people, civilians and the others always present. This mass of humanity, in an unholy chaos of tents, wagons, supplies, cannon and ammunition, was crowded into an area of little more than a square kilometre.

The camp had been laid out on the Friday. The fortifications were dug during the night. The front and sides were built up with ramparts behind trenches. The type of fortifications round the camp were called lunettes. This form of construction left the rear open, but had large triangular projections, like the sharp teeth of a carnivore. The baseline, known as the courtin, was interrupted at regular intervals, enabling a relatively rapid sortie from the fort. However, these earth causeways were also one of its weak points. The walls were mounted with cannon. In front of the ramparts were assault barricades in the form of a straggly hedge of *chevaux-de-frise*.

The camp was fortified on three sides only. The fourth side, facing east, consisted of steep sandy bluffs down to the river, almost 60 metres high. The Russians feared no attack here. A track wound down into the tree-clad vale, across the river and towards a few small earthworks on the eastern bank. From a well-founded respect for their enemy, the Russians had protected their rear and western flanks by siting the camp between the bluffs and the Yakovetski woods.

The site was simultaneously secure and highly vulnerable. If forced to retreat, there were only two ways out of the trap, and both were risky. The Russians could either go back the way they had come, north along the Vorskla, or else use the back-door route across it. To lead the whole army across the river down only one poor track would take more time than could be spared in a desperate situation. Retreating north would risk exposure to the constant threat of being thrown into the river basin. If the Swedes took up a position north of the camp the route would be cut off anyway. The camp was undeniably well-defended, but to achieve this security the Russians had squeezed themselves into a position which might prove disastrous. The question was whether the Swedes could exploit it.

The dry, steppe-like fields were covered with fine, loose earth. They were fairly level round the camp to the west and north, but sloped gradually. About one kilometre west of the camp was a large expanse of low-lying ground. Next to it was another large wooded area, the Budyschenski forest. This wood curved north-west, following the

Ivanchinski stream which trickled along in a shallow gully. At its base was a miry morass and a number of small dams. The water mirrored groves of ash and oak. Clusters of small mud cottages with straw roofs, surrounded by fences and cherry trees, followed the whole course of the stream. Many of these dwellings were now skeletal and sooty ruins.

Between the Yakovetski and Budyschenski woods was a clearing, between 1,200 and 1,500 metres broad, studded with bushes and a few groves of trees. A slight ridge ran along it. This passage between the woods was the only route open to the Swedes if they were to attack the Russian camp. There was no hope of manoeuvring large masses of troops through the woods.

The importance of the corridor was fully recognized by the Russian command, and on the Friday they took steps to block it. A line of six forts or redoubts was constructed straight across the gap between the woods. The redoubts were manned and equipped with cannon under command of a brigadier called Aigustov. The following day Tsar Peter reconnoitred the Swedish positions, and realizing that the defences could be improved, issued orders to build four more redoubts. These were to be constructed at right angles to the others, pointing in the direction of the Swedes. The whole system took on a T shape.

This was a minor stroke of genius. In an attack on the system the projecting line would cleave the Swedish battle-order like a breakwater. The redoubts would direct flank fire at troops advancing towards the rear chain in line. A frontal cannon-ball would go through four men. A perfect side hit could theoretically mow down 150. Flank artillery fire could have an appalling bowling-alley effect. If they fought their way through the whole system of redoubts and continued advancing straight ahead, the Swedes would come within range of vicious flank fire from the cannon-packed walls of the camp. If they tried a direct attack from the west, they would be flanked by the redoubts. To top it all the redoubts provided a commanding view of the anterior terrain, which would make one of those surprise attacks Charles XII rejoiced in extremely difficult to achieve. In either case, an attack through the system would cause the Swedes severe casualties, and substantially increase Russian chances of success.

Eight of the ten redoubts had now been completed, manned and prepared for battle. Work was continuing on the foremost two in the projecting line. The redoubts varied slightly in shape and size; most were square (one or two were triangular) and measured about 50 metres from side to side. They were built up with high parapets, and a trench running round them. The height from the bottom of the trench to the top of the parapet was about five metres. They were defended by the Belgorod, Natyaev and Nekludov foot regiments, 4,000 men, supported by 14 to 16 three-pounders and a number of heavier pieces. The Russians could

produce a steady stream of musket and cannon fire from all sides. The
musketeers and loaders would be in protected positions behind the
parapets and the ramparts would be difficult to storm. The forts were
surrounded by *chevaux-de-frise*.

The redoubts were about 160 metres apart, and between them could
open up annihilating cross-fire. The deeper the Swedes pushed on into the
system, the heavier and more accurate would be the fire directed at them.
Most of the Russian cavalry, 17 regiments of dragoons, 10,000 sabres
under General Menshikov, were posted immediately behind the rear chain
of forts. They were equipped with 13 two-pounder cannon. The only
approach open to the Swedes had been plugged by a substantial Russian
stopper.

The Russians worked hard to finish the last two redoubts. In the others
waiting soldiers scanned the terrain from behind the parapets. Sounds of
hewing and hammering from working men drifted across the warm fields
southwards in the summer breeze, down to the Swedish sentries, where
they too stood waiting.

# 6 · A Council of War

The mounting activity of the Russians during the Sunday morning was a cause of concern to the Swedes. The king was carried in his litter to one of the outposts which had been under attack, and ordered it to withdraw. General Lewenhaupt went out to another.

In many ways Lewenhaupt was a remarkable man. A very doughty soldier, competent, self-confident, deeply religious and intelligent. He was unusually well educated for a man of his profession (earlier he had been dubbed 'the Latin Colonel'), and proud of his learning. He had great physical courage. In battle he behaved with unflinching calm, riding wherever the bullets flew thickest. But he had a complex character. He took a dark view of life and his cast of mind was notably pessimistic. He was gauche in company and easily drawn into quarrels. His antennae for intrigues against himself, real or suspected, were hypersensitive, tending to tinge his way of thinking with paranoia. At worst, he was prone to imagine backbiters behind every tree-trunk. His face was as contradictory as his character. His features expressed both strength and weakness: large, slightly frightened eyes and heavy eyelids consorting with a long aristocratic nose and a small but determined mouth. He had been born 50 years earlier, in the midst of a blazing war, in the Swedish camp on Sjælland outside Copenhagen.

His father, a soldier with a great estate, and his mother, a second cousin to Charles X with the blue-blooded name of zu Hohenlohe-Neustein und Gleichen, had both died early. His subsequent education had been in the hands of some of the highest of the Swedish upper aristocracy, including Magnus Gabriel de la Gardie and Karl Gustaf Wrangel, Lord of Skokloster. He had studied at the universities of Lund and Uppsala, and Rostock, where he had presented a thesis.

He had intended to pursue a career in the diplomatic service. On returning from studies in Germany he discovered the prospects to be so unrewarding that he had to think again. Since a career with the quill was now closed to young Adam Ludvig there only remained that of the sword. The new order in Charles XI's army, where officers had to start at the bottom and work their way up, held little appeal for him. As was quite usual, he entered military service abroad. First he fought against the Turks in Hungary, then served nearly nine years under the Dutch flag in Flanders. After the outbreak of the northern war in 1700 he was appointed head of one of the newly raised Tremänning regiments. Lewenhaupt soon showed his capabilities in the dour battles in the Baltic. He was the only Swedish commander to be repeatedly victorious over the steadily improving and increasing Russian armies there. In 1705 he was appointed Governor of Riga with command of Swedish troops in Livonia, Courland and Samogitia. It was a rapid career, incontrovertibly based on personal ability.

He was imbued with the paternalism of the age, often showing genuine concern for his officers and men, and appreciated by them in return. He liked to speak of his affection for his poor soldiers. As a commander he was cautious, a trait often, if not always, a virtue. At times his caution verged on something closely resembling lethargy.

General Lewenhaupt completed his short round, rode back to the camp and his tent and lay down to sleep. He suffered from diarrhoea and had no appetite.

At noon the king held a council of war. To it he summoned his minister Count Carl Piper, Field Marshal Rehnsköld, and the commanding officer of the Dalecarlia regiment, Colonel von Siegroth. The position of the Swedish army was becoming untenable. The besiegers of Poltava had virtually become the besieged.

Russian pressure had steadily increased. Cut off from the outside world, the army was short of almost everything. The munitions situation was decidedly poor. There was sufficient cannon shot, but mortar and howitzer supplies were very inadequate. The greatest dearth however was of ball and powder for hand-guns, and some of what little musket-powder remained was spoiled and ineffectual. The situation was so bad that talk of the lack of powder had been forbidden. In vain attempts to remedy the dwindling stock of lead shot many officers melted down their pewter services. Ball was also cast in iron. Down by the town Swedes ran about gathering up ball fired from Russian cannon. More skirmishing would slowly but surely use up what meagre supplies remained. The army would face a well-equipped and well-supported enemy in a greatly weakened, not to say destitute, condition.

The region round Poltava was becoming more and more depleted of necessities. Foraging was hampered by the circling swarms of Russian horse. Food began to run short. The oppressive heat quickly caused what stores there were to rot, made worse by the army's lack of salt: bad gunpowder was used in its stead. The prices of those foodstuffs still obtainable rose further: a jug of spirits cost eight daler, a small piece of meat, four daler. The grey face of famine began to show in the ranks. Some units had not eaten bread for days; it was getting difficult to find acceptable drinking-water; even clothing was a matter for concern. The Swedish troops at Poltava were no longer jaunty warriors in spotless, smart blue uniforms, but weary men in worn and ragged clothing.

Fodder for the horses was another problem; by now they were being kept alive mainly on leaves. The lack of water and fodder meant that mass extinction threatened the entire stock of horseflesh, and the army could never function without horses. The problem of subsistence was even worse now that the troops were all collected together in a fairly small area. An increasing mass of men and animals would drain the ever-dwindling resources of the region. This intense concentration could only be very temporary.

The army's sagging morale was just as serious. By now many men had nine years' exhausting campaign experience. At their departure from Saxony at the end of 1707 a mounting sense of hopelessness had begun to take hold. As time went on and the army ranged ever farther east on the hunt for the elusive enemy, it had been ravaged by sickness, famine, a stubborn guerrilla war, appalling weather and doubt. The decisive moment, which was to lead to the peace increasing numbers longed for, never came. The troops cursed the evanescent foe. Letters home were testimony to the never-ending stream of adversity, and a burgeoning sense of mistrust. Carl Magnus Posse, colonel of the Guards, wrote home to his brother at the beginning of April 1708 that 'the wish of all is that our Lord should deliver the perfidious enemy into our hands, and our common hope is this, that a good peace should follow; may God hear us for the sake of Christ's suffering and death, for we begin to weary of these daily exertions, which multiply rather than diminish'. A dreadful winter had further weakened the army; continual new hardships combined with dwindling prospects of victory had meant that Swedish morale was already beginning to falter in the spring.

The martial spirit of their allies, the Zaporozhian Cossacks, had also waned. An atmosphere of outright mutiny held sway among them. Mazeppa had been obliged to ride out to the lines and deliver rousing speeches to the dejected men.

In the last six months a number of inauspicious portents and omens had been noted. Perhaps they added to the army's wilting morale; but were just as probably symptoms of it. At the end of 1708 the army had camped round the town of Romni, and rumours begun to circulate. It was whispered that it had been predicted that the king would not be defeated until he had taken Rome. The resemblance of Rome to Romni suggested the prediction was about to be fulfilled, and Charles would shortly be struck down. On earlier occasions omens favourable to the Swedes had been eagerly noted when battles were imminent: at Klissov in 1702, for instance, or Fraustadt in 1706.

Divination was well rooted in the army. A highly respectable individual like the Drabant chaplain, Jöran Nordberg, who later wrote a biography of the king, claimed a premonition of the battle of Maltitze the previous year. He had dreamt both date and outcome of the battle. Heavenly signs like parhelia, eclipses and comets were observed with awe. As recently as the 1680s comets, in particular, had been revered as auguries of the day of judgement. Their reputation was waning however: belief in comets as portents was slowly being dismantled by men of science with their new mechanistic view of the world. But superstition still flourished widely in the Sweden of this era; witch-burning had only just ceased and much of an earlier world of marvels lingered on. Faith in the supernatural was general through all classes of society. The king himself was strongly inclined to believe in it. Charles was afraid of the dark, and liked to sleep in the company of his men, his head resting on a soldier's knee. Nevertheless, efforts were made to suppress the most extreme varieties of superstition, and magic incantations and 'weapon-blunting' were strictly forbidden.

Difficult as it is to gauge an army's will to fight, it is easy to imagine how the pressures of repeated adversity, severe losses, a sense of increasing debility and growing doubts about the future sapped the spirit of officers and men. With the desperate lack of supplies, and the exhaustion caused by constant skirmishing, the army was quite simply run into the ground. Complaints were universal. Rumours that reinforcements were on their way were circulated among the soldiers to help prop up sagging morale. But desertions increased. Siegroth, the commanding officer of the Dalecarlians, told the king at the conference that he could no longer rely on his men.

The army's strategic position was bleak. The much-diminished force was bottled up in a cul-de-sac, squeezed into an area less than 50 kilometres wide between the Dnieper and its tributaries the Psel and the Vorskla. Since the bulk of the Russian army had crossed the Vorskla and dug itself in, there had been a week of feinting and manoeuvring. The Swedish command had tried without success to lure the Russians into open battle; they wanted to avoid having to attack an enemy ensconced behind strong defences. False rumours of approaching reinforcements and temporary weaknesses had been communicated to the tsar, via defectors, in order to tempt the Russians to leave their fortified lines and fight in the open. The feints had failed and the Russians stubbornly refused to accept battle on Swedish terms. Their counter-strategy was well founded. They had steadily intensified the pressures on the threadbare army.

The Swedish command had in fact worked hard to produce fresh reinforcements. Krassow's corps and the king of Poland's army were expected to march east. The Swedish minister in Poland, Wachslager, had been ordered to expedite their movement into Russia. The governor in

Wismar, Ridderhielm, had been instructed to enter Poland with his four regiments, join the garrisons in Posen and Elbing, and await further orders in Volhynia. If Turkey, and her satellite the Crimea, could be drawn into the war a very powerful force would be added. Letters had been sent to the Crimean khan and the sultan in Constantinople, via the Turkish town of Bender, at the end of March. The Swedish command entertained great hopes that these reinforcements would materialize. State Secretary Hermelin commented that 'we are now right on the route the Tartars will be taking for Moscow. They will accompany us.'

All these hopes had been dust and ashes for the last five days. On 22 June the whole Swedish army was drawn up in expectation of a Russian attack, which never came. Colonel Sandul Koltza returned from his mission to Bender the same day. With him was Secretary Otto Wilhelm Klinckowström, who came from Krassow, the commander of the Swedish army in Poland. Envoys from the Tartar khan arrived at the same time. All of these people brought bitterly disappointing news.

Krassow's corps, and the troops of the Polish king, were immobilized behind the river San at Yaroslavice in west Poland. Between them and Poltava the way was blocked at Lemberg by the Russian corps of General Goltz, allied with the Polish-Lithuanian army of Hetman Sienavski. The road from Lemberg to Poltava (the route Krassow would have to take) went via the Russian stronghold of Kiev at the passage over the Dnieper. The distance from Yaroslavice to the Swedish army was over 1,000 kilometres. In other words, any reinforcements from Krassow and King Stanislaus were out of the question.

Nor would there be any help forthcoming from either Turk or Tartar. True, the new Tartar khan, Devlet Gerai, was panting to join the fray and had equipped himself with substantial armaments; but to engage Russia in open warfare he needed approval from Constantinople. The sultan had been persuaded by advisers with well-oiled tongues, and under pressure from the Russian fleet, to adopt a temporizing, pacific stance. The Turks therefore held the war-thirsty khan in check and denied him permission to campaign. The message was that any immediate aid from that quarter was not to be counted on.

Ridderhielm and his forces in Wismar did not receive their marching orders until the middle of March. The distance between Wismar and Poltava was approximately 1,500 kilometres. No reinforcements could be expected from that quarter.

Realization that no relief was to be had was a crucial factor in the Swedish command's decision. The army would have to rely on its own resources. Further passive waiting and delay were pointless. The supply situation would soon deteriorate even more. The Cossacks were Greek Orthodox and subject to four periods of fasting during the year. They were now in the second period, somewhat alleviating the army's victualling problems. On the following day, Monday 28 June, this fast came to an end. Even if the effect were minor it implied yet another small step towards an almost total collapse in the army's provisioning. It was quite simply impossible for the Swedes to remain where they were. Rehnsköld's opinion was that they could not stay more than one or two days longer. Something had to be done.

A conventional offensive was out of the question. A strike for Moscow was impossible, mainly because of the lack of ammunition. Between them, the infantry and artillery had enough ball and powder for one major battle. After the battle they would be left with about 40,000 charges for hand-guns: three to four charges per soldier. The normal ration was 40 rounds. One option for the army would be for it to retrace its steps back to Poland. But retreat would be difficult with the Russian army intact at such close quarters. To leave the Russians 'undefeated at our back' would mean the Swedes would not be able to cross the Dnieper at Kiev. They would have to go farther south, which in turn would mean a march through vast desert wastes. The eventual likelihood was mass starvation, ending in a massacre. The only way out of this impasse was to hand the tsar's army a beating.

It is tempting to speculate that one very irrational factor influenced the king when he weighed up the alternatives. The monarch, still aged only 27, no doubt felt an unbearable burden of strain in these dark hours. Perhaps he could already feel the wing-beats of defeat and wished himself away from this enormous responsibility. But there was only one means of escape for a man of his commitment: death. Several voices in the army asserted that in the battle the king sought out the places of utmost danger and recklessly exposed himself to Russian bullets, consciously seeking death. There are indications that in certain dark moments he extended this death-wish to include the army. When told the army could no longer be relied on, he let slip a very bizarre remark. He specifically said that in that case 'neither he nor anyone else would return alive'. Could these feelings have brought him to throw caution to the winds and risk everything on one single card? Perhaps there was a vision of Ragnarök, the last battle of Nordic myth, inside the absolute monarch's head: the whole army was to be dragged down in his own destruction.

The decision was unequivocal: attack the enemy, sink or swim. If it was the bad news arriving on 22 June which forced this decision, why the delay until the 27th? Firstly, the Swedish command had repeatedly striven to bring about a battle on their own terms. Secondly, during these five days the king had suffered from a severe fever following in-flammation of his wound. At one point he seemed on the verge of death. Rehnsköld, in command during the king's illness, would not assume responsibility while Charles was languishing. The final decision was for the king to take; and today he had made a remarkable recovery.

Perhaps another factor prompted the decision. The Swedes had been able to watch the Russians continuing to dig themselves in. At least one reconnaissance patrol had been out on the Saturday evening, and gained some insight into the Russian field-works. Reports stated that yet more redoubts were being constructed. Further delay would merely mean that the position of the Russian army would become even more difficult to master. And time was on the side of the tsar.

It was now only a matter of planning the attack. Insofar as it can be reconstructed, the plan consisted of two moves: a surprise burst through the Russian redoubts, followed by an assault on the fortified camp. The first stage would be executed in the half-light of dawn. The army was simply to rush through the redoubts before their drowsy occupants had time to act. The cavalry and infantry would combine. The cavalry would first knock out the stopper of enemy horse behind the rear line of forts, then move to cut off the Russian army's only real path of retreat, north along the river. At the same time, having negotiated the redoubts, the Swedish foot would advance to attack the camp.

King Stanislaus' envoy summarized the plan as follows: 'the field marshal was to attack with the horse on the flank, the foot were to attack to the front'. The infantry would be the hammer, while the cavalry served as the anvil fixing the Russians and obstructing their retreat. If this plan succeeded, it would result in devastating annihilation. The Russian position had one clear defect: its lack of an escape route. An onslaught which followed the course sketched out would threaten to annihilate the tsar's army. Backed up against the river, with only one inadequate crossing, it would be trapped.

But there were many weaknesses in the plan. The shock advance through the redoubts was fraught with uncertainty. Much could go wrong while stealthily deploying into the initial position under cover of night. This tricky breakthrough was a risk that had to be taken.

It was also crucial for the men to summon up the momentum needed to storm the camp and hurl back their opponents. Their numerical inferiority was known, but Charles XII and Rehnsköld had the kind of battle experience against Russians which led them to believe that the odds were not hopeless. Nine years before, at Narva, they had faced a nearly identical tactical situation: a Swedish army, greatly inferior in numbers, had attacked a well fortified Russian army, and totally overwhelmed it. Since then the Russians had received repeated bloody noses (on those occasions when it had pleased them to make a stand on an open field). The Swedish command did not have a high opinion of Russian fighting skills. No doubt they thought that what had worked at Narva would work again.

However, the Russian army had progressed considerably since 1700. The Swedes underestimated their adversary: the plan presupposed a sluggish opponent who would sit still and blink while the Swedes with elegant manoeuvres wound a rope round his neck.

A third weakness was that if anything, God forbid, were to go wrong, then the Swedish troops, when past the redoubts, would be faced with a difficult retreat from the field. The redoubts would block the only route south. They would have to withdraw through the rugged wooded terrain round the village of Maly Budyschi. The character of the battlefield was such that it hampered the side obliged to retreat, regardless of nationality.

The plan was flawed and risky. But *if* the Russians let themselves be caught napping, *if* the shock burst through the redoubts succeeded, and *if* the storm assault on the camp went the distance, Tsar Peter would suffer a colossal reverse. A lot of ifs.

During the day the same taut sense of anticipation reigned within both armies. Russian troops and workmen laboured intensively to complete the chain of redoubts. Fresh fortifications rose up slowly from the mottled sand and bush-clad soil. Bands of Cossack horsemen were despatched south time and again to harass the Swedish camps and outposts. The Russian generals had been out earlier in the morning and had the Swedish dispositions under their collective eye. They had great respect for their enemy, to which their slow and cautious moves to date were eloquent witness. The many fortifications were self-protection against the enterprise of a dangerous foe. However, in the upper echelons of the Russian army the inclination was to doubt that the Swede would risk an attack in this situation.

General Menshikov wrote a reassuring letter home to his wife. He was optimistic: 'Yesterday the camp removed here, and although its site lies nearer the enemy, it appears well chosen. Our troops have built defences round it, and the belief is that our adversary will soon be forced to withdraw; whereupon we hope with God's help to make connection with Poltava. All else, God be thanked, is well, and there is no danger, for the army is wholly gathered here.'

In the afternoon the tsar mustered the Russian foot for separation into divisions. The chain of command was rehearsed. Peter Alexeivich rode about with his hat in his hand, conversing with senior officers and staff. With the latest move of the camp and the ever-intensifying clawing round the Swedish army the thumbscrews had been given another turn. The pain threshold had been reached. The Russians awaited the reaction with curiosity. Would the Swedes now back down and slink off towards the Dnieper and out of the Ukraine?

Five kilometres farther south, preparations for attack had already been set in motion.

# 7 · *Sunday Evening*

The council of war was over by about four o'clock. Colonel Axel Gyllenkrok, the army's quartermaster-general, was called to the cloister. Rehnsköld met him at the entrance and conducted him into the king's chamber, where the monarch lay in bed. The field marshal told Gyllenkrok of the decision to attack and instructed him to divide the infantry into four columns of march. Then he was given the *ordre de bataille*. Gyllenkrok remained standing quietly for a moment by the king's bed. The abrasive field marshal impatiently growled a query as to whether Gyllenkrok knew how to carry out this task, but the king interrupted him as he spoke, with a lightly irritated: 'Yes, yes, Rehnsköld, he knows well enough.' It was Rehnsköld, not the litter-borne king, who was to carry the highest command in the battle. A heavy responsibility rested on his shoulders. He reacted with sullen and touchy ill humour.

Carl Gustaf Rehnsköld was a man of pale, bloodless, commanding appearance: pointed nose, small mouth and a cold look. A skilful and experienced soldier, ruthless and zealously loyal to king and crown, he was stiff, forceful and choleric in nature. His conduct was marked by a surly arrogance. He was 57, born in Stralsund in Swedish Pomerania, where his father had been justice of the supreme court. After studies at Greifswald and Lund he had quickly taken to the career of the sword. In the Scanian war of the 1670s he had shown leadership qualities and fearless conduct in battle. Promotion had been rapid: he became a lieutenant-colonel at the age of only 26.

He was an extremely able army commander. Perhaps his greatest success had been the triumph at Fraustadt in the winter of 1706, where a corps under his command had practically exterminated a Russo-Saxon army. At this battle Rehnsköld clearly demonstrated his skill as a battle commander. He had also shown a chilling ruthlessness. After the battle he had ordered the execution of all Russian prisoners. In the battle's last stages those soldiers still standing had thrown down their weapons, bared their heads and cried for quarter. The Saxons had been spared, but the Russians were shown no mercy.

Rehnsköld drew a circle of troops round the captured Russians. A witness describes how approximately 500 prisoners were 'then quickly shot and cut down dead within this ring without mercy, so they fell over each other like slaughtered sheep'. The corpses were piled three bodies high, cut to ribbons by Swedish bayonets. A number had tried to escape this fate by turning their coats inside out to expose the red lining, hoping to pass for Saxons. The disguise had been penetrated. Another witness relates that 'once General Rehnsköld discovered they were Russians, he ordered them to the front and commanded they be shot in the head, which was a rather pitiful spectacle'.

It was an uncommonly repellent episode. Although both sides time and again had shown themselves capable, with no notable pangs of conscience, of slaughtering defenceless prisoners, sick and wounded, the massacre at Fraustadt is probably without contemporary parallel, in scale and cold deliberation. It is true the Swedes felt an intense antipathy for the Russians, which had deep historical roots by this time. But Rehnsköld's bestial order, in all probability, was not issued in passion, but coldly calculated. A number of tiresome prisoners were eliminated. Unlike the Saxons, they had no value as re-enlisted recruits to the Swedish army. He no doubt also thought he was making an example of them, as a warning and terror to others.

Now during these June days he was probably suffering fairly badly from the consequences of a wound received at the disastrous assault on Veprik in January, which would not have improved his already strained nerves.

Once Gyllenkrok had sensed the field marshal's irritation, he asked if the infantry were to march off by the right or left. 'By the left,' replied Rehnsköld. He then turned to Charles, lying in his bed, and said he now intended to organize the cavalry's march. He asked the king if he had any further orders. Receiving a negative response, he left, closely followed by Gyllenkrok. Gyllenkrok sat himself down in an adjacent room belonging to one of the lackeys and began to patch together the divisional columns.

Now, nearing evening meal-time, most of the high command were gathered outside the cloister. Lewenhaupt had left his canopy and made his way there. When Rehnsköld emerged, he called the general over and invited him to take a seat on a bench below the window of the royal chamber. The two commanders were both proud and hot-tempered; they were both capable of making enemies without really trying, and it is not surprising that by now they had disagreed sharply on many occasions. The sensitive general and the overbearing field marshal did not make a happy team, and an acute antipathy had festered between them for months.

Nothing of this showed at the moment. Both men made an effort, and exchanged courtesies. Rehnsköld moved rapidly to the matter at hand. The decision had been taken to attack. Lewenhaupt was to lead the combined infantry. He was given his orders and a copy of the order of battle. After dark, the foot-soldiers were to stand to, in four columns.

Lewenhaupt knew it would be difficult to organize the men in the dark, especially in the rugged local terrain. He asked Rehnsköld if he might deploy the regiments immediately, to order them once and for all in their columns. The request was dismissed. It was still full daylight. If the surprise attack was to succeed, the Russians were to be given no opportunity of seeing what was afoot. They parted.

Gyllenkrok finished dividing the infantry into columns. He went back to the king and gave him the papers. 'The field marshal thought ye were unable to divide up the columns,' said Charles with a smile as he received them. After a quick check he told Gyllenkrok to distribute them to the generals. When the quartermaster-general came out of the cloister Rehnsköld had already ridden off. Lewenhaupt was still on the bench below the window. With him were the infantry major-generals. Gyllenkrok handed the divisions over to him and asked him to go in to the king for further orders. When Lewenhaupt came out, after the king's personal briefing, he went with the major-generals to the royal mess-tent. There, among the shadows, they sat down to copy out the planned divisional organization.

Rehnsköld rode over the level plain to the lines of cavalry, a good five kilometres west of the town. On arrival he sought out the commanders and gave them instructions. Seven regiments were to protect the baggage-train; all the remaining horse, deployed in six columns, were to be used in the attack. As dusk approached they were to saddle up and stand ready for the command to march in column over the fields towards the Russians and their fortifications. All baggage was to be transported, in silence and good order, a few kilometres south to a point near the village of Pushkaryovka.

After issuing these orders Rehnsköld rode back in the evening sunlight to the cloister. The commander of the cavalry right wing, Major-General Carl Gustaf Creutz, conscious of the dense darkness of the Ukrainian night, made preparations for the march. Taking a captain with him, he rode out to reconnoitre and pin-point a few landmarks to follow. The commanding officers of each regiment were given copies of the divisional column plans.

At headquarters, Rehnsköld dined with the senior officers in the king's mess-tent. Charles ate his meal alone. The starter-button had been pressed. The war machine was beginning to shake and shudder. The magic word that the king had decided to advance on the Russians rapidly spread down the echelons of the military hierarchy: from commanders on the wings, and regimental colonels, on to battalion commanders and then, via company commanders, to junior officers and finally to privates, baggage-handlers, servants and all the civilians.

Round the encampments, under canvas, under the open heavens and in the chaos of the baggage-train there was feverish activity. All manpower useless in battle was winnowed out. When dawn broke, all sick, wounded, crippled, horseless troopers, baggage attendants, civilians, camp-followers and almost all artillery were to move off to Pushkaryovka. Captain Henrik Spåre, 45, from the parish of Nådendal, north-west of Åbo, sent his young son Henrik Johan with them. In his journal he commented on the farewell with a curt: 'God be his help.' It would be a long time before he saw the boy again. At the assembly-point the wagons would be formed into a defensive fort. About 3,000 Zaporozhians were detached to protect it, as well as the cavalry and artillery.

Among the many sick and wounded gathered for transportation was an ensign of 17, Gustaf Abraham Piper. He had joined the army the previous year, in time for the invasion of Russia. From the outset he had been subject to bouts of sickness, not helped by living on nothing but dry rusks, turnips, lingonberries and aquavit for long periods. Towards the new year he became so ill he had to be conveyed by wagon. On the night of December 23 the wagon jammed among the abandoned carts, entangled horses and corpses outside Gadyach. It was bitterly cold. His driver froze to death. The boy sat wrapped in cotton covers, his greatcoat over his head.

After a time he was joined by his colonel's valet, but the man went away again, failing to close the flap behind him. The icy blast whistled through the wagon. Piper sat in it until Christmas Eve, when his own servant finally arrived, and helped him to the town and the regimental sick-bay. Before long, blackened flesh began to fall from his frost-bitten feet. The toes were lopped off with tongs. He escaped major amputation, at great cost in pain: for a long time the bones had to be cut and nipped away from his heels. His crippled state had then obliged him to travel with the army like a piece of luggage. Gustaf Abraham bedded down in his wagon. With the others attached to the baggage-train he could only await developments and tensely sharpen his ears for the detonation when it came.

The watchword was passed round. In battle it could be hard to tell friend from foe. Uniforms varied greatly within the same army and visibility was often poor. It was, as usual: 'With God's help'. Aides were sent to small outposts, ordering them to withdraw and report at once to their regiments. One outpost was located at Bolanovka, a wood-girt village on the Vorskla twelve kilometres south of Poltava, where Carl Roland, a 24-year-old subaltern from Stockholm, commanded a troop of 30 dragoons from Hielm's regiment. Their task was to forage for their regiment, and hold the marauding Cossack bands in check. The village was sited at one of the better fords across the Vorskla, and by this time the troop had been in a number of minor battles.

Captain Nils Bonde, a young aide-de-camp – an extremely dangerous role in battle – rode to Bolanovka to recall Roland and his men. The order came at an unfortunate moment. Roland had not bothered to bring his hand-horses, and had no time to fetch them. All officers took hand-horses or spare mounts into battle with them, supervised by their servants. Carl Roland would have no reserve horse in the action, and the lack of one almost cost him his life.

The king finished his meal, and a sermon followed. Lying on a camp bed and surrounded by numerous attendants, he then had himself carried out of his chamber. The litter was conveyed around so he could inspect the preparations for deployment. After a while he halted on a meadow below the cloister, near the Guard's camp. The king spoke first with one, then another. His wounded foot was seen to by a group of surgeons detailed to attend it during the battle. Foremost among them was Melchior Neumann, a physician who had treated the king when he accidentally broke his leg at Cracow in 1702. Another was Jacob Schultzen. While having it bandaged, Charles rested his foot on the knee of Johan Hultman, his steward. Johan was a long-serving retainer who entertained the monarch with sagas and stories. This evening he had been entrusted with his master's essential medical dressings.

At eight o'clock a detachment of guardsmen joined the king's retinue. It consisted of 24 picked men, including a soldier named Nils Frisk, who had carried a royal litter earlier, when the king broke his leg. Frisk had marched under the white banners of the Life Guard since the beginning of the war and had received his fair share of the aches and wounds bestowed on tested veterans. He still suffered the effects of an ugly injury in the left thigh, sustained at the crossing of the Dvina in 1701. At Holowczyn in 1708 a Russian musket-ball had passed through his right hand. Musket calibre was large at this time, approaching 20 millimetres. His third and little fingers were paralysed.

Nils Frisk and his 23 comrades, with 15 more men from the Life Drabants commanded by Lieutenant Johan Hierta, were to be Charles's personal bodyguard. The Life Guardsmen's plain blue coats, with yellow facings and linings, contrasted vividly with the glittering figures of the Drabants, in their pale blue and gold. Their task was to act as a human shield round the king. In the infantry, grenadiers were usually deputed to march in front of, or alongside, their commander. Here, the Guardsmen and Drabants were to receive with their own bodies musket-balls intended for their supreme commander.

Clearly no great reliance was placed on stories that the king was invulnerable to shot. (Tales circulated of him having been rendered impervious to gunfire by a witch during his youth.) The assignment given to Frisk and his comrades was mortally dangerous: they were to be crippled and killed in his place. The king was an absolute monarch, accorded the greatest power on earth by the heavenly Father Himself. His safety and well-being, in the eyes of the generals and doubtless in the eyes of many of the soldiers, was of infinitely greater importance than the lives of a few privates. They were expendable.

The king would be carried into battle on a white horse-litter, built by carpenters of Mora company in the Dalecarlia regiment. Slung between two horses in tandem harness, the camp bed with its silk mattresses, absolute monarch and all could be lifted into it. Eight men marched on each side. The leading horse would be guided by Nils Frisk himself.

Then the waiting. The grey light thickened across the landscape. Count Piper joined the company. With Rehnsköld, he rested on the ground. Most of the general staff and senior officers were grouped round the litter. The men sat wrapped in their cloaks or tried to snatch some sleep. Their horses stood saddled and ready. As the shadows turned to dusk, and dusk to darkness, men waited in the woods and on surrounding fields, biding the signal to break camp.

The only noise heard now was the sound of desultory shooting to the north. The Vallack regiment, light cavalry under Colonel Sandul Koltza numbering about 1,000 blades, advanced along the ridge running parallel with the Vorskla, towards the village of Yakovtsi, south of the fortified camp. A major body of Russian cavalry and foot was located there. Koltza's attack was to divert Russian attention from the army's movements. Otherwise the darkness of the summer night, the waiting and the silence reigned supreme.

The sleepers were woken at eleven. A shout broke the silence: 'Up, up, time to march.' Aides went to the infantry and cavalry camps with orders to stand to. Lewenhaupt was woken by the shouts. Calling for his servants, he told them to run ahead to prepare his horses. The general's horses and men were 400 metres from his sleeping quarters. When he arrived he mounted and rode back to contact Rehnsköld.

Predictably he failed to find him. The infantry's deployment from their bivouacs quickly became disorganized. Every regiment had its appointed place in one of the four columns, but in the darkness a number of them ended up in confusion. Lewenhaupt halted the deployment soon after it began, and carefully re-started the column formation. It was essential to do this, for the *ordre de bataille* followed from the initial division into columns. To have to reorganize the battle-order when speed was wholly of the essence would be highly undesirable.

Rehnsköld materialized out of the darkness. Intensely irate at what he took as unwarranted delay, he went up to Lewenhaupt and roared angrily: 'Where the Devil have ye got to?' adding, 'Is no one to tell ye, d'ye not see all is confusion?' Lewenhaupt made excuses, blamed the darkness and the camp's disorder, and pointed out, besides, he had spent the whole evening next to the king's litter. Rehnsköld ignored this, asking what regiment was next to follow in the column. The general said he did not know, he had just arrived and would enquire.

If possible, this answer infuriated the choleric field marshal even more. He exploded into a torrent of recriminations: 'Yes, that's the way y'are, ye care for nothing. I have no help or gain from ye, never did I think ye'd be like this, I'd imagined far otherwise of ye, but I see it's all for nothing.' Lewenhaupt accepted the tirades, defended himself lamely and ventured to say the accusations were unjustified. He promised to do what was needed, if Rehnsköld would say what he wanted done and how. Cutting him off with an abrupt: 'I'll do it myself then', Rehnsköld left Lewenhaupt to sulk in his wake.

In spite of his excuses, Lewenhaupt's preparations had clearly been inadequate. Much of the delay has to be blamed on his excessively phlegmatic approach. Before the departure he had frittered hours away in supine passivity, not even getting his horses ready. After a while the regimental officers set the matter to rights. The march was ready to start. The baggage wagons and camp-followers were either already at Pushkaryovka or well on their way. A few small groups remained in the area round the cloister.

Although much valuable time had been lost, there was a pause for prayer. This was central to the vitally important psychological preparations before a battle. Those who had not recently taken communion were usually ordered to do so. There was a special prayer to be invoked 'when the field of battle or other dangerous occasions are at hand' as the Articles of War put it. 'Give all those, who with me are about to do battle against our enemies, fresh spirit, fortune and victory, so that our foes may see that Thou, God, art with us and fighteth for those who put their trust in Thee.' Just before the battle, hymn 96, verse 6, was always sung:

> In God resides our hope and trust
> Who heaven and earth created.
> Our hearts He strengthens in our breast,
> Else were our cause defeated.
> Firm is the ground we build upon,
> Secure and safe we stand hereon.
> Who then can overcome us?

The need to invoke spirit and courage, and to allay fear, was without doubt common to all in these dark hours. To be a veteran was little advantage. Great battles were fairly rare. The average warrior experienced perhaps three or four such engagements during his entire life. There could well be years between them, with little opportunity for developing well-tried battlefield routines. These short moments of prayer also re-affirmed the belief that war and battles were God's will, that His was the final decision who was to be victorious and who was to die. It was important to make the soldiers accept what was happening, so that their natural impulse to run away did not get the upper hand.

By one o'clock the prayers were ended. The infantry were again set in motion. Company closed with company. Silent drummers and pipers marched in the van, followed by a captain heading the first section of musketeers, about 50 men. Then two groups of pikemen, either side of an ensign bearing the company banner, followed by two more groups of musketeers, led by a lieutenant. This was the pattern for the full 70 companies of foot, 18 battalions, formed into four silent columns.

The first column, commanded by Major-General Axel Sparre, consisted of the two battalions of the Västmanland regiment, 1,100 men; the Närke-Värmland regiment, also two battalions, totalling 1,200 men; then followed the gravely depleted Jönköping regiment, whose sole battalion numbered a mere 300 in the ranks.

The second column, Major-General Berndt Otto Stackelberg at its head, comprised two weak battalions of the Västerbotten regiment, about 600 men; a week Östgöta regiment, 380 men in one battalion; the Uppland regiment's two battalions, 690 men.

Hard on their heels came Major-General Carl Gustaf Roos and his third column; the van taken by the two battalions of Dalecarlians, numbering 1,100 men; followed by two battalions of Life Guards.

In the fourth and last column, led by Major-General Anders Lagercrona, came two more battalions of Life Guards. In all, the Life Guard totalled 1,800 men. In the midst of the second two battalions came the king, in his white horse-litter, surrounded by his bodyguard and followed by his retinue. Last went the Kalmar and Skaraborg regiments, each consisting of one battalion numbering about 500 men. A total of roughly 8,200 soldiers marched off into the night.

Since sunset the Swedish cavalry regiments had been standing to with saddled horses. Jakob Duwall and Lorentz Creutz, the two aides sent to order them to move off, took about half an hour to ride the five kilometres over the plain. At midnight the order to mount flew out to the troopers. Everything went smoothly and silently.

There were 14 regiments of cavalry, plus the corps of Life Drabants. Eight were 'pure' cavalry: the Mounted Life regiment, the Åbo, Småland and Nyland regiments, the Östgöta, North and South Skåne cavalry, and the Uppland Tremänning of horse. The other six were dragoons: the Skåne and Life Dragoon regiments, and Hielm's, Taube's, Dücker's, Gyllenstierna's Dragoons. The 109 squadrons numbered a total complement of around 7,800 men, organized in six columns. As the march began some men noted with surprise that no prayers were held, something never before omitted. The columns rode away without sound of trumpet or drum. Grey shapes, black-framed silhouettes faded into the black night.

# THE BATTLE

I shall thunder so heaven and earth shake like aspen leaves
I shall thunder with power. The mortal hearts of men
they will tremble and gasp at it; stumble in stupor.
I am the one who mocks the world's pomp and honour.
What are the vain powers, imagined states and riches in the world
of those other poor gods, compared with my might?

GEORG STIERNHIELM, *Speech of Mars, the God of War*
from *Birth of Peace* (1649)

# 8 · 'Let Us Go Forward'

In one of the Life regiment's tents, the commanding officer's secretary lay sound asleep. Abraham Cederholm, 29, had completely missed the cavalry's departure. His elder brother Hans, a cornet in the same regiment, had been lying beside him. The departure had been so swift however that Hans never found time to speak to his sleeping brother, and so silent that Abraham had not woken. The Cederholm brothers came from a bourgeois family: their father had been a Stockholm merchant. They had been orphaned early, but Abraham had been given a good upbringing and received an education in bookkeeping and clerical duties. In 1697 he became an assistant clerk at the audit office, but soon followed his brother into army service. In 1704 he was appointed secretary to Carl Gustaf Creutz, the commanding officer of the Mounted Life regiment, and had followed him ever since. Abraham had come to know the face of war during these years. He had witnessed orgies of plunder and seen enemy soldiers burned alive. He had lived in fields resembling abattoirs, with corpses lying in troughs between the tents.

The cavalry had vanished into the night when Abraham's servant woke him and told him the regiment had left. Abraham, a fair-haired man with a broad nose and thick lips, dressed hurriedly and ordered the horses to be saddled. From his baggage he picked out his most valued possessions, including four silver-gilt beakers given to him by Mazeppa as thanks for helping save a sizeable portion of the hetman's property during the winter. The objects were strapped to his pack-horse, a handsome Danish colt. Anyone who had anything of value ran grave risks leaving it at camp; it was better to take it into battle. This is what made corpse-robbing so widespread and so rewarding. Abraham took with him as much as he possibly could and in his greed ended by stuffing more than 1,000 ducats in gold down his roomy trousers. Straining somewhat, he hauled himself up on his elegantly caparisoned horse, also a gift from Mazeppa. His servant was deputed to lead the Danish animal; together the overloaded pair of them set off across the plain to chase after the army.

The long line of battalions snaked on through the dark. On the march the officers reminded the men of the battle at Narva nine years before, where a well-entrenched and numerically superior Russian army had been defeated. As the stolid, purblind columns worked their way north the men became more and more aware of their adversaries. To their right they could see the flickering lights of the Russian camp-fires. Soon they heard the noise of strenuous labour on the line of redoubts: ringing sounds of axe and pick flew on the wind through the night, south to meet the Swedes. At about two o'clock the first units reached the place selected by Rehnsköld as the start-line for the attack, approximately 600 metres south of the southernmost redoubt.

The columns made their appearance one after another, marched up next to each other and halted. The soldiers were ordered to lie down in the dewy grass. Even though still well before dawn, it was desirable to minimize the risk of discovery. The darkest hours of the night were past. The king and his retinue cruised between the battalions: broad carpets of soldiery either sitting crouched or lying down. They halted next to the Västmanland regiment, in the van of the leading column. The bed was lifted from the horse-litter and the king's foot attended to. He drank a little water offered by the obliging steward and then lay down to rest.

The king was accompanied by a sizeable entourage. Besides the bodyguard of guardsmen and Drabants it included Rehnsköld and his staff, Lewenhaupt, Gyllenkrok, Siegroth and a horde of adjutants. There were also a string of foreign envoys and military attachés: the Prussian, von Siltmann; the Poles, Poniatowski and Urbanovitch; the Englishman, Jeffreys; and two defectors from the Russian high command, Schultz and Mühlenfels. The latter was to meet a singularly atrocious fate in the course of the next days.

Then there was the whole of the royal household, under supervision of the Lord Chamberlain, Baron Gustaf von Düben. One of its members was Chamberlain Carl Gustaf Gynterfelt, who had both hands shot off at Klissow in 1702 but who had travelled to France and there ordered 'two strange machines, which partially replaced their loss'. It also included Gustaf Adlerfelt, the king's historiographer. Adlerfelt, a gifted boy, had been born on a farm outside Stockholm. Sent at the early age of 13 to Uppsala university, he had studied languages, history and law. In 1700 he was introduced to the king, who gave him a position at court. Soon afterwards he started to record the campaigns and battles of Carolus, an undertaking sanctioned from on high. Adlerfelt worked on his opus all the time. He had his own library with him and functioned as the army's chronicler. His most recent entries had been made only two days before: the manuscript was now carefully stowed away in one of the baggage-wagons.

Also in the retinue were the lofty Court Chaplain, Jöran Nordberg, with his awe-inspiring beard, and the Court Apothecary Ziervogel, as well as physicians, stewards, lackeys and pages. The field chancellery, too, followed the army out on the field of battle. Its administrators included Registrar Hirschenstjerna and Olof Hermelin, the adroit Secretary of State. Hermelin was in an unusually subdued mood. It was rumoured he had already burnt all the secretariat's documents.

The time was nearing half past two. A problem had arisen: the cavalry had failed to appear. Invaluable time was beginning to slip away for the Swedes. To set off without the cavalry was unthinkable: it had to be at hand now that the break through the redoubts was imminent.

Surprise can be completely decisive in war. Apart from the tactical advantages it confers, surprise can have a devastating effect on enemy morale. But truly effective surprise is often extremely difficult to achieve. A cleverly conceived operation easily founders on small unforeseen incidents; and this was patently about to happen here. Rehnsköld rode impatiently to and fro. A stream of aides were sent off to locate the missing cavalry and get them to move along. For every minute that went by the dawn crept closer and the risk of discovery increased. If the Russians caught sight of them, surprise would count for nothing: the shock burst through the redoubts would turn into a normal attack, for which no plan had been prepared. The horizon was now just a thin film of grey. Where were the cavalry?

Both wings of the cavalry, the left under Major-General Hamilton and the right under Creutz, had lost their way – in spite of their reconnaissance. They had used a star as guide, but the march had not been long under way before Creutz lost contact with several of his regiments. He ordered a time-consuming halt to set things right. The left wing had veered about a kilometre too far to the left of the assembly point. They discovered their mistake quite suddenly when they found themselves facing Russian outposts at the verge of the Budyschenski woods. In what must have been a couple of exceptionally tense moments the squadrons pulled away to the right in the utmost silence, leaving the Russian sentry-posts in blissful ignorance behind them. Rehnsköld's aides caught up with the strays and put them straight.

A sense of uncertainty began to infect the Swedish command. During the nervous wait for the cavalry 50 soldiers under Major-General Wolmar Anton Schlippenbach, a 51-year-old Livonian, were sent out to reconnoitre. Gyllenkrok also set off, accompanied by two non-commissioned officers from the fortifications. They rode away towards the sounds of men at work. Veils of mist rested over the depressions on the plain; the contours of the nearest redoubt began to rise up out of the grey light and formed an outline against the reddening morning sky. The eye of dawn was opening.

The right wing of the cavalry arrived at the assembly point and the silently waiting infantry. Creutz's men joined the recumbent battalions, and he sought out the king. Rehnsköld, Lewenhaupt and the prime minister, Piper, were grouped together next to the king's litter. Creutz reported his columns in place, drawn up in formation as directed. Rehnsköld mounted his horse and rode back with Creutz to inspect the new arrivals under the feeble grey light. The major-general asked if they should form up in line, or deploy on the flanks of the infantry. Rehnsköld's reply was vague and evasive: 'Ye'll get orders no doubt.' Creutz stayed close to his regiment and his columns, awaiting further orders. Shortly afterwards the rest of the missing cavalry rode up: silent columns of men and horses swung into place.

All troops were now in place, but they were well overdue. The time schedule had long been shattered. It began to grow light. The foot soldiers and some of the cavalry converted from column to line of battle formation. The cavalry on the right wing probably did not ride out into line because of the nearness of the Yakovetski wood and its ravines, and the consequent lack of room on their side. Two lines of infantry hastily came into being. The aim was to strike as quickly as possible, before the Russians had time to notice them.

As he rode over the field Gyllenkrok caught sight of the two foremost redoubts. Men were hard at work on them. He turned his horse, rode back and soon met Rehnsköld riding up on his own. The field marshal received the news about the two redoubts in total silence, and turned back. Gyllenkrok stayed behind and continued looking in the direction of the forts. He saw the men moving between them, unprotected by ramparts of any sort. It could only be a matter of moments before they discovered the Swedish troops massed silently in front of them.

The moment came. A horseman broke away from the shadows round the redoubts. He held a pistol in his hand, and the crack of one shot from it smashed the silence into a thousand fragments.

The report coursed like a jet of blood through the landscape; past the little mud houses at the verge of the Yakovetski wood, over the mist-covered plain undulating down to the silent Swedish units. Its echo reverberated past the completed redoubts, through the throng of the Russian cavalry's tents and up to the great camp. The drums began to beat their timpani. The drum-roll of alarm bounded over the bivouacs and fortifications and was answered by a swelling return of new rolls of sound from new tymbals, until the air was thick with their blunt, rolling clangour, mingled with loud shouts and thundering shots of warning.

The Russian had sighted the Swedish troops. Possibly he had glimpsed the long pikes of the foot soldiers as the rising sun glanced off them. Schlippenbach's roving scouts had also been spotted, and the Russians realized that something was afoot. Surprise was no longer to be hoped for. Through a clattering racket of drums, shots of alarm and echoing Russian passwords, Gyllenkrok rode back to Rehnsköld and the king. The field marshal was berating Siegroth and another of the column commanders, Sparre, for being 'all in confusion'. Sparre tried to answer. Rehnsköld fiercely cut him off with: 'So y're cleverer than I am.' The formation into line of battle may have been hurried. Perhaps it had been executed without orders from the high command. The reason for the move was obvious: an attack was about to be launched very shortly. Gyllenkrok asked Siegroth wherein the 'confusion' lay: Siegroth did not know but remarked that 'everything here proceeds oddly'. The field marshal apparently did not want the men in line. Asked how they were to form up he answered: 'They are to stand in column as they have marched.' Gyllenkrok rode back with Siegroth to order the units to re-form in column.

The Swedish command hesitated, not knowing exactly what to do. Rehnsköld, the king and Piper stood a little apart from the rest. Charles had already been lifted up into the litter. The three of them conferred at length on whether the attack was to go ahead or whether the whole thing should be cancelled. The element of surprise had lapsed: there was no question now of a swift burst through the system of redoubts. They would have to fight their way through. But there had been no preparations: in the original plan there had probably been no thought of storming these fortifications. The ditches and ramparts were difficult to surmount. An assault demanded assault-ladders, bundles of brushwood – fascines – for filling up the ditches, ascent ropes fastened with stakes, hand-grenades. These were aids the troops would have had to prepare well in advance and bring with them. And to storm the redoubts the ideal requirement was for heavy artillery supporting fire. There was none to be had.

The entire strength of artillery the Swedes were taking into the battle consisted of four three-pounder cannon and four ammunition wagons, attended by about 30 men: gunners, constables, warrant officers and drivers, dressed in the nondescript grey coats of the artillery, with blue stockings and black hats. They were commanded by Captain Hans Clerckberg and an ensign named Blyberg. Clerckberg had previously served in the navy. As a young man he had travelled in Holland, France, England and Spain and picked up a knowledge of navigation and pyrotechnics. The army career of his henchman had been more conventional. Jonas Blyberg, a 40-year-old from Södermanland, had joined the artillery as long ago as 1687. It was a scant band with scant resources which stood waiting to support the infantry's attack.

This weakness is very surprising. The part played by artillery was on the increase, and artillery, well applied, could decisively affect the outcome of battle. Field artillery consisted mainly of relatively light pieces, usually between three and six pound calibre, exceptionally rising to 12 pounds. The projectile which a piece was capable of firing was measured in pound

## Map 3 · Initial Position

### SWEDISH FORCES (A–F)

A. 8,200 infantry (18 battalions); 4 pieces of artillery
B. 7,800 cavalry (109 squadrons)
C. The Vallack Regiment: 1,000 irregular cavalry (12 squadrons)
D. Siegework troops: 1,100 infantry (2 battalions); 200 cavalry (4 squadrons); 2 cannon
E. Baggage-train: 2,000 cavalry (25 squadrons); small detachment of infantry; unknown number of Zaporozhian Cossacks; 28 pieces of artillery
F. Various detachments off the map by the lower Vorskla: 1,800 cavalry (16 squadrons)

### RUSSIAN FORCES (G–L)

G. 25,500 infantry (51 battalions); 73 pieces of artillery
H. 9,000 cavalry (85 squadrons); 13 pieces of artillery
I. Line of redoubts: 4,000 infantry (8 battalions); 16 pieces of artillery
J. Outpost at Yakovtsi: 1,000 infantry (2 battalions); 1,000 cavalry (8 squadrons)
K. An unknown number of Cossacks
L. Poltava's garrison: 4,000 infantry; 28 pieces of artillery

### THE OPENING MOVES

1. The Vallack Regiment launches a preliminary attack in Yakovtsi.
2. The Swedish army march up. The cavalry rides astray and is delayed.
3. The Swedes are discovered. The Russians sound the alarm. Russian cavalry prepare for battle.

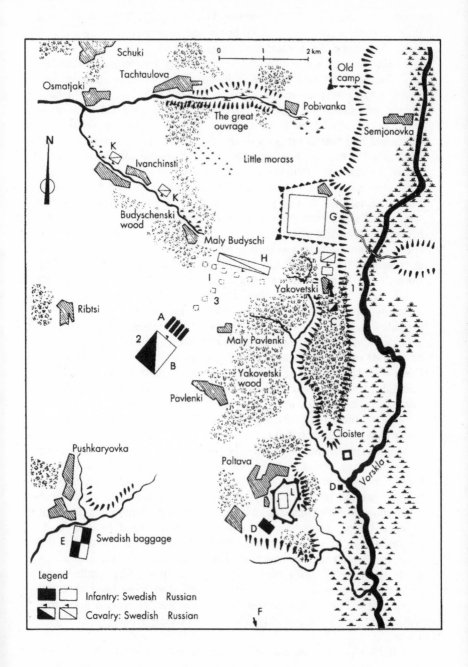

weight. A three-pound ball weighed about 1.5 kilos. The cannon were short, muzzle-loaded and smooth-bored and only used for direct fire at quite close range. Their maximum range was over 1,000 metres, but fire at such a distance was ineffective since accuracy was minimal. Random long-distance fire could be used to get large, massed units to move, but effective range was around 300 to 500 metres. The rate of fire of light cannon was fairly high. Small three-pounders, using special ammunition, the so-called 'geschwinde' shot (a sort of combined powder canister and ball bound up in cloth covers), could deliver a great number of rounds per minute. For bigger pieces of 12 pound calibre or over the rate of fire was low: about ten rounds per hour.

At over 200 metres the ammunition was primarily solid ball of iron. Men were told not to aim too high, in case the rounds flew over their target. Fire was directed at the enemy's knees or under the bellies of the horses, to take full advantage of ricochet. These iron balls flew at a speed of about 200 to 250 metres per second and were visible as they approached. They could do terrible damage. They easily smashed through the tightly packed lines of upright soldiers: one single ball could maim and kill more than 20 men at a time. Their effect was appalling: arms, legs and hands would be instantly sheared and heads exploded into atoms. The soft body of a human being, with its delicately connected sinews, cartilage and muscle, would be split in two or mashed to pieces when hit, leaving nothing but a mess of meat and bone. The kinetic energy of the cannonball diminished as it flew, but this did not make it innocuous. At best, a man grazed by a falling ball might escape with an ugly contusion or broken bones. Spent balls, rolling over the ground like black marbles, were capable of crushing any foot which tried to stop them.

At shorter distances, especially under 200 metres, canister or grapeshot were just as terrible, and searingly effective. Canisters were containers made of board, wood or iron, filled with lead balls, chips of flint or any old bits of metal like broken, rusty nails and screws and other choice rubble (this was known as scrap-shot). Grapeshot consisted of an envelope, preferably of cloth, filled with round balls of lead, resembling a bunch of grapes. When firing these barbarities the piece functioned like an enormous shot-gun, time and again injecting thick showers of projectiles into enemy ranks. They killed and wounded many more than the round ball, and were used at every opportunity. The almost machine-gun like impact of cannon firing this sort of ammunition was highly effective in beating off or supporting an attack.

A third type of ammunition was the grenade: a hollow ball of iron primed with a charge of gunpowder and a fuse to make the contraption explode at the required distance. Grenades were mainly employed at sieges and seldom used in battle. They were nearly always fired by mortar, very stubby pieces of large calibre; or howitzers, a sort of halfway house between cannon and mortar.

Artillery had only one great disadvantage in the eyes of the field commander: its poor mobility. Twelve-pounders weighed about 1.7 metric tons and needed a dozen horses to be pulled along. The barrel had to be transported separately on a four-wheeled carriage. Russian field artillery had poorly constructed gun-carriages and was very slow-moving: their 12-pounders weighed 2.5 tons and required as many as 15 nags to shift from the spot. When heavy guns had once been deployed they usually remained in place for the duration of the battle. Light artillery was much more flexible. The three-pounders were pulled into battle by a team of three horses, or 12 men wearing a special kind of harness. They were used in close co-operation with infantry, often in the gaps between battalions. The horses and ammunition-wagons would then be drawn up out of range or behind cover.

Why had the Swedes only mobilized four small cannon in this utterly decisive hour? Back with the baggage at Pushkaryovka there were 28 fully serviceable pieces: 16 three-pounder cannon, five six-pounders, two 16-pounder howitzers and five six-pounder mortars. There were also a couple of two-pounders, looted from the Russians, and some three-pounder mortars, but these lacked ammunition. There was enough ammunition for the others, however. The 16 three-pounders had over 150 rounds of ball and canister per piece; the five six-pounders had 110 rounds; and the two howitzers rather less, 45 rounds per piece, but nevertheless a useful supply. Only the supplies for the six-pounders were meagre: 15 grenades per gun.

The field artillery, commanded by Colonel Rudolf von Bünow, a 58-year-old Pomeranian the king used to call Grandad, was perfectly battle-worthy. That was not where the shoe pinched. The reason all these pieces of ordnance had been left behind was probably a combination of two different factors. First, the plan had been constructed on speed and surprise. The Swedish command probably felt that all these heavy cannon and wagon-loads of canister would delay the troops during their swift attack. A few light pieces would cause no problems. Second, the decision was certainly influenced by ingrained ideas: a tendency to underestimate the value of artillery. Swedish tactics subordinated fire-power to the *armes blanches* attack. The king favoured rapid manoeuvres, with firing reduced to a minimum: swift, decisive, frontal attacks, where there was no time for artillery. He positively disliked using cannon in battles on open fields. Artillery was for use at sieges or to support advances across difficult rivers or through passes. Some flatly stated that the king felt contempt for artillery. An almost doctrinaire mistrust of firepower was cultivated in the Swedish army, a mistrust which was to cost them dear during the next few hours.

This contempt for artillery did not exist among the Russians. Tsar Peter's attitude was almost the complete opposite: he regarded artillery of paramount importance in battle. In the intensive reformation of the Russian army since the beginning of the war much of the most radical reorganization had concerned artillery. The new munitions industry which had been hammered out of the soil was creating large units of artillery. Production was immense: between 1702 and 1708 the Russian army was supplied with 1,006 metal pieces of ordnance and countless iron cannon. By 1708 the demand for ammunition had been covered for a long period into the future: over 3,800 tons of gunpowder had been manufactured. The Russians had overwhelming resources, and since May had been steadily increasing their artillery supplies to the battle zone. These came mainly from their central base in Belgorod, but also from large depots in Moscow and Voronesh. An endless stream of cannon, ammunition-wagons, cannonballs, canisters, bombs, grenades, gunpowder and hand-grenades flooded into the Russian army. Meanwhile, Swedish supplies were rapidly drying up.

The Swedes had mustered four three-pounders for the battle. The Russian artillery numbered, all in all, 102 cannon, not including the three-pounder pack-horse hand-mortars attached to the cavalry. Seventy of these Russian pieces were light, rapid-firing three-pounder cannon; the rest consisted of 13 two-pounder cannon attached to the cavalry; 12 eight-pounders; two 12-pounders; two howitzers, one 20-pounder, one 40-pounder; one 20-pounder mortar and two 40-pounders. The Russians had more ammunition than they could possibly ever consume.

Numerical superiority apart, the organization and tactics of Russian artillery gave a further advantage. It was structurally divided into siege, fort, field and regimental artillery. The Swedish artillery regiment controlled all the cannon in the field; sometimes it might second light pieces to other units. Each Russian regimental commanding officer, however, had his own cannon, a feature which greatly improved the stability of regimental artillery. In battle, Russian regimental cannon could be employed in an adaptable and attacking manner, mainly supporting both cavalry and foot with canister fire. The cavalry also had their own cannon and their gunners were mounted. This was a great innovation, making their pieces highly mobile and capable of accompanying the horse in nearly all manoeuvres. Field artillery would have a somewhat less mobile and less attacking role, mainly because the poor gun-carriages of the heavier pieces made them difficult to move. Their purpose was to achieve massive, concentrated fire. The waiting maws of the 102 Russian cannon represented an immensely powerful strike-force.

As the light of dawn advanced, the morning greyness blanketing the fields gave way to greater detail and colour. The Swedes could see the redoubts and, beyond them, the swelling ranks of the Russian cavalry preparing for battle. The Russian gunners in the redoubts began to sight in their cannon on the silent shadows ahead of them. Front and back sights did not exist. They aimed along the barrel, over the high curve at the rear, the chamber, and towards the bulb at its muzzle, the trumpet. Elevation sighting was achieved by wedges which were inserted below the rear of the barrel; directional sighting by rocking the cannon to left or right with the help of special levers. The range was great, perhaps too great, and there would be no question of any very precise target-shooting.

A Russian gunner set the fusee's glow to the touch-hole, and the first round thundered towards the Swedish troops. The cannonball described an arc through the air and crashed down on the ranks of the Life Guard. Two guardsmen fell to the ground, their heads severed from their bodies. The first men had fallen in the battle of Poltava.

More cannonballs began to drop among the Swedish troops. Captain Carl Johan Horn stood in front of his men, the Östgöta regiment of foot. He had started his career in Dutch service, become a lieutenant with the Östgöta men in 1700, been promoted to second captain in the summer of 1702 and five years later elevated to first captain. His father, Christoffer Henrik Horn, also a soldier, had fallen in the Thirty Years' War. Captain Horn was married. He and his wife Sophia Elisabeth had several sons: Carl, Adam and Jacob, aged two. Another cannonball dropped near by, ploughed a furrow through the Östgöta men, knocked four musketeers to the ground and killed Captain Horn.

Next to the king's litter two guardsmen were killed by one ball. The cavalry units were also struck by random shots. The Russian guns were shooting at their greatest range and the effect of their fire was slight.

A decision was pressing, further delay would only mean more pointless deaths. The off-stage conference between the king, Piper and Rehnsköld had to come to a rapid conclusion. Should they take the risk and launch an attack, or withdraw back to the camp, and think again? The army's desperate lack of supplies argued strongly against the latter course. Rehnsköld turned to Lewenhaupt, who was standing some way off. 'What is your opinion, Count Leijonhufvud?' he asked, using the Swedish version of the general's name. Lewenhaupt was still sore from the thick ear the field marshal had dealt him earlier, and answered curtly. He was in favour of attack. 'I hope, with God's help, it will go well.' 'In the Name of God then,' said Rehnsköld, turning back to Piper and the king, 'let us go forward.' The final step had been taken. It was exactly 0400 and the dawn sky was growing red. A beautiful day was in prospect.

# 9 · 'Give the Enemy No Time'

The Swedish infantry began its attack just as the dazzling sun rose over the line of the horizon, dividing night from day. As one battalion after another lumbered into forward motion the fire from the redoubts intensified in fury. The thundering cannonade came so thick it sounded like musket-fire.

One of the Swedes marching in the Jönköping regiment, a unit at the far rear of the first column, wrote a poem some years later, probably recalling his memories of this day. It is not a work of any particular note, but nevertheless gives a good impression of the beginning of the engagement, and the sounds of weapons, wagons, men and beasts which filled the air:

> A rumble, a roar and a cry, a din, tumult and clamour
> From horses and wagons, from clattering hosts up in arms
> That meet on the plain in the morning, at first light of dawn:
> The signal is given for battle with thundering cannon report,
> Volleys starting to sound, the musket-balls flying like hail,
> And burning grenades hurled out mid the ranks of brave men.

The advance was confused from the start. There was an acute shortage of time, mainly because the cavalry had ridden astray; and the command had hesitated to the last on whether actually to launch the attack. Moreover, it had not been exactly clear how the troops were meant to form up and several battalions had not completed their formation when everything burst into action.

Lewenhaupt had been instructed to draw up his men according to the *ordre de bataille*, but on the right wing they were so close to the edge of the Yakovetski wood that there was no room for all the battalions to form into line. It was a complicated business: time was short and space was cramped.

A far more serious matter than the confusion and delay was that many of the commanders did not have a clear idea of the purpose of this initial phase. The order to attack had been sent out in the greatest haste to the column commanders, who then relayed it on down to their subordinate regimental and battalion commanders. It is highly unlikely there were any thorough, detailed briefings; some officers merely received rough instructions which cannot have been easy to interpret. Siegroth rode with the order to Major-General Roos, commanding the third column; his troops were to attack the nearest redoubts. Shortly afterwards Stackelberg, the leader of column number two, beside Roos, also sped past and confirmed that they were to attack.

As the simple order was passed on down, some kind of distortion took place – rather as in the old parlour game. A number understood it to mean that they were to fight everything they encountered. Others realized that although they were to attack the redoubts, on finding an opening they were to pass through. The fortifications were merely to be skirted. The plan must have been for the two central columns simply to neutralize the dangerous flanking fire of the projecting line. Covered by their attack, the third and fourth columns, and the battalions to the rear of columns one and two, were then to quickly reach the back redoubts and either completely avoid them or fight their way through.

The attack on the redoubts was a side issue in every sense. They were only an obstacle to be surmounted on the way to the real objective, the Russian camp. Ignorance of this plain fact was to cost the Swedes extremely dear.

The advance of the central columns was disorderly from the beginning. The units soon drifted apart, but in spite of this the forward battalions pressed rapidly ahead. The nearest redoubt, still uncompleted, lay on a slight ridge by some bushy outgrowths. Four Swedish battalions engaged it on two sides. They were supported by the four squadrons of the Life Dragoon regiment, who attacked the small Russian force stationed in the gap before the next redoubt. The Swedish onslaught washed over the redoubt, meeting no resistance. Its occupants, presumably mostly labourers, were quickly cut down to the last man. The only ones to escape with their lives were the panic-stricken few who managed to scramble over the rampart and run back to the next redoubt. No prisoners were taken. All Russians who fell into Swedish hands were shot, stabbed or beaten to death.

The attack rolled on behind the firing and the billowing clouds of smoke. The captured fort was left behind, unoccupied. The two battalions of the Dalecarlia regiment pressed on into the T-shaped system. A long blue hedge, tipped with gleaming bayonets and swaying pike-points stamped forward over the sandy soil. It approached the next redoubt. But the battalions began to slip yet further apart in the confusing roar of battle. The two Guards battalions at the rear of Roos's column, under command of Carl Magnus Posse, turned off to the right, and joined up with the other battalions of Guards in the fourth column. This column aimed to avoid the redoubts completely. The Västerbotten regiment, which had taken the first redoubt in concert with the Dalecarlia regiment, quickly lost contact with it and kept straight on towards the rear chain of defences, together with the Guards battalions. Roos was mystified by the sudden disappearance of half his column.

The king, with his numerous escort and the general staff, was out on the right wing. Charles lay on the horse-litter with one spurred boot on his good foot. With his long sword in his hand he commanded the nearest troops in his forceful manner. Here on the battlefield the king was in his natural element. He was an accomplished and charismatic army commander who radiated immense power: a near-total transformation of the diffident young monarch took place when battle was joined, a strange and terrifying transformation which in an almost spell-binding manner struck fire and lust for battle into those who saw and heard him. One of the participants in the war, Captain Peter Schönström, later wrote that the king, 'when he sat mounted to horse before his army and drew his sword, had a mien quite different from the other he used in society, aye, a mien which was near supernatural to implant courage and desire to fight in those one might hold the most faint-hearted'.

Charles was well aware of the power of example, and rarely hesitated to risk his own life in battle. He deliberately ate and dressed in the plainest manner so that, as Schönström put it, 'the rank and file should endure the more'. Much of his asceticism seems to have been a calculated act for the gallery, a way of manipulating the men into silent and patient acceptance of hardship and starvation. It is understandable that this strange king came to stand in such high regard in the eyes of his contemporaries. Stories circulated that he was both invincible and invulnerable. One soldier said the rank and file believed they could not lose when the king was with them. Carolus was a talisman of victory: and hence the consternation caused in the army by the news that he had been wounded ten days earlier.

The troops on the right aimed to circumvent the whole system of redoubts. They paid little attention to the screaming, whistling fire felling men in their ranks, and advanced rapidly in the soft morning light. To their left they could see the first redoubt stormed by Roos's men, and the Russians fleeing for their lives. The cannon in the other bastions fired unceasingly. Solid iron balls smashed bloody furrows through the Swedish ranks. Swedish artillery should now have been present to open fire in response. But there was no heavy support of this sort for their advance. According to Lewenhaupt, 'for our common soldiers their courage began to fail, when they apprehended that they were sustained by no cannon'.

As they advanced they could see that the woods on the right gave way to gently sloping meadows. The spreading field offered more space for circumventing the redoubts. To exploit this, Lewenhaupt pulled even further to the right. The speed of the manoeuvre made him realize that he was likely to lose contact with the other battalions if he did not pull up. As

Rehnsköld came riding past, Lewenhaupt turned to him, saying: 'Your Excellency, we have drawn off to the right and are marching too fast, it is impossible for the left wing to catch up if we do not make a halt.' The field marshal rejected this request with: 'No, absolutely not. We must give the enemy no time.' Major-General Stackelberg rode past alone, agreed with Rehnsköld, and repeated in German that the adversary was not to be given any time. Lewenhaupt's battalions continued their march to the right of the backward line of redoubts. Beyond them lay the waiting Russian camp.

Thrusting on through the projecting line, the Dalecarlia regiment reached redoubt number two. This one was better prepared. The assault force was somewhat smaller, making this second attack more difficult and causing more casualties than the first. But the redoubt was taken and, as before, everyone in it unable to escape was slaughtered. Anders Pihlström, a 32-year-old ordinary second lieutenant with Orsa company, regarded as a solid and reliable man, relates that 'we cut down every bone we found therein'.

This brutal conduct, where all were refused quarter and killed without mercy, was fairly common. The relationship between Swedes and Russians was often extremely bitter. Nor was there the faintest hint of a Geneva convention: no tacit right to imprisonment. It was common practice on both sides to threaten a besieged fortress with total massacre if it did not surrender. This appeared to cause no one any ethical qualms. War was war. Possibly the Swedish soldiers saw the redoubt as a kind of fortress which had refused to surrender and whose garrison they therefore had a right to slaughter to the last man.

Massacres in action were frequent. Troops would run amok and flatly refuse to take prisoners. Sometimes men seemed gripped by a wild intoxication during battle: when the time came to slow down and take prisoners the killing would continue of its own momentum. Often it seems to have been a crude thirst for revenge, spoken of as 'embitterment' or 'revanche'. The Russian campaign had grown ever more ugly, cowardly and dirty, and atrocities of all kinds became more and more common on both sides. At Holowczyn the Swedes massacred almost all the Russians who tried to surrender. After the battle a number of officers urged that even those prisoners taken in spite of this should also be killed, since they considered that guarding them would only be an extra burden on the men. At the battle of Dobroye prisoners were also killed. A senior Swedish officer had spared a Russian lieutenant-colonel in order to try to extract some information from him, but a Finnish private rushed forward, shouting: 'No quarter, sir, none of that, my good sir', and thrust his sword straight through the defenceless man.

The attitudes the belligerents adopted towards each other are difficult to define, projecting contradictory impressions. Even though hostility some-

## Map 4 · The Infantry Breakthrough

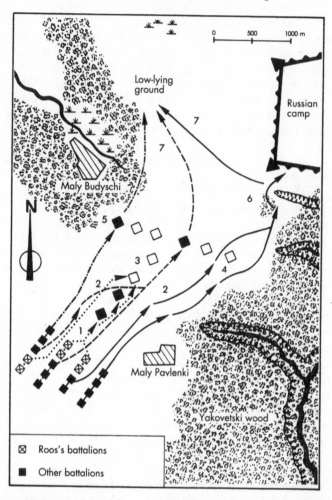

1. The Dalecarlian and Västerbotten regiments under command of Major-General Roos storm the first redoubt. The Dalecarlians then take the second.
2. Lewenhaupt's battalions on the right gain more space. There is a general drift to the right by the foot-soldiers.
3. A series of battalions – finally numbering six – attempt in vain to storm the third redoubt.
4. Supported by the cavalry, the battalions on the right push past the back line of redoubts.
5. The Västmanland regiment storm a redoubt and pass the line.
6. Lewenhaupt marches his battalions up to attack the encampment, but receives a counter-order to regroup.
7. The Swedish forces that have gone through the redoubts reassemble on low-lying ground to the west of the Russian camp.

times seemed to break all bounds, there were tendencies the other way. As a rule, relationships between officers in opposing armies were probably better than those between the rank and file. Some felt it would not do to let soldiers on opposite sides of the front line meet during a truce, for they were 'disposed to fight'. It was different for the command. It was perfectly possible to make friends with the other side. Officers could conduct polite, animated small-talk in no-man's-land, meet at dinner or exchange gifts. Courtesy and chivalry might extend right into the smoke of battle. Their concept of their adversary was unlike our own. Physicians might be seconded, refreshments supplied or even trade take place across the front line.

Most officers had something denied the soldier: the possibility of communication. They often spoke the same language, German or French. They also had a natural point of contact by virtue of their class, since the great majority were noblemen. Their professionalism gave them a considerable set of common values – they were all in one sense or other a kind of mercenary. The military tradition of professional brotherhood across the firing line lived on for a very long time. A famous instance was the fraternization on the Western Front at Christmas, in 1914. This incident is usually thought of as an eruption of brotherly love and burgeoning pacifism between nations, but was just as much a highly traditional expression of the officers' simple professional fraternity.

While the Dalecarlians were storming the second redoubt and cutting down the men in it, the seven battalions of infantry on the left were moving forward to the rear chain. With the right wing beginning to pull further and further to the right, the left wing was tending to drift with them. As a result, they were drawn straight towards redoubt number three in the projecting line. This was a large and well-armed triangular bastion, surrounded by a ditch and a barricade of *chevaux-de-frise*. In it a battalion of Russian infantry from Aigustov's brigade, five or six hundred men equipped with cannon, awaited the Swedish assault. If they failed to repulse the advancing blue waves they were certain to meet the merciless fate of their comrades in the redoubts already taken.

The first battalion of the Närke-Värmland regiment, led by Lieutenant-Colonel Henrik Johan Rehbinder, 37, from Södermanland, went into the attack. Assault tactics had been thoroughly drilled into the men by countless interminable exercises. The battalion commander gave the order: 'Make yourselves ready.' The four companies were drawn up in one long line, four deep and 150 men wide, giving a front of about 130 metres. In the middle of each company stood about 50 pikemen who, at the command to get ready, swung their five-metre long pikes up to the high port. Taking a firm grip of the pike's lower end, they braced it against the shoulder and pointed it straight at the sky. On each side of the pikemen marched the musketeers, about 100 men per company. The musketeer's flintlock musket, weighing fully five kilos, was more reliable and functioned better in rain than earlier firearms but it still misfired at approximately every ninth shot. It had a higher rate of fire than the previous musket: a well-trained marksman could load, aim and fire within 30 seconds. Practical range was 150 metres. The calibre was large – 20 millimetres – and the big gunpowder charge produced a powerful recoil. The musketeer would place the stock against the right-hand side of his chest, rather than his shoulder, to avoid dislocating his arm.

Small sections of grenadiers were stationed farthest out on the company wings. Their peculiar tall caps replaced the normal wide-brimmed three-cornered hat, which would have impeded them when they slung their muskets before lobbing their hand-grenades. The grenades were small hollow balls of cast-iron, lead, earthenware or glass, with a diameter of about eight centimetres and a weight of between 1.5 and two kilos, equipped with an explosive charge and a touch tube which was lit before throwing. Grenades were little used on open ground; their main value was in battles at forts. Grenadiers acted as a sort of bodyguard for commanders, and also functioned as marksmen.

On each side of the sections of pikemen and musketeers stood non-commissioned officers armed with halberds. These weapons were not much use in battle but were good for keeping order in the ranks and rapping those privates who failed to keep in line. Immediately in front of each company stood the drummers and pipers of the band, their leader, the company commander and the ensign, who carried the colours. Above each company the banners slapped and flapped in the warm wind. The banners of the Närke-Värmlanders were blood-red, with two crossed yellow arrows within a green wreath. The soldiers and command bore the regulation blue Carolinian uniform, but with red collars, lining and cuffs. The privates had red stockings, the non-commissioned officers blue. The long line of men, weapons and wind-stroked flags was a blaze of colour.

The battalion stormed towards the large redoubt. The air was rent with the roar of musket and cannon. The bastion vomited projectiles. Through the smoke and fire the men reached the ditch and the edging of *chevaux-de-frise* was hurled aside. The battalion welled down into the ditch. There, the avalanche of men met a solid wall of bullets and pelting rubble, dashed against it and was washed away. The Närke men recoiled in confused disorder. At the same moment the lone battalion of Smålanders comprising the Jönköping regiment, sent in to reinforce them, also attacked the redoubt. The fleeing met the advancing and collided: the way forward for the Smålanders was barred. The time was about half past four.

In this confusion the Närke-Värmland regiment split into two parts. While the first battalion made their assault, the second battalion slipped rapidly past the redoubt on its eastern side, and eventually closed up with Lewenhaupt's group.

The first Närke battalion reorganized its ranks. So too did the 300 men of the Jönköping regiment. A concerted joint assault was launched. This was also repelled, with many severe Swedish casualties the only result. Numerous dead and wounded Swedish soldiers were already lying at the bottom of the ditch and on the soil around the redoubt, their bodies sprawling or thrown up in heaps.

## 10 · 'Cavalry Forward'

Out on the right wing Lewenhaupt's battalions marched on. Behind the rear line of redoubts glittered the greater part of the Russian cavalry in battle array: 9,000 horsemen, 85 squadrons, their mobile mass stiffened with horse-drawn light artillery. They were commanded by Cavalry General Prince Alexander Menshikov, one of Tsar Peter's favourites. So far the Russians had contented themselves with pouring an even stream of ball and scrap over the advancing Swedes. Now they made their first counter-movement. A number of squadrons spurred forward through the gaps between the rear line of redoubts.

The danger of the situation increased at a stroke; the Russians threatened to fall on the flank of Lewenhaupt's infantry. The Swedish battalions coming up on the left had not had time to close with the rest, and the line was not in good order.

Clashes between cavalry and infantry tended to be haphazard affairs. If infantry battalions were to repulse the shock of horsemen they had to be well formed up: disorganized foot soldiers were liable to be lost in a pure bloodbath. The best way of meeting enemy cavalry was with one's own cavalry. As yet very few of the Swedish horse had seen action. The sight of the Russian squadrons made the ranks of infantry uneasy: a call for cavalry support was passed along the file. By the time the order reached the horse on the far right of the infantry it was distorted into a cry for help: 'Cavalry forward, cavalry *forward*, in the name of Jesus!' The squadrons spurred forward. Great crush and confusion developed as frenzied masses of men and horses surged towards their Russian adversaries. In the van rode the premier élite, the king's Drabants, closely followed by Småland's cavalry regiment, the Life regiment and the rest in their column order. Over the plain the Swedish cavalry streamed forward in the milky morning light: their fringed standards were flecks of colour above the dark flood of silent riders. Drawn swords darted flashes of reflected light from the low sun and the bodies of the horses laboured rhythmically. A thundering cascade of hoofs swept past the Swedish battalions and turned off to the west, towards the Russians.

The cavalry were armed with sword, pistols and musket or carbine. A

Swedish squadron of 250 men always formed for battle in line, two or three men deep. The riders closed up tight in a massed cluster, knee locked behind knee, in a wedge or plough-shaped formation; then aimed themselves at the enemy, charging as fast as possible, at a canter or gallop. For opposing cavalry units to ride straight into each other, in close formation, was as rare as for infantry to meet with bayonets in open battle. Either one of the squadrons would break through after a brief clash of swords or, more often, one side would veer off without a fight at the sight of the surging wall of hoofs and swords. The nerves of both horse and rider were factors of the greatest importance. The less resolute side would lose. One single clash would not normally settle the issue. There would be a series of charges with brief hand-to-hand fighting. A squadron repeatedly thrown head over heels would eventually be totally ripped apart. The force of the cavalry shock depended on its speed and compactness. The troop able to squeeze the greatest number of riders into the shortest front would gain a natural numerical superiority. Swedish cavalry was extremely densely packed, and highly manoeuvrable.

The squadrons met. There was no room for a continuous Swedish line, and the squadrons charged unit by unit, without mutual support. The foremost squadrons recoiled, the Life regiment bearing the initial brunt. Finally they were all forced to turn, pull back and re-form. Again they charged, again they recoiled. They rode back to recompose themselves, out on the wings of the infantry.

The Russian command, following the battle in front of the line of redoubts, judged the time ripe to withdraw their cavalry. It was unlikely to withstand the entire Swedish army in the long run, and would be needed for more than this preliminary fencing. The tsar's horse had suffered badly during the winter and was still not entirely restored. Cavalry was the one arm where the Russians did not have clear numerical superiority.

At this stage the Russians were patently still not planning to risk an encounter in the open field, but expected to face the Swedes from behind the walled security of their fortified camp. Nor could they know if the attack on the redoubts was not merely a diversionary manoeuvre. They feared that the real attack might come along the heights by the river, which was why they had deployed a large outpost there. However, it was becoming more and more apparent that the attack on the redoubt system was in deadly earnest.

Menshikov was ordered to withdraw his cavalry from the redoubts, and immediately retreat to the encampment. Dizzy with success, he was unwilling to comply. The aide bringing the order was sent back with the message that the battle was going well; and they were so close to the Swedes that an about-turn and retreat could put them at risk. Instead, he asked for reinforcements: a couple of regiments of infantry and he would bring the

Swedes to a complete halt. Tsar Peter turned a deaf ear to this. Menshikov merely received renewed and, no doubt, somewhat irate orders to return. Meanwhile the Swedish cavalry had been repulsed yet again. Menshikov refused to contemplate retreat. He now sent the tsar a number of captured Swedish standards as proof of his success, stubbornly insisting that if his cavalry was withdrawn, the redoubts would fall.

During the first cavalry charge Gyllenkrok suggested to Lewenhaupt that the infantry should halt, to remedy the disorder in the Swedish line. The general told him he had already asked Rehnsköld but received no answer. He added sullenly that the field marshal 'handled me today like a lackey'. Gyllenkrok was welcome to try. 'Willingly,' said the quarter-master-general, 'as my Lord General commands me', and set off to find the ferocious field marshal. On the field he rode past the Life Guard's grenadier battalion, wandering aimlessly. Its commanding officer, 29-year-old Captain Libert Rosenstierna, a former student at Uppsala who had worked his way up from pikeman, asked where they were to go. Gyllenkrok told them to follow the other battalions. At the same moment Rehnsköld came riding over the field and called to him. Pointing at the bastion in front of them, he asked Gyllenkrok if he thought they ought to attack it. The quartermaster-general felt they should rather attack the enemy forces on the field. The field marshal agreed, and set spurs to his horse. Keeping up with him, Gyllenkrok requested permission to halt and reorganize the disordered infantry. With a brusque 'That will be satisfactory' the field marshal rode off to the cavalry, regrouping for a renewed charge. Gyllenkrok returned to the waiting infantry.

The cavalry charges had given the infantry time to reorder their ranks. The long lines of men started forward again. The Russian cavalry slowly backed away. Snipers emerged from their lines, felling men with fire into the advancing battalions. The Swedes answered in kind: men were sent forward with sporting rifles, marksmen's guns regarded primarily as weapons for officers. Their accurate fire succeeded in making the Russian cavalry fall back further. The Swedish cavalry completed their regroup-ment and once more charged. In face of the combined pressure of foot and horse the Russian squadrons withdrew in good order, through the gaps between the earthworks.

Clouds of gunpowder smoke mingled with the dust thrown up from the sandy soil by the thousands of men and animals. The dust whirled and rose, intermittently reducing visibility to zero: from time to time men found themselves fighting as if blindfold. The dust settled over the soldiers and covered them from top to toe: the colourful uniforms disappeared beneath the thick coating, and the black powder left a greasy black film on sweaty skin. In the chaos of battle it was frequently difficult to distinguish friend from foe.

A troop of Life Dragoons clashed repeatedly with the Russians. When the troop re-formed again, they made an astounding discovery. Six Russian horsemen had neatly slotted into the Swedish squadron, strictly according to regulation: two in the forward line and four in the rear. The back four were discovered first and immediately killed. The two in the front line, realizing their mistake, tried to escape. One broke loose and rode straight at the squadron's commander, Captain Robert Muhl – a 26-year-old veteran with a series of battles behind him, who had started his career as a volunteer in the Life Guards at the age of 15. Muhl, his back to the troop, did not see the Russian plunging towards him with his great sabre drawn, ready to slash. Shouts from the troopers made him spin round. He ducked beneath a sweeping cut directed at his head and thrust his sword through the Russian. The man tumbled from his horse and thudded to the ground with a bloody wound in his belly. His comrade came spurring past a second later. One pistol-shot, and a lead ball smashed into his head.

In a fog of powder-clouds and white dust the Swedish cavalry followed hard on the heels of the Russian. Too late, the Swedes saw they had reached right up to the fire-belching bastions. But, as one Life regiment cavalryman, 24-year-old Thure Gabriel Bielke, later put it, the step had been taken and had to be followed through. Bielke was a rather typical representative of his class: a high aristocrat, a count, a knight of the Prussian order De la Générosité. In his childhood he had been *given* a whole company of soldiers from his father's regiment, in the Dutch service. He had studied at Leiden, Oxford and Angers.

The intervals between the redoubts measured only 150–70 metres. Each gap was swept by heavy cross-fire. Every unit attempting to squeeze between them was exposed to intensive short-range fire from front, rear and flank. Mingled with the retreating Russians, they rode through a screaming hail of shell and ball.

In the North Uppland company of Bielke's regiment rode second quartermaster Lorentz Gustaf Lillienwald. He was 27, born in the village of Kälinge in Tibble parish in Uppland. As a 15-year-old he had signed on as a trumpeter. Present at most of the major actions since the landing in Denmark, he had been wounded many times. At Holowczyn he had fought 'a single combat duel with a fearless Russian officer', as he put it. He had taken a shot through his left leg. Another ball had sheared the stock off his carbine and struck him in the chest, where his cuirass saved him. As he now rode forward past the forts he felt a ball hit him in the back, on the left shoulder-blade. The ball spun upwards and bounced into his hat. Virtually unharmed, he rode on. He had been lucky again.

The infantry fell in and advanced behind their cavalry. Several battalions evaded the forts by skirting them, but the terrain made this impossible for others. Two Guards battalions, led by Erik Gyllenstierna and Hans Mannersvärd, were forced to go between the redoubts, losing a number of men, and the battalions on the left wing, which had drifted to the centre, also had to fight their way through. The Uppland and Östgöta infantry regiments took redoubts by storm. These were gory affairs, especially for the Upplanders, who had started the battle with only 690 men. Among those wounded in these assaults was an Östgöta officer, 28-year-old Captain Carl Fredrik Toll from Uppland. He had been badly wounded at the siege of Thorn, six years earlier, since when he had campaigned with a permanent bandage. Now he received another wound, this time in the left leg, but hobbled on into the battle. The captured redoubts in the rear chain were left unoccupied, like the others.

The sound of the thundrous firing was wafted on the gentle morning breeze all the way down to the baggage-train. The first salvos could be heard as the battle began. As the noise became more and more subdued and softened by the distance, those waiting by the baggage took it as a favourable sign.

While the Swedish cavalry's right wing had struggled, their colleagues on the left, led by Major-General Hamilton, had met with greater success. There was only one infantry unit out on this wing, the Västmanland regiment. The rest were either caught up in the assault on the projecting line of redoubts or had united with Lewenhaupt's group on the right. The left wing was made up of seven regiments of cavalry and dragoons, 56 squadrons in all. They rode rapidly towards the rear line of redoubts. A number, presumably the majority, went round the redoubts to the left and passed through the foliage of the Budyschenski wood and the little village of Maly Budyschi. Inside the wood the advance was difficult: the Russians had thrown up substantial barriers, and the Swedes were hampered by felled trees at every turn. It got worse as they moved on through the razed village, with its demolished houses. Concealed pits in the ground and collapsed cellars were death-traps for the horsemen as they dropped into them. The squadrons were broken up, but pressed raggedly on.

The rest of the cavalry burst through the line of redoubts. They ran the gauntlet of Russian fire and suffered fairly substantial losses in both men and chargers. Once through the missile hurricane, they found themselves facing the Russian cavalry on this flank, ready for battle. The Swedes charged. After a brief hand-to-hand bout the Russians retired and were pursued northwards, away from the redoubts. The infantry out on the right could see the Swedish horse clashing with the Russians in the distance, and driving them before them through a small grove of trees. The pursuit was slow however since the Russians kept breaking off their retreat and re-forming for battle, withdrawing only when the Swedes made a direct advance. But the forceful pursuit finally caused the orderly Russian retreat to collapse. With the flight of the enemy cavalry the Swedes had achieved their first real success: joyful cries of victory and triumph rose up from their ranks. But now the whole affair was beginning to resemble all the other battles they had seen in recent months, where the Russians had consistently withdrawn. Wounded horsemen were heard to swear that not even today would it come to a major battle: the Russians were again going to deny them the decisive action which, with a little luck, would mean a quick end to the hardships under which the army was wasting away.

Through the smoke and dust the Västmanland regiment followed the cavalry. The regiment was strong, numbering 1,100 men. They advanced straight ahead, stormed one of the redoubts and the advance continued. With no time to be carried to safety, the most severely wounded soldiers remained lying where they had fallen when the regiment moved away. One of these unlucky men was a lieutenant-captain with the Life company, Niklas Norin, a 25-year-old from Örebro, son of an iron-founder. Norin had abandoned the career mapped out for him in the collegiate of mines, to study gunnery and military fortifications. He entered the army as a volunteer of 17 in 1701. A fair-skinned young man with melancholy eyes, he had since then fought in many battles and been wounded many times. As the redoubt was being stormed, Niklas Norin was wounded in both arms, in the thigh and in the stomach: seven times in all. When the regiment marched on he was left to die, lacerated and drained of blood and strength.

Apparent success continued to attend the cavalry attack on the left. The fighting was violent: a cavalry officer on this wing, Lieutenant Joakim Lyth, called it 'a murderous and bloody fencing, and heated shooting'. The Russians suffered severe losses and remnants of shattered units made vain attempts to surrender, but were mown down. The hard line of the Swedes continued to apply: taking prisoners in the middle of an engagement was impracticable. Under pressure from the seemingly irresistible Swedish advance panic began to spread among the irregular Russian troops. The Skåne Dragoon regiment received a note from the leader of a group of Cossacks, offering to come over to the Swedes with 2,000 men, if the king approved. This request was passed on by Lyth to his regimental commander, Prince Maximilian Emanuel of Württemberg. The prince opined, in truly bureaucratic spirit, that he was not empowered to sanction such a thing. 'Whilst our gracious king has been separated from us during the action and is now not to be reached, his gracious will in this matter cannot be ascertained'. The Cossack messenger was sent back with this answer.

It was now about five in the morning. On the left wing everything seemed to be going to plan. Gyllenkrok, to their right, could see the Swedish pursuit. The long chain of Västmanlanders were following close on the heels of the cavalry. He rode toward them along the line of battalions which were now through the rear redoubts. As he passed the Uppland regiment he spoke briefly with its commander, Stiernhöök. The Upplanders had just taken a redoubt. Stiernhöök complained that the action had been brisk and that he had lost his best men. Gyllenkrok responded 'There's no helping it, God stand by us yet.' After expressing his pleasure at Stiernhöök's own survival he rode on.

Next in line was the second battalion of the Närke-Värmland regiment, and its colonel, 52-year-old Georg Johan Wrangel, a real old war-horse, marching at the head of his men. Born in Reval in 1657, the son of a rural councillor, Wrangel had been commissioned second lieutenant at the age of 17. In 1678 he became adjutant to the Duke of Birkenfeld, then employed in the French service. In the same year he entered Dutch service with the guard of the Prince of Orange, and in 1680 had gone into Swedish service. Wrangel, like many of his soldiers, had only a few hours left to live. Gyllenkrok greeted him as they met. He was uneasy about the confusion on the Swedish side and said in German: 'God be praised, all goes well, would God only grant we were rightly ordered.' Gyllenkrok answered very briefly: 'Amen to that', and rode on past the long lines of men and banners.

On the right, the pursuit of the Russian cavalry led north. Command had passed from Menshikov to General Bauer. Some of the Russian squadrons succeeded in finding safety in the fortified camp, but most just thundered past in great clouds of dust. When the pursuing Swedes rode past the camp they were met by a fiery cannonade from the packed artillery behind the ramparts. Ball and canister scythed through the lines; grenades exploded among horses and men; wedges of fire belched from the walls and in the fumes and dust tattered figures tumbled over on the dry soil.

Despite the heavy fire, the hunt continued farther and farther north. The situation now became highly dangerous for the retreating Russians, whether they made a sharp right turn past the camp and collected there, or continued northwards. In front of them was the deep and marshy rain basin called the 'great ouvrage', and to their right were steep ravines leading down to the Vorskla. They were liable to be forced into a position where farther retreat would be impossible. They would then have to stand with their backs to the wall and either be ripped apart in battle, forced down into the rain basin or over the steep bluffs down to the river.

They bolted farther north, towards the great ouvrage. The distance dwindled until only about 1,000 metres remained. The trap was about to snap shut. Then came an order: the Swedes were to halt their pursuit. Most of the packed mass of Russian horsemen struggled over the marshy rain basin and ranged themselves on the other side. A few isolated Swedish squadrons were so hotly engaged in the dusty chase that the order to halt failed to reach them. They followed the Russians over the ouvrage but were soon obliged to return. Their fate indicates what might have happened to the fleeing Russians. In their headlong retreat many Swedish horses sank into the marsh and remained standing. The Russians were quick to exploit this advantage and mounted a rapid counter-thrust; the Swedes were forced to leave their horses and valuable trappings behind them and flee. A number failed to get away and were cut down.

The order to stop the pursuit originated from Rehnsköld himself, and had gone out to both cavalry wings. He must have been extremely unwilling to lose control over his cavalry, a permanent hazard when squadrons set off on wild pursuits, which were apt to go on for leagues. The highly confused state of the infantry at the present moment meant that it was advisable to keep a firm grip on the cavalry. In any case, the cavalry were essential to the battle-plan: their task was to build a mobile barricade against any eventual northward Russian retreat from their camp. In the wisdom of hindsight it is clear that Rehnsköld's order saved a large section of Russian horse from a very tight corner; but from his viewpoint the decision, if not over-inspired, was strictly correct.

By this time the ten infantry battalions on the right flank had completely passed through the rear line of redoubts. Lewenhaupt was fixedly set on pushing forward to launch an attack on the Russian camp. He had been urged on by Rehnsköld, and the main objective of the battle-plan was, indeed, a direct attack on the camp. From where he now stood the ground sloped gently upwards, and he could see the camp's left rampart. It loomed up at a distance of less than 1,000 metres, and to the general it seemed invitingly sparsely manned. It also looked as though the Russians were beginning to harness horses to sections of artillery, and to their supply-wagons. Some reports indicate that a few units had already crossed over the Vorskla. Possibly their task was to secure the route over the river. Russian nerves were clearly somewhat shaken, and not without reason: the Swedes had penetrated the protecting line of redoubts, and sent most of their cavalry flying. What Lewenhaupt saw was presumably not a direct retreat, but Russian preparations for that eventuality. In spite of everything the battle had begun anything but well for them.

The rows of blue-coated infantry moved towards the camp. A bare 100 metres from the ramparts, among a few cherry orchards, they halted. The way forward was barred by a steep rain fissure cutting through the terrain like a deep wound: it was only about five metres wide, but very deep. In order to get into position for an assault they would have to go round it. Meanwhile they were exposed to artillery fire from the camp.

Battalions that had fought their way through the line of forts were tending to lag behind the Guards, leading the van. The grenadier commander, Rosenstierna, who had earlier asked Gyllenkrok for directions, was either given inadequate orders or just misunderstood them, and led his men straight towards the camp. For a time they stood before it on their own, missiles sizzling through their ranks, irresolutely awaiting further orders. Many of their men were killed and wounded before they joined up with the other Guards battalions.

The king, with his suite of Drabants, guardsmen, courtiers and attendants, was in the vicinity of Lewenhaupt's ten battalions. During the break through the redoubts they had kept somewhat behind the battle front, but had then been attacked by Cossacks swarming around them on all sides. These were not a major danger since, true to form, they had contented themselves with lobbing a few shots from a distance, to the accompaniment of shouts and yells. Nevertheless, a Drabant corporal, Bror Rålamb, was sent off to find more men to reinforce the king's guard. Rålamb was 40, an educated man once articled to the court of appeal, who had turned soldier and composer of doggerel royalist verse. The unit he requisitioned was Robert Muhl's Life Dragoon squadron – the same that had recently discovered Russians in its ranks. When they galloped up the Cossacks veered off and disappeared.

After this little incident the king and his entourage passed through the line in extreme danger. Following the route of the cavalry, they were caught in cross-fire from the redoubts. The leading horse carrying the king's litter was shot dead. The bodyguard was already filling its role as human rampart. Three Drabants and a number of guardsmen were killed. The first Drabant to die was 54-year-old Jacob Ridderborg, born in Stockholm and married since 1679 to Anna Laurin, daughter of a cleric.

The motley royal escort remained exposed to heavy fire as it reached the area round the Russian camp. A cannonball smashed the right-hand shaft of the king's litter. A soldier ripped a pole from one of the surrounding fences to replace it. Motionless, out on the open field, they endured continuing violent fire as the litter was being repaired. More of the men and horses round Charles were shot dead, or maimed. The steward Hultman's horse, heavily loaded with various possessions and a bulky valise, was killed. The king and his decimated escort finally closed up with Lewenhaupt's ten battalions, by now regrouped.

Lewenhaupt's advance towards the ramparts began again, to the accompaniment of dull thuds from the camp's fire-belching cannon. They had not progressed far before the general was reached by an order to cease the attack immediately. He was to withdraw from the camp and march westward. He obeyed.

It is possible that here yet another opportunity slipped through Swedish hands. Lewenhaupt later maintained that the Russians were starting to withdraw from the ramparts as his men advanced. He believed Russian morale would have cracked in the face of a vigorous attack. They would have fled the field, and were already showing clear signs of so doing.

Impossible to tell: an attack now would certainly have come at a very advantageous psychological moment. But it might equally well have ended in exceedingly gory failure. This order, too, had its logic: an attack by the collected Swedish infantry, with co-ordinated cavalry support, would presumably be more likely to succeed than Lewenhaupt's plucky but totally unsupported assault. While waiting for the rest of the infantry there was little point in exposing his ten battalions to Russian fire.

They marched away, north-west over the broad plain towards the Budyschenski woods. Lewenhaupt could not then know why he had been ordered to break off his assault. He had his misgivings however, and these were soon confirmed. The command had lost contact with part of the infantry. Six whole battalions were missing. Major-General Roos, Colonel Siegroth and one third of the total Swedish foot were as if swallowed up by the earth. It was inexplicable.

# 11 · 'Shot Dead in Vain'

The two battalions of the Dalecarlia regiment succeeded in storming the second redoubt. All its occupants, except for those who fled, were killed. By the time the mopping-up process was over all the other units had long ago gone past. When the soldiers raised their heads they saw neither Swede nor Russian. The battlefield was suddenly empty and deserted. The clatter of weapons had stilled and an uncanny silence took its place. Neither Siegroth, the regimental commander, nor Roos, the column commander – now left with two battalions from his original column of four – knew where to make for next. No other units could be seen, no guiding sounds of battle were heard and there was little to indicate what direction they ought to advance in. They were now going to pay for their ignorance of the original plan.

Siegroth drew up his men in battle formation. The Dalecarlians were one of the army's finest regiments, about 1,100 strong. They were an élite, looked on as a kind of unofficial guard. Siegroth was an experienced soldier, who had seen French service and had a long series of battles behind him. The king had great confidence in him. The regiment's senior officers were Lieutenant-Colonel Fredrik Drake, 49, from Småland, and Lieutenant-Colonel Arendt Johan von Gertten, Drake's junior by ten years. Gertten's unit had originally been the Helsinge regiment, one of the many so badly mauled at Lesnaya that it had been disbanded and merged with others. A number of Helsinge men filled out the ranks of the Dalecarlians this morning. They reorganized, and moved off in a north-easterly direction, deeper into the system of redoubts.

When the large third bastion in the projecting line came into view, the Dalecarlians were presented with a remarkable scene. The first Närke battalion and the Jönköping battalion had just attempted to storm the redoubt, and been repulsed. They had been reinforced by the Västerbotten regiment, consisting of two weak battalions numbering 600 men in all. The addition of the Västerbotten men had been of little assistance. Their commanding officer Fock, together with lieutenant-colonels Sass and von der Osten-Sacken, had been wounded at the assault on the first fort. As the Dalecarlians now approached them the four battalions stood silently waiting near the bastion. Not a shot was heard: both sides lay low, unwilling to waste ammunition. Each foot-soldier carried only about 25 charges of powder into battle, which meant that muskets were only fired when absolutely necessary.

Siegroth felt he could not just march past without coming to their assistance. He ordered his men to attack. The two long rows of Dalecarlians strode towards one of the corners of the fort. To their right the other battalions closed up with them. At a range of about 200 metres the fort exploded into life. Rubble and shell-splinters lashed the Swedish ranks with metal. One of the first hit was Siegroth, who was gravely wounded. Shortly afterwards Drake was also hit. Still the assault continued.

Soon they came within musket-range. Rumbling volleys slammed into them, and many fell. The blue-coats pressed forward through the shower of projectiles, past the *chevaux-de-frise*. When the long chain reached the corpse-bestrewn ditches most of them faltered. Some few continued stubbornly forward a few strides more, and rushed up to the rampart. There they came to a final stop. Every man who climbed the wall was shot, or stabbed to death by Russian swords and bayonets.

This gory failure did not prevent a new assault from being quickly mounted. The ranks were re-drawn and storm-wave after storm-wave swept up to the Russian fort, only to tumble back again somewhat sparser than before. The fort would not yield. Nakedly exposed to its fire, the Swedish battalions were being shot to pieces. Men died in droves. They were being made to pay dearly for having neither assault equipment nor supporting cannon. Without ladders, their attempts to scale the ramparts degenerated into a simple bloodbath. At times, their superior numbers proved more of a hindrance than a help as they impeded each other.

A battalion primed for battle was a long and unwieldy instrument. Six long rows of men pressing together round the bastion made it impossible to avoid congestion. And the assaults were badly co-ordinated: some attacked while others merely looked on. The densely massed soldiers offered packed, easy targets. Musket-balls and scrap rattled down, killing or wounding clusters at a time. A carpet of fallen Swedes covered the soil round the fort. The battle for this third redoubt turned into a massacre.

Proportionately, those worst hit were the officers, who led the van in the assault. The Dalecarlia regiment quickly lost its two senior commanders: Siegroth was dying and Drake was already dead. Of the regiment's 21 captains, soon only four were left standing. The other units suffered similar losses. In this boiling cauldron the soldiers' fighting morale began to melt away: individual men, frightened sick of the mortal danger, broke from their companies and ran from the blood-soaked field round the redoubt. The shot-crippled wounded crawled on hands and knees towards the verge of the wood, off to the right of the redoubt. Others were carried away on improvised stretchers. A few lines from the poem by Harald Oxe, of the Jönköping regiment, describe the terrible scenes:

> Some cry: I am shot, in the arm, in the hand, in the thigh,
> In the head, in the neck and in chest, in side, leg and foot;
> Help, help me now, dear comrade, to the surgeon for treatment!
> Some take to their heels, leaving bonnet and hat in their wake . . .

In each regiment the regulation personnel for care of the wounded was one surgeon and three orderlies. The Dalecarlians' field surgeon, Jacob Schultzen, was a 28-year-old East Prussian who had been deputed to attend the king. The art of surgery was in a generally primitive state. With alcohol the only anaesthetic, the wounded soldier had a choice of surrendering to the mercy of the surgeon, with his saws, curved scissors, trepanning drills, bullet-extractors and cauterizing-irons: or death.

Some unfathomable power seemed to be drawing one unit after another into this meaningless and bloody maelström round the large redoubt. There can be no doubt that the assaults were utterly senseless. The attack on the redoubts had been a side issue from the outset, a means of diverting the Russians' attention while the main body of the Swedish army hurried past. With this achieved, the assaults served no purpose at all. The troops in the redoubts were confined there, and constituted little threat once they had been skirted. The stubborn persistence of the officers in calling up one storming attack after another can really only be explained by their inadequate briefing at the start of the Swedish advance. The point of the attack was quite simply not clear to those involved.

Moreover, Roos, the overall commander of these six battalions, remained inactive. The assaults were allowed to carry on without question or command from him. Events seemed to overtake him like a natural phenomenon following its own strange laws, and quite beyond control. Roos was an experienced but rather unimaginative soldier: he may have been influenced by his experiences at the battle of Narva, where he had commanded the Närke-Värmland regiment. With them, he had rolled up swathes of Russian fortifications, bastion after bastion. After the battle he boasted that half his regiment were either dead or wounded. He himself had been wounded in the arm, had his hat shot off by a cannonball and his clothes drilled through by Russian bullets. He may have thought to repeat the feat.

One more factor most probably helped to create the tragedy of the third redoubt: the inflexible tactical doctrines of the Swedish army. The entire military establishment was permeated by an intensely powerful spirit of attack. The weaponry, the manner of fighting, the strong emphasis on naked steel, the bayonet attack and the cavalry charge, were all suffused by a near-fanatical belief in attack as the universal key to victory. The army was institutionally offensive. It was an instinctive assault machine which had one unvarying response to every threat in the field: attack, attack and yet again attack. The formula had been remarkably successful to date, but now these battalions were facing an unfamiliar situation. Their strength was insufficient to take the bastion, and without orders or more intelligent direction the assault machine did what it had been designed for, and ground on mechanically.

The losses swiftly mounted. At the end, 1,100 men had been killed or wounded: a good 40 per cent of the original force. The very high officer casualty figures made it difficult to control the battalions. As the hopelessness of the attempt filtered down to the men, their will to continue fighting quite naturally began to sag. Lieutenant Olof Pommerijn, a 31-year-old Dalecarlian with two brothers in the regiment, left the futile débâcle by the bastion to look for Roos. Having found him, he put it to him that the attempts should cease and that they should retire. The situation is faintly absurd, and a comment on Roos's lethargic leadership. A lieutenant approaches a major-general and practically demands a halt to the proceedings. Roos, realizing there would be no more reinforcements, acceded. Better retreat than 'further let the men be shot dead in vain.' By now all other units had vanished, no one seemed to know where.

If they were to locate and re-join the army a number of courses were open to them. As a first step, Roos decided to gather up and reorganize his bloody bands, and ordered the men to march to the verge of the wood near by, where wounded Swedes had already collected. There had been a lull in the fighting, but as the Russians behind their ramparts saw the Swedish foot assemble and march away, they re-opened fire. In farewell salute fresh missiles rained on the backs of the retreating men and a few more fell to the ground.

Within the wood's cool shade the arduous task of trying to reorganize the tattered units began. Roughly 1,500 men were left of the original 2,600. The high casualty rate among the officers meant there was a serious lack of command to give the right orders, supervise and drive the men on. It also took a long time. The companies had to be formed up before they could be ordered into battalions. Siegroth had been carried out of the action on an improvised stretcher of pikes. He was in severe pain, and dying. However, he grasped enough to realize that the men were just standing still at the edge of the wood. Through his final torments the colonel continued to voice his concern and urged them to press on and join up with the main strength of the army.

The question remained of where it was to be found. The noise of battle had died down, apart from regular volleys directed at Roos's men from nearby Russian artillery. Cannonballs occasionally dropped through the trees, but their precise origin was uncertain.

Among the men at the wood's edge was Abraham Cederholm, the secretary with the valuables. In the light of dawn he had caught up with his regiment, just in time to see a cannonball whistle into one of the squadrons and kill two horsemen. During the confused cavalry engagement he had been separated from his unit, and had then joined Roos's group. The cannon fire worried him, and he decided he would probably be safer riding out on the field. The fire, after all, was being directed at the troops by the verge of the wood.

He rode out towards one of the half-finished redoubts stormed earlier. When well out on the field he was quickly made aware that something was wrong. A cannonball bounded straight towards him. Abraham had an incredible stroke of luck: it passed between his horse's legs. The startled colt bucked, and he realized that the fire was coming from the fort. Finding it unoccupied after the assault, the Russians had re-taken it. The Swedes had even omitted to take the elementary precaution of spiking the guns, by driving nails into the touch-holes to make them useless. Now they were in action again. Cederholm galloped back to the wood.

By now the sun had begun to climb the sky and was beaming warmly on the summer fields. The day was getting hot. Roos was unwilling to march off with no fixed objective: first he had to find the rest of the army. A number of officers were sent out with orders to discover its exact location. They would have to be quick about it. Time was getting short.

## 12 · 'Would God Roos Were Here'

It was now about six o'clock in the morning. The shocking realization that one third of the total Swedish infantry were missing spread swiftly through the main body of the army. Riding west past the foot soldiers, Gyllenkrok met an aide who asked him: 'Does my Lord Colonel know that Major-General Roos is to the rear with several regiments of foot?' Gyllenkrok burst out with an astonished: 'How in the name of Jesus has this come about?', turned his horse and rode back to the right wing. He met Rehnsköld and asked him if he knew of what had happened. The field marshal did know, and had already taken steps. Gyllenkrok suggested a short halt by all troops, but Rehnsköld greeted this with silence.

By this stage Rehnsköld had ordered the commanding officer of the Västmanlanders, Sparre, to return to the redoubts with his men, find Roos's force and pilot them back to the main body. Hielm's dragoons were seconded to them, and aides and Drabants were also sent on the same errand. One of the aides was Nils Bonde, by now back from his long ride to Bolanovka to instruct Carl Roland's outpost to withdraw and rejoin the army.

A little later Gyllenkrok encountered dragoons on their way to the area round the redoubts and exchanged a few words with their commander, Colonel Nils Hielm. Hielm was a scarred 42-year-old Smålander who had fought in the Dutch service at Mons, Pont de Pierre, Huy, Namur and elsewhere. Since the beginning of the war he had served under Swedish colours and been ennobled in the course of it. The colonel let it be known that he had been sent to fetch Roos's men. Gyllenkrok exhorted him to hurry and 'get Roos to us.'

It was a matter of urgency now for the command to consolidate their scattered bands. An immediate Russian counter-attack was highly unlikely, but could cause the Swedes great problems if it came at this time, hitting them when both foot and horse were split into several small groups. It was impossible to collect the forces in front of the fiery mouths of the Russian heavy artillery. The camp contained 20-pounder mortars, 20-pounder and 40-pounder howitzers, and massive eight-pounder and 12-pounder cannon, infernal machines with a range of 1,000 metres. A good point of reassembly was chosen. The regiments were marched to a large depression in the ground, immediately east of the Budyschenski wood, concealing them from sight of the Russian gunners.

The foot soldiers trudged down to the meadows in the shallow dale. One battalion closed up with the next. The cavalry began to collect at the same place. The king and his escort joined them, near the blue lines of the Östgöta regiment of foot. The infantry gathered at the north end of the hollow, halting at a spot facing a patch of marshland – the 'little morass'. The king's litter was lowered to the ground, and Carl Piper sat down on a drum next to it.

Piper was the king's premier minister, the only member of the government to follow the monarch out into the field. He directly supervised the chancellery, and attended any conference of importance. This plump 61-year-old man held an extremely high position as one of the king's foremost advisers, and faithful executor of a variety of absolute edicts. Of bourgeois birth, with a successful career in public service behind him, he had been one in the progressive circle of lesser nobility which had once rallied round the king's father, Charles XI. Now he was a count, and by virtue of a good marriage, skilful business dealings and a healthy appetite for bribes, had built up a great fortune.

An ebullient and swaggering attendance on the king now ensued. Officers flocked round the litter, offering congratulations on the success so far, and expressing good wishes for 'further progress'. Gyllenkrok joined the chorus, adding: 'would God Roos were here', so the battle might be concluded. Charles was sanguine: troops had been sent to fetch Roos and 'he will doubtless soon be here'.

The cavalry were not yet fully reorganized. Gyllenkrok rode over to discover why the squadrons were still not in line. He pointed the matter out to the commander of the cavalry left wing, 41-year-old Major-General Hugo Johan Hamilton. Hamilton was a man of resolute appearance, with thick bushy eyebrows, a pronounced Roman nose and full lips. He came from an ancient family of Scottish warriors which had arrived in Sweden, via Ireland, in the middle of the 17th century. His own military career had begun at the tender age of twelve. The major-general's wing was in order: he did not know what the problem was on the right. The squadrons on the right had been engaged in the hardest fighting and were also involved in the most violent pursuit. No doubt they needed longer to re-form.

Time passed. Nothing was heard from Sparre, Hielm, Roos, nor any of the many aides and Drabants sent off to find him. As the battalions gradually came into line, the men had time for some well needed rest. Many of them were numb with fatigue. None had slept long the previous night. The infantry lay down in their rigid formations. The cavalry dismounted. But where was Sparre? Where was Roos?

The Swedes were not alone in their awareness of the missing battalions. The Russian command, informed no doubt by reports from the redoubts, had also realized that a major section of Swedish infantry were separated from the main force, and were swift to take advantage of this opportunity to deal the Swedes a major setback. Five battalions of infantry, the Tobol and Kopor regiments, and half the Fichtenheim regiment, were despatched out of the camp under command of Lieutenant-General Rentsel. They were supported by five regiments of dragoons, seconded from the left wing, commanded by Lieutenant-General Heinske. Their objective was to attack and defeat Roos's isolated force, and also to make contact with the besieged Poltava garrison.

Schlippenbach, whose small section had been sent out to scout before the battle broke, had earlier joined up with Roos. The section now set off to try to find the rest of the army. Unfortunately for them, they soon rode into the Russians now on their way to attack Roos. After a brief skirmish Schlippenbach's men were overwhelmed, and he surrendered. One of the officers with him, a 23-year-old infantry captain called Carl Palmfelt, nevertheless managed to escape and continued his aimless search for the army.

The ten Russian regiments began a pincer movement. Rentsel's infantry marched straight towards Roos's battalions, while the cavalry rode in a wide arc through the line of redoubts to reach a position behind them.

It had been a long wait for Roos's shattered men. Some had lain down to sleep. A certain order had been re-established, but the heavy losses had obliged the two battalions of the Dalecarlia regiment to merge into one. The Västerbotten men were also now united into one thinly manned little battalion.

The dearth of officers was serious. Officers had two main functions on the battlefield: they led the fighting and supervised the men. They had to lead by personal example, almost always marched in the van, and so suffered the highest percentage losses in action. The rank and file were more liable to suffer starvation, sickness and hardship on campaign. Private soldiers usually met death in a filthy camp and not on the field of honour. The supervisory role meant that officers not urging the men on in the front line were to bring up the rear and, 'with the non-commissioned officers, see that the soldiers do not slink away, and keep the ranks closed when they are to fire'. Soldiers trying to flee action were to be summarily killed. As the ordinance put it, the command in such cases 'is empowered to knock such mutineers to the ground, for the word is either to fight and die facing the enemies of the realm, or to fall by retribution of their superiors'. If the whole unit broke down and fled, the articles laid down that every tenth man was to be hanged.

The style of command was rather brutal. Obedience was enforced by violence. One officer's account describes how he drove the lower ranks before him with cuts and blows. His colonel, a witness to this, had remarked that 'every officer ought to do likewise'. Once the men had been threatened that 'whoever I see turn his back and offer to depart, I shall thrust through or shoot dead', his orders had been obeyed. Giving the men a whack with one's sword was a natural part of leadership. Charles XII himself had been known to reach for his long blade, to invigorate excessively sluggish subjects.

The shortage of officers in Roos's battalions was extreme. With the motive power absent there was a risk that whole units would collapse under pressure. The situation was so bad among the Dalesmen that non-commissioned officers had to function as company commanders.

Some time after seven, Roos's men noticed a long line of cavalry coming up behind them, near the redoubts stormed earlier. Fully convinced they would be Swedish dragoons, Roos sent his aide, 22-year-old Ensign Bengt Sparre from Närke, to meet them. The relieved major-general was optimistic that these horsemen would provide clear directions on the whereabouts of the main strength. He was to be unpleasantly disappointed.

Sparre was soon seen to swing his horse round and spur at full stretch back across the sun-baked plain. He reported that the cavalry was Russian: Heinske's five regiments of dragoons. Ironically, moments later an aide from headquarters arrived, with all the information they had been starved of. Nils Bonde had broken through. Bonde reported to Roos and offered to guide him and his men to the king.

Almost simultaneously, yet another foe hove into view. In front of them, Rentsel's battalions were advancing straight for the Swedes, with Cossack support on their left. At their back, Roos's men could see Heinske's long chain of men and horses drawing closer. The trap was about to snap shut: it was past the eleventh hour. Bonde would have to defer his guidance, since Roos could not move before repelling the Russians. He turned to Bonde, saying: 'It does not appear that we may march before we receive them.' In the greatest haste, he began to make ready for battle, now wholly unavoidable.

A few of Heinske's squadrons, without firing, swept up at a gallop and wheeled away. After a short pause they repeated the manoeuvre: it was clear they were inspecting the Swedish dispositions.

Captain Johan Ahlefeldt was sent to reconnoitre the woods. The captain, a former deputy gamekeeper and now acting major with the Närke Life battalion, returned to report that yet another Russian battalion was advancing through the trees, in line with those on the field. The Russians were about to outflank them. Roos regrouped his men, sending the Närke battalion to face the new threat approaching in the wood. He hesitated on how to draw up the remaining three battalions. Extending the line would bring it far too close to the large redoubt, exposing the men to dangerous fire from this and the other forts near by. Deployment in one simple line facing the infantry attack from the north would allow the Russian cavalry to take them in the back. He decided on a kind of open square: setting the Jönköping battalion at right angles to the Närke. Next came the Västerbotten battalion, with the Dalecarlia battalion deployed farthest out on the left. The left wing of the Dalecarlians was pulled back, buried in a little copse of hazelnut trees, to prevent the Russian cavalry, steadily drawing nearer, from attacking the rear.

This arrangement was purely defensive. Roos had attempted to build up flank protection, but the risk of being surrounded had not really been dispelled. To strengthen his defences further, Roos interspersed the pikemen between the second and third ranks of the musketeers, stringing them out along the whole of the front instead of grouping them in the centre of each company, as was usual. This weakened the impact of a musket volley, but gained a continuous firing line. Spreading the pikemen the entire length of the line made it, hopefully, more resilient against a cavalry charge.

The pike was a weapon of debatable value. It was mainly thought of as a defensive counter to cavalry, and performed this role reasonably well. The bayonet was beginning to make it obsolete, however. Every musketeer could now turn his weapon into a miniature pike. Although the pike was slowly disappearing from the battlefields of Europe, both Russians and Swedes were still armed with this ancient weapon. One-third of each battalion was composed of pikemen.

It was rather doubtful whether this interspersion was really going to help, since many of the Swedish pikes had been shot and broken in the battles for the redoubts. The men awaited the Russian onslaught with their fists firmly clenched round splintered stumps.

Redeployment took time. The distance to the advancing enemy dwindled rapidly. The movement had barely been completed before the Russian infantry swung into line before them and attacked.

The Swedes could repel the Russian attack with fire, ideally combined with a counter-attack launched at exactly the right moment. Careful troop control was vital. Fire was delivered in volleys, line by line; and loading, aiming and firing were executed strictly on command. With a maximum range of 150-200 metres and a firing rate of about two shots per minute it was possible to fire three or four salvos at an attacker before contact. Barriers in the terrain, as here, where some of the Russian foot were advancing through trees, or a temporary break in an advance to return fire, would delay the approach and allow more volleys. The heavy smoke produced by black gunpowder made firing more difficult and reduced the rate. Pauses were frequent, to give the smoke time to disperse. On a calm day an almost impenetrable fog of billowing white smoke could cover the front line and had already added to the chaos round the redoubts.

The soldiers' aim was always fairly poor. There were even theorists who asserted that aiming was completely unnecessary, since it lowered the rate of fire. Muskets were not designed for precision firing. The ball's trajectory was parabolic. Volley fire required the soldier to act mainly as a support for his gun: a unit functioned as a sort of crude machine gun which intermittently spewed out a hailstorm of ball against the enemy. Most of the musket-balls missed completely: volley fire could be wasteful. Calculations indicate that the hit rate might be one in 300. But the spread meant that a few balls would always hit home. Given that the target was a concentrated mass of upright human beings making little effort to get away or seek cover, the effect also varied greatly with the range.

Long, protracted exchanges of fire were very costly, achieved little result, and were avoided. Volley firing was also very difficult to stop once into its stride: commands would be lost in the deafening roar. The first salvo, when the muskets were at their best, was the most effective. As time went on the barrels would foul; fear and confusion distracted the men and loading would grow ragged. The objective was therefore at most one or two volleys at the shortest possible range. The Swedish king did not want his men to fire, said one of them, 'until they saw the whites of the enemy eyes'. The longer the fire could be delayed, the greater its effect. The officers' task was to control this delay.

The Russian battalions drew closer. The muskets were silent. Before the steadily advancing Russian lines the nerves of some of the Swedish soldiers gave way. A few isolated, ragged shots were loosed, whereupon panic firing took over. Against orders, the rear ranks in the Swedish battalions began firing wildly, and too soon. The range was too great. A short fire-battle was fought out. Hardly had the Swedish fire rung out before it received a thundering echo in the form of a very heavy Russian answering salvo. Then the foremost Swedish ranks also fired. The Russian response was immediate: a fresh volley lashed the Swedish lines. They swayed, fell into disorder, and the soldiers started to falter back.

The Russians seized the opportunity created by their heavy preparatory fire and rushed in with naked weapons. Lowered bayonets, pikes and swords came charging through the bushes: the Russian battalions fell on the Swedes like a landslide. The hand-to-hand mêlée was short, bloody and confused.

The blades are drawn from scabbards, and sabres bend and flash,
They cut and thrust, advance, land blows on every side now,
Here heads and legs fly off, there lie the horseman and his horse . . .

as Harald Oxe puts it. A couple of battalions, the Dalesmen, stood firm before the assault. The others gave way. Sergeant-Major Wallberg of the Dalecarlians wrote that 'all was in vain as the pike-points of the enemy were at us to the body, so the majority were wounded to death by them'. A few moments more and the whole of the Swedish line imploded. The men streamed back in panic, defying the desperate threats of the small number of officers, and their pleas to stand and fight. The battalion commanders were killed or taken prisoner, one by one. Most of the bunched mass of soldiers suffered the same fate. Wallberg was captured by some Russian grenadiers and plundered of all he possessed: soon he was standing stark naked. Johan Ahlefeldt, Roos's forest scout, was severely wounded during the battle, then captured and stripped to the skin.

The Dalesmen, deployed to the rear and left, prevented the Russian cavalry from tying the knot in the sack. Their stand kept an escape route open to the south for the men trying to save themselves by flight. Most of those not killed or captured were washed away in a feverish general bolt down a large and many-branched ravine, running immediately behind the initial defensive position.

In the chaos one or two individuals managed to slip away in other directions. Captain Conrad Sparre, aged 28, of the Närke-Värmland regiment, had only recently recovered from a wound sustained in a skirmish in February. He had nearly bled to death at the time, but the wound had been sewn up and cauterized. The subsequent gangrene had been mastered after several operations. He had mounted his horse in good time for the battle. Somehow he managed to evade capture after the brief struggle at the wood's edge; perhaps because he took a piece of equipment from a dead Russian officer, perhaps because his red-cuffed uniform resembled the Russian, or most probably because the uniforms of neither side could be seen below the thick layers of dust and spent powder. In any case he passed unchallenged through the Russian ranks and made off south, away from the corpses on the battlefield, over the level plain towards the Swedish baggage-train.

Abraham Cederholm also escaped death. He and his servant, both mounted, slipped away through the wood, the servant still leading Cederholm's pack-horse, heavily laden with valuables. Cossack horsemen pursued them. The servant released the pack-horse and the Cossacks were on to it at once. Abraham looked back in despair as his collected wealth was now snapped up. A great loss, but he was faced with losing liberty or life itself if he failed to make good his escape. As more and more Russian soldiers and horsemen found their way into the woods and down the large ravine only one way out was finally left, across a small quagmire. This boggy bridge to salvation was highly dangerous; many Swedes had already sunk in it. Cederholm was heavily weighed down by his thousand ducats. If he fell off his horse he would never be able to pull himself back into the saddle without help. But there was no choice: he had to risk the passage over the mire. Miraculously enough he made it across and, leaving those stuck in it to their fate, he rode away, much the poorer but still alive.

About four hundred Swedes, including Roos, managed to scramble down into the ravine. They were by no means saved. Some of the Russian troops turned back to their camp, but others under Rentsel continued to pursue those still alive. Dark clouds of cavalry surged down the ravine in front of the fleeing men. Hard on their heels followed foot soldiers, brandishing bayonets. The Russian battalion which had clashed with the Närke men in the woods continued to plunge on through the vegetation, threatening to fall on the dwindling remnant from the flank. Again the Russians threatened to surround them.

They would have to fight their way out. The Swedes sprayed fire at the Russian horse who turned aside and kept their distance. The battalion in the trees was a permanent menace. The exhausted men fled on, worked their way across the ravine and hauled themselves up over its rim, inside the wood. Roos led them south, towards their camp of the night before. He nourished a forlorn hope of finding relief.

The men's wilting morale now began to fold completely. Battle casualties of 20 per cent are reckoned heavy: for a unit to survive losses of 50 per cent is almost unheard of. Casualties sustained over a short space of time are also much more demoralizing. In the course of a couple of hours Roos's battalions had, incredibly, lost more than 80 per cent of their original strength. Many of the soldiers cried despairingly that they should lay down their arms and 'demand quarter'. Roos, stiff-necked, refused: 'No man of honour would do that', he shouted back and tried to encourage them: 'We will soon meet up with the army.' The mobile battle continued south, as the swarms of Russian horse and foot grew denser.

The struggle was meaningless: their spirit was broken, but iron bands of discipline still bound the soldiers together and made them obey orders more or less by force of habit. Perhaps Roos's words gave them energy for a last desperate physical effort. Concepts of honour, hammered into them over the years, also made them fight on, in spite of their terrible casualties. Gallantry, courage and a fathomless contempt for anything resembling cowardice was cultivated in the army. To flee, to retreat and especially to surrender were fundamentally wrong. To stand firm and never to give in were shining ideals, frequently and eloquently extolled. It was better to fight a hopeless battle 'than to have the name, that one had readily fled'.

Enemy troops that capitulated without resistance – thereby serving their own best interests – would be subjected to humiliating treatment.

Courageous enemies, who had caused great trouble and inflicted heavy casualties, would be highly respected, and often given preferential treatment. The high hymn to courage was sung by both sides. Swedish units might receive good terms of surrender if they were judged to have fought well. The consistent application of these ideals was an expression of the martial ethos found in the officer corps. It was an echo of earlier epochs, shades of a mediaeval cult of chivalry cross-fertilized with the *gentilhomme* ideal of the new age.

The Swedes continued their blood-soaked Calvary through the woods, halting now and then to confront their pursuers. The soldiers were tolerably well organized. Ragged volleys were loosed off in every direction, then all was set in motion again. Nils Bonde, the aide from headquarters, had been separated from Roos in the smoky turmoil of battle. Roos was still ignorant of the army's whereabouts. Hence the faint hope that relief, possibly even the king, might be found at the old camp area. This was extinguished upon arrival: no one was there, except the relentlessly circling Russian cavalry.

They stumbled on, eastwards now towards the high ground by the Vorskla. The king and a number of regiments had been quartered there. Would they find succour, or was the remaining fragment of Roos's six battalions to be totally wiped out?

# 13 · 'They Are Leaving Their Lines!'

The Russian command was puzzled by the Swedish army's delay. Since its disappearance from their sight, hours had slipped by without a hint of action. The Russians were planning to meet the anticipated assault from behind their ramparts. But, as a further defensive precaution, 23 infantry battalions had been ordered out to positions on both sides of the camp, 13 on the north side, ten on the south. The Swedish thrust would be met from behind a cage of iron, with heavy fire from the camp parapets. The doubled lines of foot to each side were intended to close in on the flanks of the attacking force.

Most of the Russian cavalry were busy sorting out their tangled lines north of the great ouvrage and the Tachtaulova rivulet. To their west stood the greater part of the Cossack irregular horse under command of Hetman Skoropadski. Originally posted round Maly Budyschi, they had been forced back, like all the other Russian cavalry units. The irregular horse had been badly shaken by the initial Swedish momentum, and their fighting qualities cannot have been great. The only parts of the Russian army that had been in direct physical contact with the Swedes were the troops under Rentsel and Heinske, still engaged in pursuit of Roos's remnant. The initiative still seemed to lie with the Swedes. Tsar Peter waited impatiently for their next move. It seemed a long time coming.

Down in the low-lying ground two hours elapsed with no sign of the lost battalions. When, finally, some infantry were spotted in the distance the Swedish command were sure that here at last were Roos's missing men.

Their apparent approach prompted the command to complete the army's deployment for renewed attack. The plan now must have been to thrust forward with both foot and horse, from a start-line north of the small patch of marsh. From there, most of the Russian cavalry, well north of the camp, could be separated from the forces more closely surrounding the fortifications. An attack launched from this more northerly position would cut off the Russian avenues of retreat rather better than if launched from the depression they now occupied.

The Swedish command probably had it in mind to defeat each Russian sector separately, from a more central position: first driving off their cavalry, then turning towards the forces practically immured in and around the encampment. The early hours of the morning had given painful proof of the strength of the Russian defences, however, and the Swedish command felt the need for reinforcements. An aide was sent south to Pushkaryovka to fetch up the troops and artillery located there. This would be time-consuming: it would take the reinforcements at least six hours to reach the battlefield. An attack on the camp could not be contemplated until some time in the afternoon. The immediate aim was probably to take up the commanding central position, by advancing in the direction of the Russian cavalry. By now the command must have been growing impatient. In order not to waste further precious time they decided to wait no longer for the missing battalions – thought in any case to be on their way – and ordered the infantry north without delay, over the little morass.

The soldiers stood up. Their rest was over. The battalions formed into columns and marched across the patch of marshland, unit by unit. The king followed with most of his entourage. During the waiting period Carl Piper had left the drum by the litter and settled down under the shade of a tree in a garden, a short distance away. After a while he was woken by Secretary Hermelin, who informed him that 'His Royal Majesty has had himself conveyed from where he was resting'. Piper, who was tired and wanted to sleep on, replied 'no haste for us' and stayed put, under his tree. The army had not yet been drawn up in battle-order.

The short march was led by the second Närke battalion, still ignorant of the fate of their comrades in the Life battalion, with Roos. They marched forward slowly, in the direction of a small clump of trees on the other side of the Tachtaulova stream. Near the trees they could see Russian cavalry stationary in the shimmering heat, ready for battle, drawn up in two lines. To their left, a little farther back, stood part of Skoropadski's Cossacks.

A few shots rang out suddenly. The slowly marching soldiers were being fired on at close range. Cossacks in the nearby gardens were directing well-aimed fire into the long lines from behind the fencing. Fifty men were sent to drive the creeping snipers off. With the return of the smell of gunpowder the leading battalion more or less instinctively altered formation. The column swung into line, still facing the trees across the stream. The advance continued. The left flank of the Närke battalion moved a little farther ahead: if the enemy over the stream were to launch an attack it would have to be met quickly.

The Swedish cavalry were already drawn up in readiness on the northern side of the small morass. While waiting, they clashed with retreating enemy squadrons, sweeping past very near them. Some of the Swedes set off in pursuit, but Rehnsköld immediately ordered them to halt. His cavalry had to be kept collected and ready; not split in pursuits of isolated

## Map 5 · *From Regroupment to Final Battle*

1. Roos breaks off his attack on the third redoubt and retires to the verge of the Yakovetski wood.
2. The Russians launch a two-pronged attack on Roos with infantry and cavalry. The Swedes are overwhelmed and flee towards Poltava.
3. The Swedish command assume they are about to be reunited with Roos and begin deploying to attack the camp.
4. The Russians advance from the camp with their entire force, threatening to cut off the army's contact with its supply-train.
5. The Swedish army has to counter this threat. It is ordered to retreat.
6. The remnants of Roos's fleeing group are pursued to Poltava. Their attempt to reach the siege works is foiled by a Russian attack.
7. Roos's group take refuge in an abandoned fort. The Russians pursue. The Swedes capitulate.
8. The Russian forces at Poltava attack the Swedish units in the siege works.

enemy units. Carl Gustaf Creutz, commanding the right-hand wing of the cavalry, rode up a small rise to have a look round. A middle-aged man with a round face, moustache, aquiline nose and squirrel eyes: brave and dutiful, he was a soldier to the core, but unimaginative and lacking initiative. Two years after his birth in Falun, in 1660, he had been entered as a lieutenant in the Mounted Life regiment, the unit which he now commanded. These absurdly early enrolments were quite usual in certain families of the nobility and illustrate yet again the rigidity of career mapped out for scions of the upper classes. Creutz peered across at the fortified camp to see what the Russians might come up with in this situation.

Rehnsköld walked his horse down the long snake of battalion columns. He reined in at their head and turned to Gyllenkrok, who had followed the Närke battalion and helped direct the march. Rehnsköld asked him irately if he did not know 'how to march in column?' 'I am marching with the whole battalion facing in line,' replied Gyllenkrok, 'and will move on up to the trees.' The field marshal, uninterested in any further explanation, cut him off with a surly 'march, march', and rode back. The advance continued a little further until a surprising command to halt was passed down the line. Gyllenkrok told Wrangel, at the head of the Närke battalion, to ride back and check the order.

The Swedish command had been confronted with the painful truth that Roos's battalions were gone for good. The infantry glimpsed in the distance had been Russian: parts of Rentsel's force returning to their camp after defeating Roos. The news was brought by Captain Anders Gideon Gyldenklou, a 34-year-old Stockholmer, the aide sent down to Pushkaryovka to fetch reinforcements. On his ride south he rode into Rentsel's returning men. As he approached he made the startling discovery that they were Russian. Throwing his horse around he had galloped straight back to report.

A few moments later reports arrived from the detachments sent to find the missing men. Neither the Västmanlanders nor Hielm's dragoons had been able to make contact with Roos. The dragoons had engaged the Russian irregular horse and cut their way through, to no avail. By then the Russians had reoccupied the redoubts: the holes bored in the fortification system with such great loss of Swedish blood had now been repaired, with minimal effort. It had just been a matter of moving in again when the blue battalions marched away. From a distance, however, the Swedes had seen Roos's shattered battalions and followed their death-throes at the green verges of the wood.

No help either that Carl Palmfelt, the captain who escaped when Schlippenbach's detachment was torn apart, had finally reached them with good information on the whereabouts of the lost battalions. Vigorous Russian counter-moves had nullified all attempts to reunite Roos with the main army.

The surgeons examined the king's wound and re-bandaged it. Hultman ran about looking for water and proffered some for Carolus to drink from a special silver beaker. Major-General Sparre, returned from his abortive attempt to relieve Roos, went over the situation with the king, describing what he had seen. He had not been able to make his way through 'for force of the enemy' but said 'Major-General Roos is standing in a wood, and defends himself well'. Listening to Sparre's report, Gyllenkrok was of the opinion it boded ill: it would be better if Roos's men 'were here'. Sparre sensed veiled criticism and retorted angrily that if Roos 'will not defend himself when he has six battalions, he may do what the devil he likes, I cannot help him'.

Worse surprises were in store. The little conference was abruptly interrupted by Rehnsköld with sensational news. 'The enemy infantry are advancing – *they are leaving their lines!*' The Russian foot, to a man, were starting to pour out of their camp in a mighty river. Twenty-two thousand men organized in 42 battalions of pikes, bayonets and musket-barrels, were forming up in line of battle.

Repeated urgings had been necessary before Rehnsköld could be brought to grasp the situation. First to notice the menace was Creutz, from the vantage point of his hillock. He had reported it when Rehnsköld rode by, but the field marshal's reaction had been dismissive. 'Do not concern yourself,' he had answered, and returned to the king. Charles had not been so sanguine and thought Rehnsköld was being negligent. The king muttered to him, as he leant against the litter: 'Field Marshal, you have not reconnoitred well today. Send someone up to the high ground to observe what is happening.' Rehnsköld was deaf to advice. 'There is no need,' was his answer. 'I know the situation. I know this terrain like the back of my hand.'

A moment later another report arrived saying the Russians were in full march. Again the king asked Rehnsköld to see if it was true, again the field marshal stubbornly declined. It was impossible, such boldness was un-Russian. Rehnsköld's confidence was rooted in a tragic misjudgement of the Russian army. He underestimated the Russians' will to fight and their ability to take the initiative. The original plan had assumed they would remain passive while the Swedes executed their elegant tactical pirouettes. The field marshal may also have brushed aside these first reports because he imagined that they referred to the deployment of Russian infantry on the flanks of the camp. In his arrogance he may have thought inferior capabilities had misinterpreted this purely defensive measure.

Charles ordered Lieutenant Johan Hierta of the Drabants to ride off and establish the accuracy of these alarming reports. Hierta returned, and confirmed them. Rehnsköld, still sceptical, had then gone to make sure with his own eyes. He rode up the hillock Creutz was standing on, and gazed across the sun-baked plain. Battalion upon battalion, in an apparently endless line, was streaming out on the field in front of the Russian camp, and forming up.

Ever since their departure from Saxony, in the late summer of 1707, the Swedish army had attempted to bring the Russians to a decisive battlefield encounter. Time and again the Russians had smoothly evaded a major engagement, to the great odium of the Swedes. Now this confrontation, so keenly desired, was staring them straight in the eye. It was a moot point whether the moment was well-chosen.

Creutz turned to Rehnsköld and said: 'It will be necessary to form up.' He pointed to the terrain near where they were standing. 'There is an evil morass here,' he said. The field marshal gave him a curt answer and rode down the slope to the king. The hour was at hand.

# 14 · 'Not My Men But the King's'

Roos's pulverized detachment continued its death-march through the trees and the cherry orchards growing on the hillside, up towards the high ridge along the river. Russian horsemen circled them constantly, picking them off with their fire and steadily reducing their number. They gained the ridge, with its beautiful view over the winding Vorskla. On its summit, they were mocked again. There were no compatriots to meet them there: only a large swarm of hostile Cossacks riding down from the north; from Yakovetski and the fortified camp. The Swedish bivouacs around them were deserted. Heinske's dragoons had got there before them, and were now busy plundering the empty camp-site. The situation was quite desperate. Wherever they turned they met Russian bayonets and sabres. Salvation would have to be sought elsewhere. The one possibility still remaining was Poltava itself. Roos knew there were still Swedish troops in the siege-works round the town. He decided to risk making for Poltava and ordered his men south.

They followed the high ground until they reached the cloister at its point, where finally they found some fellow Swedes. A small group only. A few people left at the camp area had barricaded themselves inside the building and sealed the doors and windows with bricks. Roos went up and called to them to come out and follow him, or be taken by the pursuing Russian troops. They refused, and he and his men continued south. When they emerged on the slopes facing the town their hopes of reaching the siege-works crumbled. They were about 1,000 metres from the Kharkov gate, through which ran the main route to Kharkov. Four battalions of Russian foot, supported by horsemen, flooded from it, formed a line and advanced towards them, on the long slope dipping down to the Vorskla. By a marshy patch near an alder wood, they drew up facing Roos squarely in front of the town. The way to the siege-works was closed.

The demoralized Swedes had no hope of fighting their way through. They numbered about 400 men, including wounded. Down by the marsh waited more than 2,000 Russian soldiers, not including the horsemen. The Swedes were being followed by strong Russian units. To attack the Russian line standing at the bottom of the depression, about 500 metres in diameter, would be to descend into a cauldron surrounded by enemies on all sides.

It was the beginning of the end of their Via Dolorosa for the Swedes. Roos saw nothing for it but to make for one of the fortified earthworks by the banks of the Vorskla, now abandoned. The nearest of these, only about 500 or 600 metres south-east of the cloister, was what was called the great guard-bastion. Here they would be able to defend themselves against their pursuers, and perhaps hold out until some relief came. The soldiers made an about turn and tramped past the ridge point down towards the river. They entered the fort shortly before nine o'clock.

The bastion they occupied was the largest in the network of Swedish fortifications by the river. Rectangular in shape, it measured about 120 by 140 metres. Round it ran a small ditch, and its rampart was crowned by a palisade and had a couple of fort-like projections. Immediately east of it were the charred remains of a burnt bridge which had crossed the tributary rivulet. Long defence-works connected it with other siege-works nearer the town. In an attempt to delay their pursuers and deny them access to these defences, the Swedes set fire to fascines and the basketwork used to construct the connecting passages. Wreaths of smoke ascended to the blue skies. Inside the stronghold the 400 men, many of them wounded or weaponless, prepared themselves for final battle. After their prolonged struggle they were very short of ammunition. Roos had the ramparts manned, and detailed a reserve strength, in the desperate hope that they could hold out until relief arrived.

Peace, of a sort, had reigned in Poltava since the early morning. The Swedish siege-works, manned by the Södermanland and Kronoberg regiments, lay mainly south-west of the town, a good distance away from Roos's force. The regiments were organized in two battalions with a total strength of about 850 men. They had two little half-pounder cannon, sited far forward in a battery on a captured part of the town's ramparts. They were supported by a small detachment of Life Dragoons led by 34-year-old Major Anders Strömsköld, and a number of Zaporozhians. Two more small detachments, one to the north-west and another due east of the town, maintained the illusion that Poltava was surrounded. Immediately outside the burnt suburb's low wall of earth there was a sentry-post of about 30 horsemen guarding the gate. Down by the Vorskla, where the Kharkov road crossed the river, was a star-shaped fort manned by Second Captain Jesper Hård and 40-odd soldiers. Hård suffered from a rather unusual injury. He had been wounded 'in the privates', as the record discreetly puts it. All in all, the Swedish force now containing Poltava was not particularly strong. Their task can only have been to keep the garrison more or less in check, to ensure they did not cause any trouble for the baggage-train or the main army.

Colonel Kelen, the garrison's commander, had been keeping his forces in readiness since the early morning, waiting for a suitable opportunity to join the battle to the north. Nothing happened until they saw the battered remnants of Roos's six battalions emerging from the edges of the Yakovetski wood near the cloister, surrounded by Russian cavalry. Kelen ordered the sortie to block the Swedes' route to safety in the trenches on the other side of the town. His battalions did not remain stationary, biding their time, after the Swedes retired to the guard-bastion. They turned, and advanced on the little star-shaped fort with its 40 occupants. Hård, a pragmatist, seeing little future in further resistance, accepted the terms the Russians offered him. He and his men laid down their arms.

Kelen began to scent success and ordered another advance, directed against the troops in the siege-works. The Russians threw themselves into an assault but were repulsed. More men were needed.

The men who had just secured Hård's surrender were ordered up the steep slope south of the town. They were to surmount the Masurovka heights and then fall on the flank of the Swedes in the trenches. One hundred and forty foot soldiers from Kronoberg's regiment, commanded by a young Pomeranian, Second Captain Carl von Rango, were posted north-east of the town, towards the river. They pulled back before the packed Russian bayonets and were chased to the heights above the wooded slopes. Simultaneously other Russian forces, with Cossack support, stormed the little outpost north-west of the town and swept it aside without difficulty. More Russian units sallied out past the town ramparts.

The colonel of the Kronoberg regiment, Johan Cronman, ordered von Rango's outpost to return immediately to the siege-works. The Swedes collected their forces and addressed themselves to defending the trenches below the walls of Poltava. The attacks had to be repelled on two fronts: forces from inside the town were storming their forward and left flanks, while the four battalions mentioned earlier attacked them on the right. When the long green lines of gleaming weaponry and charging men reached the siege-works a form of trench warfare set in. Groups of men stumbled to and fro through the warren of trenches, connecting passages and parallels, and shot or cut each other to death. Attack and counter-attack followed in quick succession. The Swedish battery on the ramparts was stormed and the two cannon fell into Russian hands. The commanding officer of the Södermanlanders, Gabriel von Weidenhaijn, was killed by a cannonball fired from one of the block-houses abutting the wall. The Swedes defended themselves desperately; after a time the attacks ebbed away. A lull ensued. The only Russian success was the capture of the battery: in other respects the Swedes had maintained their positions.

Two kilometres away, north-east of the trenches, the vain hopes of relief in the great guard-bastion were beginning to dwindle. More and more

Russian units began to gather round the stronghold: but no hint of any Swedes to the rescue. Two figures detached themselves from the Russian ranks. A drummer and an officer approached the rampart. The drummer sounded a roll on his drum and the Swedes waited, silently. The Russian officer called out, asking them not to shoot. He was allowed closer. Roos climbed up on a ledge on the rampart to hear what he had to say. The officer saluted politely: His Tsarist Majesty sent greetings and was pleased to offer the Swedish commander his clemency. If Roos would surrender with good grace, not only he, but all with him would be permitted to keep everything they had and would 'be as honourably treated as any prisoners in the world.' The Swedish major-general up on the ledge asked who was in command of the opposing forces. The answer came back: Lieutenant-General Rentsel. Roos then histrionically requested the officer to greet Rentsel, saying that 'he knew they were not my men but the King's that I had with me, which I ought in no way give up in this manner.' Nevertheless, he asked for a period of grace until evening to consider the offer.

The Russian officer made his way back to his battalions, waiting in battle-order opposite the bastion. The Russians rolled a few pieces of artillery down from the town and began to dig a battery position. These preparations increased the psychological pressure. The officer returned and repeated Rentsel's offer. But he was unwilling to agree to such long delay. He pointed out the cannon. The bastion was 'paltry', and would cost little effort to take. Roos assured him, with a show of bravado no doubt, that while that might be so, they would 'at least take with them as many as they were themselves, and more, before they would be removed.' He repeated his demand for a period of grace. He was content to reduce it to two hours, but still demanded that during this period his opponents should cease their preparations for assault and that no one was to approach the bastion. All the Russians were to lie down. The spokesman rode back to Rentsel with this latest message, and then returned again. Rentsel agreed, but he was only willing to give the trapped men half an hour's respite. Roos asked if the spokesman had a watch. Both men pulled out their watches and compared them. The time was a little past nine.

Once more the Russian rode back. An order went out to the soldiers who, after a while, lay down on the ground. Perhaps some relief, Roos hoped, might arrive in the time thus gained. It was a minuscule hope by now, and shrank further as fresh reinforcements swelled the numbers round the bastion. Of course the Swedes wanted to avoid captivity, but they were faced with being stormed and totally annihilated. There was no real choice: out-and-out fanaticism was relatively rare in this era. Battle tended to be waged only up to a certain point; and when further resistance became patently meaningless the white flag would be unfurled. Bombastic harangues about battling to the last man, and the last drop of blood, nearly always proved to be bubbles of empty rhetoric.

In many ways the whole thing was a balance of power between professionals, practitioners of a trade created by the existence of standing armies. These soldiers were not mediaeval warrior castes formed from a base of feudal ties, nor private entrepreneurs selling their swords to the highest bidder. Elements of the knight and condottiere type of warrior lingered on; but the soldiers, and particularly the officers, were state servants with good positions, salaries and career prospects. As professionals, they were only to some marginal degree driven by ideological-theological motives able to call forth that kind of resistance to the last man which is as pathetic as it is fanatical. Nevertheless, capitulation was always a blot, if not a disgrace, especially for the man in command. It is not surprising that Roos tried to drag the whole thing out, and avoid selling himself too cheap, if only temporarily. In order to justify an eventual compromise it was important for him to show he had not given in too quickly, and not until absolutely necessary.

Not long passed before the intrepid spokesman again rode back to Roos. The Russians clearly wanted to make sure that the beleaguered men were coming to the right decision. To increase the pressure with additional threats he began with an assertion which must have descended on them like an icy shower. The whole Swedish army, he maintained, had been routed. They could expect no relief. He added that if they did not give up with good grace they should reflect that the Russians' intention was immediately to storm the bastion, and he guaranteed that not a man among them would be spared. They would all be slaughtered.

It was high time to decide. Roos vacillated. He summoned the remaining officers, to hear their views. Probably he was more interested in involving them in the decision than in hearing what they had to say. They would share the responsibility if it now came to a shameful surrender. The Russian's assertion that the whole army had been defeated might easily just be a ruse to persuade them to give in. However, some of them pointed out that since more and more Russian units were collecting round the bastion, all could not be well. The Russians had been reinforced directly from the fortified camp, a good five kilometres north of them. In any case, the situation was hopeless. There was no food and no water; and lack of water was especially serious in the suffocating heat. Large numbers of wounded needed treatment if they were not to die. There was little chance of withstanding an assault supported by artillery: many of the men had no weapons, and there was very little ammunition left. They had been fighting since sunrise, nearly five hours earlier. 'The lads had shot all away.' The likelihood of relief within the foreseeable future was judged to be nil. The officers voted to surrender.

Roos also decided to hear what the soldiers had to say – a rather strange step since no one otherwise ever cared what the rank and file thought. This was probably just another attempt to off-load responsibility for the decision; Roos and the officers wanted an opportunity to blame the men. Many soldiers, during their bloody flight through the foliage, had already demanded that they should surrender. Now that their opinion was being sought they too were inclined to give themselves up. In common with the officers, they judged the terms of surrender to be good. Roos decided to give in.

When the Russian next approached the bastion the decision was conveyed to him. Roos wanted the terms of surrender in writing, however, undersigned by Rentsel. Via the intermediary, Rentsel replied that he had neither paper nor ink at hand, but Roos could rely on his gentlemanly word: every promise would be as piously kept as if it had been written on a hundred reams of parchment. Roos was obliged to content himself with this. But he added yet another condition: the wounded must be taken indoors and tended to. He also requested that he and his officers be allowed to retain their swords.

This was a part of the ritual. So that the name and honour of those surrendering should not be humiliated more than necessary it was generally thought important for the surrender to be decently conducted, and follow certain unwritten rules. These occasions were often attended with an impressive ceremonial, martial music, fluttering banners, guards of honour at attention and thundering salutes. A standard demand at the surrender of a stronghold was for the garrison to march out with flags, music, bullets in their mouths and fusees burning; defiant indications that they did not consider themselves completely defeated. Military honour was intact. The retention of weapons, at least the swords of the officers, reveals an archaic trait in the mentality of these combatants. The noble gesture of returning his sword to a defeated but gallant opponent was a relic from mediaeval days of tournaments and chivalry in heavy armour.

The spokesman rode back to his own side. Rentsel was a punctilious professional soldier and agreed to tend to the wounded Swedes. The question of the swords was a slightly more delicate matter. Only the tsar could sanction something of this nature. Rentsel offered a compromise: his adjutant would gather up the swords, and later, when they had gone up to the camp, he would try in person to secure this favour on their behalf with Peter Alexeivich. Roos went along with this.

The bastion doors opened. Through the palisades and over the shallow ditch stumbled a blood-stained vestige of the original six battalions. Of the 2,600 men facing the redoubts at dawn, 85 per cent had fallen, been massacred or taken prisoner. Practically all the regimental and battalion commanders had been killed or wounded: the commanding officer of the

Dalesmen, Siegroth, had died of his wounds; Georg von Buchwaldt, commanding officer of the Jönköping regiment, was gravely wounded and his life ebbing away; Gideon Fock, commander of the Västerbotten regiment, was wounded. Four of the seven lieutenant-colonels had fallen, two were wounded, and the seventh had been captured earlier. One third of the total Swedish infantry had been ground down to a tiny fragment in the course of a few hours, and to no purpose whatsoever. Their sacrifice was meaningless. Salvation had been little more than two kilometres away, but it might just as well have been on the moon.

Some of the Swedes left their weapons inside the bastion. The remainder laid them down before the Russian battalions. The terms of surrender were observed in every particular. The wounded were taken care of, and the prisoners were not plundered. Sections from the du Bois or Bieltz grenadier regiments mounted guard over them. The new prisoners of war were herded north, up the long ridge they had fought their way down an hour or so earlier. Their path followed the high ground, through the wood, towards the village of Yakovetski and the fortified Russian camp a little beyond it. As they marched, the captured Swedes heard a familiar sound, coming from the north-west: the rolling, reverberating roar of long, thundering volleys. The main battle had begun.

# 15 · 'Sheep to Sacrificial Slaughter'

The Russians waited, but the Swedish army seemed as if swallowed up by the earth. The expected attack never came. The Russian command began to fear that their opponents had taken it into their heads to break off the battle and return to Poltava. Eventually mounted scouts returned to report that the Swedes really were still there, and deploying for attack. Possibly not until this phase did the Russian command gain a clear picture of the force confronting them. They may have overestimated the strength of the Swedish army at the beginning of the engagement, and as a result acted with excessive caution. The Russian general staff held a council of war. Encouraged by their local success against Roos, and the apparently passive and hesitant behaviour of the Swedes, they decided on counter-action. A wholesale sortie from the encampment was indicated.

The Russian general staff, with Sheremetev and Peter Alexeivich in the lead, left the tsar's tent. Peter's uniform resembled that worn by several of his officers: black tricorn hat, black boots and green coat with facings and lining in red. He also wore the blue silk ribbon of the order of St Andrew. The tsar stepped up to his favourite horse, Finette, a dun-coloured Arabian given to him by the sultan, and swung up into the saddle, which was embroidered with silver thread on green velvet. He rode through the lines of waiting infantry and artillery. The troops were mustered, and the march began. One unit after another filed past the ramparts and out on the field. As they left they were sprinkled with consecrated water.

Most of the battalions emerging from the camp joined up with the 23 already deployed on its flanks. The total complement of 42 battalions were manoeuvred hither and thither in front of the camp, facing the low-lying ground and the little morass. The rows of green and grey-clad soldiers formed up in two close-knit lines: 24 battalions in the first line, 18 in the second. The Russian front was unbroken, the soldiers standing elbow to elbow, except for small gaps of about ten metres between battalions, where regimental artillery was rolled into place by red-coated gunners. About 55 three-pounder cannon were deployed in this manner, in accordance with the latest military theories.

The cannon were extremely well supplied with canister and ball.

Snorting dray-horses and service sections stood behind them. The field artillery was mounted behind the camp's western ramparts. If a retreat were necessary it would function as support. It consisted of 32 pieces, ranging from small three-pounder cannon to 40-pounder howitzers. The heavier pieces, especially the mortars and howitzers, whose higher trajectories meant they could fire over their own troops, would support the men in the field with long-range fire. The commanding officer of the artillery regiment was a Colonel Günther.

Nine infantry battalions, under Colonel Boy, were also left as an all-purpose reserve, with orders to stay concealed behind the ramparts. Overall command of the forces left in the camp was held by Günther, who as a gunner counted senior in rank to the infantry colonel. Three further battalions were detached under Colonel Golovin to move south to occupy the cloister. This was important for maintenance of communication with Poltava. The Swedes barricaded within it had clearly managed to give a sufficiently good account of themselves for the Russians to send a special detachment to take it.

The Russian cavalry was deployed mainly on the flanks of the infantry. The right wing, commanded by Lieutenant-General Adolf Fredrik Bauer, consisted of ten regiments of dragoons, Kropotov's mounted grenadier regiment and what was called the general's squadron. All in all they totalled about 9,000 men: 45 squadrons deployed in two lines, 23 in the front, 22 in the rear. Following the morning's initial fighting there was no longer any cavalry out on the left. The terrain was cramped by the Yakovetski wood and its deeply scarred system of ravines. The Russians created a left wing by moving cavalry over from the big group north of the camp. Six picked dragoon regiments under Menshikov rode behind the infantry and lined up on their left. They were also ranged in two lines, 12 squadrons to the front, 12 to the rear. The left wing was considerably weaker than the right, numbering only about 4,800 horsemen.

The tsar also seconded six dragoon regiments under Major-General Volkonski to support Hetman Skoropadski's Cossacks, round Tachtaulova. This was a defensive measure. If the Swedes were to start retreating, Volkonski's dragoons were to assist the Cossacks in pursuit. Otherwise they were only to wait and observe, and not attack on their own account. This precaution caused brief dissension in the Russian command. Sheremetev, egged on by the infantry general, Repnin, opposed any weakening of the Russian right. Both wanted the greatest possible numerical advantage. The detachment of Volkonski's horse meant a fairly substantial weakening of the available cavalry: almost 5,000 men were being removed. Peter was adamant, however, and the question is why. Presumably he wanted to ensure that Skoropadski's Cossacks would not be completely overthrown, give up or even change sides if exposed to a resolute Swedish charge. Their morale was low. During the early morning battle there had been a number of attempts at mass desertion among them. The irregular horse needed hand-holding, not to say supervision.

These unexpected moves by the Russians gave rise to some discord within the Swedish command. The king had already been less than satisfied with Rehnsköld's reconnaissance. Now he considered they ought to attack the cavalry standing near by: the Russian right wing under Bauer. Charles clearly wanted to exploit the advantage the Swedes had gained by virtue of their central position north of the little morass. He asked the field marshal whether 'it were best we went at the cavalry and drove them away first?' Rehnsköld rejected the suggestion. 'No, Your Majesty, we must advance towards them.' By 'them' he meant the Russian infantry, forming up their lines a bare kilometre away. The king gave way. 'Well, well, do as ye wish.'

By this time Roos's force had probably been written off. In any case there was no hope of any immediate reunification. But it was impossible to ignore the Russian deployment, which threatened to cut the army off from its supplies at Pushkaryovka. The Russians might secure a central position of their own, enabling them to strike at the vitally important Swedish supply base with the army powerless to intervene. Besides, the Russian moves were liable to sew them up in a sack: Russian forces were now closing in on three sides. The transfer of Volkonski's horse to support Skoropadski could also have been a conscious reinforcement of the north side of this sack.

The Swedish command decided to retire south again, out of the sack, back to the old assembly area on the low ground by the Budyschenski woods. Battle would be joined with the Russian infantry from there. Part of the cavalry left wing would be temporarily left behind as flank cover. All other units were ordered to return.

The long snaking coils of men and horses turned about and started back the way they had just come. It became a race. The Swedes had to get into place and draw themselves up in line of battle before the Russians completed their deployment and began their onslaught. The side ready first would have an advantage. The Swedish columns hurried across the plain, back over the morass, by now thoroughly trodden down and difficult to cross. The minutes passed as one after another of the chains of blue-coated soldiers squelched their way through the mire.

The Russians were going to win the race. All their battalions fell into place on the other side of the plain. Under the spacious vault of the blue June sky the lines thickened into a compact wall with a roof of black hats. A beautiful kaleidoscope of hundreds of banners waved above their heads. In the brief gaps between the battalions, the muzzles of the three-pounder cannon stared one-eyed over the level expanse, away towards the lines of

men and horses they could glimpse over the crest of their horizon. This
wall of soldiers, glittering bayonets and cannon, with its forests of pikes
and standards, measured over two kilometres in length and was, to say the
least, an impressive sight.

The tsar made a short speech. Then the wall came to life. Like a
ponderous river of lava it started to well forward in the direction of the
Swedish army.

The intended right wing of the Swedish cavalry followed the foot
soldiers as they marched back. They rode on the inner side of the infantry
and when over the morass found themselves squeezed between the
marching men to their left and the Budyschenski woods to their right.
There was not enough room for Creutz to line up his full complement of 52
squadrons on the right of the infantry. The wood, its groves and patches of
swamp, crowded them out. For the time being Creutz was ordered to draw
up his units on the cramped field *behind* the infantry battalions, now
beginning to fall into place immediately opposite the Russians. It was
simply a matter of expediency.

When Lewenhaupt saw that the cavalry were not being ranged on the
flank of his infantry, but behind it, he says 'there was a pang within my
heart, and it was like the sting of a knife'. He and his men would have to
attack completely on their own. Rehnsköld had ridden up to him just
before this, and ordered the infantry to face the Russian front, now less
than a kilometre away. The battalions at once changed formation from
column to line.

Unlike their adversaries, they were obliged to create substantial gaps
between battalions. There were over 50 metres between each unit. In spite
of these wide intervals the Swedish line was much shorter than the
Russian: not more than 1,500 metres long compared with the Russian line
of over 2,000. Lewenhaupt, from where he stood, made a crude estimation
by eye that the Russians out-flanked his men by a factor of three. This was,
however, a patent exaggeration. Another eye-witness comments that the
Swedish line of foot was like 'a few inches to an ell'. They needed cavalry to
extend their line, and to provide flank cover, if they were not to be totally
enveloped in the embrace of the enemy. Their cavalry were now being
crushed behind them, and the chaos mounted as more squadrons surged
across the little morass and pressed into them.

Time began to grow short. The turn into line was a simple manoeuvre.
When complete, Lewenhaupt politely asked the field marshal 'whither His
Excellency desired' them to move. Rehnsköld gestured to a little clump of
about ten trees to their right. In the haste of the moment Lewenhaupt
misunderstood his instructions, ordered the men to right turn (reverting to
column formation) and set the long line in motion towards the trees.
Rehnsköld rushed up in a raging fury, and demanded to know 'where the

Devil' Lewenhaupt thought he was going. Was he going to leave no room
at all for the cavalry? The field marshal must have meant the line to move
*level* with the trees and not *towards* them. The infantry threatened totally
to close up the cavalry's only narrow exit from the crowded field behind.

It was a clumsy manoeuvre. Rehnsköld handed the general a thorough
dressing-down. The touchy Lewenhaupt, who had already received
several thick ears from his choleric master, did not understand what he had
done wrong and considered himself gravely maltreated. He says he became
'in my spirit utterly vexed and wished myself rather dead' than to serve
under such a command. This may seem an excessive reaction, but a public
rebuke of this kind must have cut deeply into the soul of an aristocrat
conditioned since childhood to follow a strict code of behaviour, where
everything was permeated by a ceremonious courtesy and where any
breach could lead to violence, even death. Lewenhaupt managed to
compose himself. He loudly commanded the men to halt and face the
enemy. He offered his excuses to the field marshal: he thought he had acted
according to orders. If the infantry had moved too far to the right he
offered immediately to turn left and go back. Rehnsköld must have
managed to halt the men before they had marched any distance. He
contained himself, and replied: 'No, let them stand.' He rode off.

The disorder in Creutz's cavalry increased. The squadrons were crushed
in a confused mess in the cramped, unfavourable terrain.

Among the many civilians following the army out on the field this
morning was a fair-haired man with pale eyes and an engaging, somewhat
childish appearance. Josias Cederhielm, 36, secretary of the chancellery,
had studied at Uppsala. Then he had taken up a successful career in the
civil sector: steward at the peace congress of Ryswick 1697, registrar at the
chancellery 1700, secretary for about a year. Cederhielm had been present
at Narva, where he learned what it was like to be shot at. In that battle he
had single-handedly captured a Russian lieutenant-colonel. From that day
on he had owned the man's pistols and sword. Since his appointment as
secretary he had worked on translations and letter-drafting, and been
entrusted with certain diplomatic missions. Josias was opposed to alliance
with the Cossacks since he felt (like the children of Israel) there was a risk
of incurring the wrath of God by mingling with the heathen. He was well-
read, well-informed and hard-working, favoured with good humour and a
lively mind: a careerist of the kind which formed the backbone of the
remarkable Swedish imperium.

Josias noticed the chaos. He was told by a pair of Cossacks that the bad
terrain could be avoided merely by going round the nearby village of Maly
Budyschi. With this vital information, he rode off to look for Creutz.
Creutz, who had received similar reports from Zaporozhians, had already
raised the matter with Rehnsköld. The field marshal had not reacted

noticeably and, as usual, merely answered brusquely. Still, Creutz thought Josias ought to find Rehnsköld and inform him of the way round the village. Josias had no doubt learnt not to confront the forbidding field-marshal more than absolutely necessary, and refused point-blank: 'That I won't do.' 'Then ask Count Leijonhufvud,' said Creutz, 'to tell him.' Cederhielm trotted off but could not find Lewenhaupt. The minutes slipped away.

The Russian wall moved slowly forward. Gradually the distance between the two sides narrowed.

The Swedish infantry were as ready as the limited time allowed them to be. As ready as they were ever going to be. A thin blue line, one and a half kilometres long, had been drawn across the hot plain. This line consisted of 4,000 men, organised in ten battalions. Badly mauled by the battles round the redoubts, the battalions now only averaged between 300 and 400 men per unit. The line was continuous, severely stretched and sparsely manned, with large gaps between each battalion. Directly opposite them, less than one kilometre away, a massive wall advanced towards them. The Russian infantry consisted of roughly 22,000 men; 42 battalions in two lines, with minimal gaps. They were supported by approximately 100 barrels of artillery; the regimental cannon rolling forward beside the foot, and the heavy pieces back in the camp. From their wide muzzles, roaring grenades were already mounting to the sky, describing an arc over the plain and splintering with a cracking, whistling sound. The Swedish artillery consisted of four small three-pounders.

The Swedish infantry actually numbered 12 battalions, but the Väst-manlanders still had not had time to get back after their attempt to fetch Roos. Their two battalions were quite near, however, immediately behind the left wing.

Since the dawn, 18 battalions had dwindled to the ten now pitted against the 42. The decisive engagement was about to be fought. Most of the Swedish foot were going to spend the rest of their lives marching one mile across a dust-blown plain.

Numbered from the right, listed in the order they crossed the morass, the unit *ordre de bataille* of the Swedish infantry was as follows. On the far right stood the 1st battalion of the Life Guards, commanded by Captain Gustaf Gadde. Gadde was 29, born in Vekelax parish, Viborg county. He was brave and reckless to the verge of foolhardiness, favoured with kindly, good-natured features and dark close-set eyes. He had enlisted in the Guard at the age of 14 and worked his way up. At Narva he and his men had seized several Russian flags, but it had been touch and go; surrounded, he had been slashed in the arm but succeeded in breaking free. At Klissow in 1702 he had been wounded in four places; twice in the chest, once in the arm and once in the leg. As the custom was, he had been plundered naked and left bleeding among the dead. Someone had found him in the evening and taken him to a surgeon. Two bullets remained in his body as souvenirs. He had broken from the battle-line on his own at Klissow and paid a high price.

Then came the Life Guard's Grenadier battalion, which had wandered through the redoubts and stood for a time alone in the missile rain outside the Russian camp. The Guard, recruited from a peace-time base in Stockholm, were not localized like other infantry regiments. They were a career unit, a sort of school where budding officers received training before going on to new commands out in the realm. The Guard were an élite. The officers' uniforms were particularly magnificent. The rank and file dressed in the normal blue regimental uniform with yellow facings, cuffs and stockings and the familiar black tricorn hat. Corporals had velvet collars to their coats with gold and silver braid. Drummers, pipers and shawm-blowers wore colourful clothing with masses of fine braid and decorative tinsel. Above them flapped their beautiful white banners, eight in all. Today the two battalions included officers and men from the regiments which had formerly been part of Lewenhaupt's corps.

Next to the grenadiers stood the single Skaraborg battalion. It was commanded by Colonel Carl Gustaf Ulfsparre, a scarred warrior who had seen service with the French, the Dutch and elsewhere. The soldiers wore the standard blue uniform. Their neckerchiefs were blue or white instead of the usual black. The colonel's banner was white, with the quartered arms of the king and the realm in blue and gold. Fluttering in the warm wind, the company banners depicted Skaraborg's lion leaping on a field divided diagonally from corner to corner; the upper part black, the lower yellow.

Fourth came the Kalmar regiment, like the Skaraborg, shrunk from an original two battalions into one during the campaign. They too wore the regulation blue uniform. Their hats and stocking seams were trimmed with blue and white twisted beading; the facings of the drummers' coats gleamed red. Their banners were red with yellow tongues of fire licking inwards from the corners and edges towards the badge of their province, a standing lion holding a crossbow in its claws. Their commander was Colonel Gustaf Ranck, another old war-horse, who had fought in Brabant in the 1690s.

Next in the thin blue line came the two remaining battalions of the Life Guard: the 2nd under Captain Hans Mannersvärd and the 3rd under Major Erik Gyllenstierna. Erik was 30, born in Stockholm, the unmarried son of General Lewenhaupt's sister. The white banners of the Guard streamed above them.

Next to the 3rd Life Guards came the two battalions of the Uppland regiment. These were numerically weak and together totalled a little under

700 men. The regimental commander, Colonel Gustaf Stiernhöök, commanded their 1st battalion. Aged 38, born in Stockholm, he had started his career as a court page. The 2nd battalion was commanded by Lieutenant-Colonel Arendt Fredrik von Post. Their blue-coated ranks were crowned with white and russet-coloured flags, bearing the arms of Uppland, the orb of the realm.

The regiment's eight companies were ranged in a line a little over 200 metres long. The Life Company numbered 108 men under Captain Mårten Appelbom. The Lieutenant-Colonel's Company was commanded by Captain Per Rosensköld. Rosensköld had served his way up from the bottom, starting as a private with Jämtland's dragoons in 1685. The Major's Company numbered 88 men under Captain Carl Fredrik von Redeken. Rasbo Company numbered only 44 men, led by Captain Nils Fehman, 46, son of a lawyer. Sigtuna Company was commanded by Captain Carl Gustaf Silfverlåås, an Upplander, 36, who had begun his career at 18 as a volunteer with the guard. Hundra Parish Company, commanded by Captain Georg Zacharias Grissbach; Bälinge Company, commanded by Erik Kålbom; Lagunda Company, under Premier Captain Johan Jakob Greek, made up the rest. These are a few of the names of the 700 rank and file, musicians, non-commissioned and commissioned officers, most of whom would be dead within half an hour.

Left of the Upplanders came the Östgöta regiment, another unit reduced in the past year to one battalion of only 300 men. Their non-commissioned officers wore red neckerchiefs, blue facings on their regulation blue uniform, and blue stockings. Their standards were red. Their commander was a colonel in early middle age, Anders Appelgren, who had led them only since January. His predecessor had died on 12 January in Zekowa from wounds received at the mismanaged assault on Veprik. Appelgren had been appointed two days later.

On the far left, close to the patch of marshland, stood the 2nd battalion of the Närke-Värmland regiment. The unit was probably still not properly ordered, since it was last in the long line which had marched across the thoroughly trampled morass. The regiment had split in two during the break through the redoubts. The 1st battalion had disappeared without trace along with the regimental commander, Roos. Command of the 2nd battalion was held by Georg Johan Wrangel, the man Gyllenkrok had spoken to earlier, and who had expressed his concern over the lack of organization. The soldiers were in blue, and their facings, cuffs and collars were red. The banners flying above their heads were also red, emblazoned with the Närke arms: crossed yellow arrows within a green laurel wreath.

The lines of infantry were resplendent in strong, glowing colours. It may sound bizarre to compare the *ordre de bataille* to a work of art, but an early 18th century battle-order can be thought of as resembling a ballet, with a structural and dramatic function. The actors were dressed in beautiful costumes and carried banners with an obvious aesthetic appeal. The stylized steps and movements of the ballet corresponded with the strict formal drill of the infantry. The units moved about according to well-rehearsed patterns, and executed a variety of artistic and highly complicated manoeuvres such as right and left inclines, wheels, counter-marches, interspersals, split battalions, halved and doubled ranks, columns, squares and so forth. All were characterized by the obsessive geometric forms of the baroque. The martial ballet was not performed in silence but to the constant accompaniment of music. Each regiment had its corps of shawm-blowers, pipers and drummers, usually dressed in highly ornamented uniforms with lavish braid, beading and trimmings of silver or camel-hair. The units spun round on the battlefield and performed their intricate gyrations to the echoing, silvery tones of the musicians' *marcia pomposa*.

A regiment drawn up in full array also reflected the structure of a feudal society. The formal hierarchy, with mainly aristocratic officers ranged at the head of a rank and file drawn from the lower orders, created an impression of obedient masses, sternly directed by a small number for the general good of all. Even the play of colour carried a message. The hierarchy was indicated by a complicated system of uniform details, where braid, beading, gorgets, perukes and boots announced the wearer's position in the pyramid of rank. The uniform blue, and the regimental colours with the king's cipher on a white field proclaimed that the army was a national investment and no longer a raffish collection of entrepreneurs. They were all the king's men, bearing his uniform and following his flag.

All these colours, costumes, decorated banners and artistic movements to the sound of music were an embellishment of war. War was given an aesthetic, war became a work of art. Even a modern onlooker would probably be sensible of the grim beauty in a line of men arrayed for battle, full of colour, music and motion, a sort of grotesque many-faceted work of art. This aesthetic emanated from a mentality other than our own, for which cosmetic considerations were more important than for us, in our own utilitarian age. All the elements listed had certain practical aims: the flags were signposts intended to unite the men; the music helped them keep in step, signalled to them and guided them. Ideally, the colourful uniforms distinguished friend from foe: but they also enforced discipline. By making the soldiers striking to the eye the intent was to inhibit desertion. The striped clothing of the convict fulfils the same purpose.

The same tendency to beautify, or trivialize, war was apparent in the language of the officers. This was spiced with euphemisms and facetious circumlocutions. To shoot an adversary would be referred to as 'delivering a few blueberries'; the artillery 'played a merry tune' and the enemy provided 'entertainment'. Opponents would be 'beaten out of the bushes' or 'drummed up'; a hard battle might be called a 'brisk and merry bit of sport'. It all served to conceal a sad and dirty reality, and make it more bearable. The dream of the aristocracy was fair and virtuous war incarnate. But silken banners would be spattered with bits of brain and scraps of flesh, and elegant breeches soiled with blood and faeces.

Rehnsköld had only parted from Lewenhaupt a moment after their latest altercation, when he turned back. He had made his decision. He seems to have been conscious of his own surly humour and now made an effort to show a more amiable side. He grasped the general by the hand and said: 'Count Leijonhufvud, ye must go and attack the enemy. Act now as an honest man in the service of His Majesty, we will now unite in friendship and brotherhood together.' The prickly Lewenhaupt was surprised by this civility, and had time to reflect suspiciously that it originated from a mounting lack of confidence in victory. Perhaps Rehnsköld was being so friendly because he was now giving him an order which, in all likelihood, meant he was being sent to his death.

He returned the courtesy, nevertheless, declaring ornately that 'as God in His grace has provided that I have always been enabled to show myself a faithful servant to His Majesty, so have I yet the firm expectancy in God that in His mercy to me in this pass He will grant me grace to continue a faithful servant to His Majesty.' Whereupon he asked the field marshal directly 'if the wish of His Excellency were that I should now presently advance upon the enemy?' The answer was short: 'Yes. Now, at once.' Lewenhaupt responded with: 'Then, in the name of Jesus, may God stand mercifully by us.' Rehnsköld rode off to the right, towards the cavalry.

Lewenhaupt gave the order. The drums rolled. To their dark music the thin blue line pulled away, moving forward, towards the solid mass of Russian infantry spread out on the plain before them. Four thousand men had been ordered into an attack on 22,000. All of them could see the massive enemy lines and the way they out-flanked their own. Many, perhaps the great majority, must have realized at this moment that this could never succeed, that they were now going to die. Lewenhaupt was not particularly sanguine. He later used these words to describe his assignment: 'Advancing with these, as one might say, poor innocent sheep to sacrificial slaughter, must I go to attack the whole infantry of the enemy.'

The time was a quarter to ten. The encounter was unavoidable.

# 16 · 'No Musket-ball Will Hit'

Despite their five-fold inferiority in numbers the Swedish command had thus decided to launch their infantry into an attack. This desperate attempt to regain the initiative was more or less the only remaining course of action.

The decision was not quite so stupid as it seems. The battle-tactic of the Swedes was extreme aggression: their constant, overriding aim was to strive for victory by means of an attack, advancing towards the heart of the enemy and forcing him to give way before the play of bayonet and pike. Exchange of fire played a minor role compared with the get-up-and-go attack with *armes blanches*. It would have been quite contrary to ingrained tactical thinking and even counter to regulations to meet the Russians standing still. This would have allowed them to exploit their overwhelming fire-power and, at short range, literally shoot the stationary Swedish battalions to little pieces. The Swedes, with their poor powder and their pitiful four cannon could not compete with fire. Their only chance now lay in attack: an attack with cold steel.

Not that *armes blanches* were particularly effective, technically speaking – quite the opposite. Bayonet, sword and pike caused comparatively few injuries in battle. Many more battlefield casualties arose from shot; fire was by far the most effective killer. It was very rare for bayonets to clash. This usually only happened when neither party could easily escape, when fighting in confined areas, in fortresses or during an assault under cover of darkness. There are a number of romantic preconceptions about protracted hand-to-hand bouts with fixed bayonets and musket-butts as normal practice. Nothing could be more misconceived. Drawn weapons were relatively seldom actually applied in battle.

The bayonet was probably most commonly employed when pursuing the fleeing, and killing off wounded opponents. If bayonet-to-bayonet fighting occasionally did occur it was usually of little consequence, only lasting a few confused moments. Nevertheless, if it did come to hand-to-hand combat the equipment of the Swedish soldier gave him a certain advantage. The sword that every Swede carried was probably the best naked weapon that has ever existed, as well suited for thrust as cut. The Swedish bayonet had a more stable fitting than was otherwise normal. It was a considerably better weapon for thrusting than that of many other armies, whose bayonets tended to fall off, or remain embedded when muscle, skin and bone closed round the blade.

The popular image of a battle is of two large masses of humanity crashing straight into each other, like two stampeding herds: a wild struggle of man against man. This happened extremely rarely. Usually the battle was decided before there was any chance at all for hand-to-hand combat. Battles tended to consist of each side approaching the other slowly, reluctantly, and often in a disorganized manner. Within suitable range there would be an exchange of fire. If the attacker was not stopped by the defender's volleys, then in nine cases out of ten the defender would flee. Before bayonets crossed, therefore, one or other of the parties would have left the field.

For one side to back down did not imply defeat in the physical sense of being broken by intensive fire. Even if this sometimes happened, fire itself was not particularly effective. Exchanges of fire might well be costly and long-lasting, often ending in no directly decisive result. Troops gave way mainly because their courage faltered in face of a determined advance. They would be beaten psychologically. The same was true for the attackers, who quite simply might come to a halt before a steadily unbroken defensive front and become rooted in one of the prolonged fire battles field commanders were so keen to avoid.

The will to fight in each individual man, his readiness to get to grips with his enemy, his ability to endure, has always had and will always have a deciding influence in battle. The forcefulness of the Swedes depended on morale, not technique. Swedish tactics were founded on the will to win and faith that the enemy's nerve would be the first to crack. The attacker always had a certain advantage. It is axiomatic that offence elates while defence depresses. More importantly, an attack with cold steel automatically increases the soldier's will to fight. The phenomenon is known as the 'flight to the front'. If a soldier advances towards an enemy defending himself with heavy fire, and is prevented from replying in kind, there is only one way he can end the danger: to push the attack home, to charge. The practice in the Swedish army was always to restrict firing, so the men would be forced to resort to an assault with *armes blanches* in order to gain respite.

The impetuous Swedish bayonet charge worked extremely well, so long as the enemy was less well-disciplined and less resolute. This was the kind of opponent encountered during the entire war so far, and one battle after another had been won in this manner. But this style of combat had a rather low technical efficiency. Faced by an enemy with high morale, strong discipline and greater fire-power, who did not back down but stood firm and continued to pour on the fire, the storming assault would turn into a bloodbath.

If the Russian was going to be beaten, however, it had to be an attack. An attack would also give the almost hopelessly enmeshed cavalry behind the foot soldiers some time, and sorely needed space, to reorganize their entangled lines.

The infantry had not fully completed their formation into line before the order to attack was given. Before them stretched the dusty, sun-baked plain. They had approximately 800 metres to cover before they closed with the compact Russian ranks. The first 600 metres would be taken at the normal pace of 100 strides (75 metres) to the minute: a duration of about 8 minutes. The last stretch would be covered at a significantly higher speed, the standard procedure when attacking a rapidly firing enemy. This would take a round minute. In all, the assault would take nine minutes. Nine very long minutes.

The line was already within range of the Russian heavy artillery. Weighty projectiles flew in long curves towards the Swedes. At the start they would do little damage. Volume and accuracy would increase the nearer the approach. The real hell would break loose when the Swedish battalions had only about 200 metres left. Then the Russian cannon would begin to fire grapeshot and scrap. A little farther on, and the line would be within musket-range.

The thin blue line had not advanced far before it was obvious that its alignment was poor.

After Rehnsköld had ordered Lewenhaupt to attack he rode off to Creutz on the right wing. He remarked: 'Do you see the enemy infantry far outflanks ours? What is to be done?' Creutz answered that 'there is no other course, but when our infantry begin to get their bayonets in play, that I should see to it to go in on the right'. Rehnsköld was satisfied with Creutz's intention to act. He sped on towards the cavalry left.

Confusion still reigned among the cavalry, with troops blundering hither and thither without purpose. Creutz succeeded in gaining control of a few squadrons and drew them up in the limited space, but was obliged to range them in file, one after another. The original grouping had collapsed; the troopers now being organized by Creutz came from three different columns.

In the van were squadrons from the Life regiment, commanded by Captain Johan Blum, a Livonian. Behind them came the North Skåne cavalry, totalling 600 men organized in eight squadrons. One of their units was Landskrona Company, consisting of two cavalry captains, one being the company's commander, Jonas Ehrenklo; one lieutenant, two cornets, four corporals, one trumpeter and 49 troopers. Back with the baggage were a corporal, the provost, four troopers, nine baggage boys and four sick: a lieutenant and three troopers. At full strength the company should have numbered 125 men, but frost and sickness had rent gaping holes in its ranks. There had even been a case of suicide. A sick trooper, Johan Hägg, had shot himself. Behind the Scanians came a portion of Hielm's dragoons. Carl Lewenhaupt, a lieutenant-colonel born in Stockholm, 32 years old, led the regiment in the absence of the commanding officer, Colonel Nils Hielm. These units, in tight succession, were to cut their way into the Russian infantry, supporting the attack of their own foot.

On his rapid ride to the left Rehnsköld passed the king and his retinue. The field marshal reined in his horse and reported to Charles in a harassed manner that 'now the infantry advance rapidly towards the enemy', then sped on. Not long had elapsed since the infantry had passed them, and Gyllenkrok burst out in surprise: 'How can the battle possibly be starting already?' The king replied calmly: 'Now they are marching.' Gyllenkrok composed himself, bowed low and expressed the hope that 'God's angels should preserve His Majesty'.

The angels were to have some help, nevertheless, from the Drabants, a number of Life dragoons and that part of the North Skåne cavalry not engaged with Creutz out on the right wing. They closed ranks round the king, as he was raised up in his litter and conducted up to a little knoll with a view over the plain. Gyllenkrok mounted his horse and rode out into the field, towards the backs of the receding Swedish infantry.

Plump Piper was not left to sleep long under the shade of his tree. Hermelin, waved away shortly before by the somnolent minister, now came riding back. He reported that 'the enemy are in full march forward to engage us, and are only a couple of musket-shots away'. Piper, in a daze, clambered up on his charger. From his saddle he could see the long Russian battle-order stretching away across the plain. His eye then fell on the chaos behind his own infantry. Apprehensively he turned to Hermelin and said: 'God will have to work miracles, if it is to turn out well for us this time.' He threw his horse around and rode towards the right, to make contact with Charles.

On the opposite side of the plain the Russian wall halted. The tsar, who had been riding ahead of the line, in front of the bunched group of generals, lieutenant-generals, major-generals, brigadiers and colonels, now stopped. He made a gesture with his sword, as a blessing on his men. Then he handed command over to Field Marshal Sheremetev and rode Finette towards a division in the middle of the line he intended to lead. Sheremetev ordered the senior officers to take command of their units. The cannon were set in place in the small gaps between the battalions, and opened fire.

The range was still fairly great, about 500 metres. The bombardment began with cannonball. The balls fell at an even rate like muffled hammer-blows. The solid iron globes had a diameter of 7.7 centimetres. They were hurled off at a speed of 220 metres per second. Each met its mark a good two seconds after being fired, again and again and again.

The missiles cut blood-spattered avenues through the steadily advancing battalions, but did not halt them. Men were ripped apart, crushed and maimed. An ensign with the Skaraborg regiment, Sven Kling, was one of those hit. From a position probably just behind Sven – in a unit drawn up for battle the band would march immediately behind the ensign bearing the standard – trumpeter Anders Persson from Ärteberg in Härja parish saw the cannonball strike. The ball hit Sven in the crotch and practically split him in two. The ensign fell, dying almost instantly, without a word.

> But see Mars, see the fiery thundering pipes of Mars,
> what is their work? Fire-vomiting dragons and serpents,
> weighty cannon, and horrible mortar wide-gaping, and others
> like these: grenades filled with poison and rubble,
> sly petards and gruesome, earth-scattering mines.
> What is their work? When these start to rumble, to spit,
> to whistle and whine, you see heads and arms in the air
> spring like hail, you see soldiers and horses in heaps
> fall and tumble each over the other . . .
>
>                                        G. STIERNHIELM

The soft summer breeze blew into the faces of the Swedish soldiers and swept through their ranks in a powder-stinking haze. The smell of spent black powder was reminiscent of the odour of rotten eggs. Visibility became more and more restricted.

Stride followed stride. The steaming field between the two sides was being eaten up by tramping feet. The sun beat down. The long green-dappled wall of Russian infantry stood motionless, surmounted by the waving flecks of colour of innumerable banners. A never-ending stream of rumbling, reeking, fiery threads emerged from the smaller field-pieces. Great tumbling clouds of smoke grew ever bigger and thicker before the flame-barbed front. Small black balls etched their sudden scratches across the dusty air, fully visible.

On the other side of the plain the thin blue line advanced rapidly towards this wall. The wind-whipped banners fluttered. The weaponry and harness clattered. High-flying musket-balls and shrapnel ricocheted off bayonet and pike-point with ringing sounds, adding to the dull beat of the drums and the thin whine of pipe and fife. Loud shouts, fierce orders, and rasping, inhuman death-rattles filled the louring smoke-dimmed air. Men slipped, stumbled, staggered, fell and dropped or were hurled down upon the warm earth. Blood gushed from severed limbs. Dusty bundles twisted on the ground, swaddled in scarlet. Almost unidentifiable pieces of humanity squirmed stickily among spilled entrails, in large pools of gradually blackening blood. Still the thin blue line continued its advance into the embrace of the thick swirling smoke.

Far out on the right wing, in the ranks of the Grenadier Battalion of the Life Guards, Oxenstierna's Company, marched Pike Corporal Erik Larsson Smepust, 28, born in the village of Oxberg in East Dalecarlia. Under his command were ten unranked pikemen: Eric Järnberg, Swarthufwudh, Drabitius, Erick Berg, Thomas Swan, Mattz Graan, Oluf Ellg, Johan Hiellmar, Mattz Stockenström and Lars Bergwijk. Corporal Smepust thought the Russian fire sounded like 'an even thunder-roll'.

With 200 metres remaining, the Russian cannon switched from round-shot to grape-shot. The hail became a hurricane. Load upon load of lead ball, flakes of flint and jagged bits of iron were pumped into the line of blue-coats. The line continued its resolute advance, marching straight through the whining shower. Now, perhaps, the thoughts of each man, in his apprehension of death, dwelt on the truth of the assertion that 'no musket-ball will hit a man', whether he walked erect through the hail of lead, or sought cover, unless God willed it.

If this was true, then clearly God wanted a large number of Swedish soldiers to die now, during these terrifying moments. The volleys smashed through the thinning ranks. Companies and battalions were ground down, root and branch. The Swedish line of foot was like a wagon-train crashing at speed, shattered and splintered but still, by its own massive inertia and the rolling pace of its advance, continuing forward. There was surely something mechanical about this insane charge. During these few minutes the grape-shot worked its most terrible effect.

The fire storm made an ineradicable impression upon those that survived it. Stilted descriptions in diaries and memoirs convey the appalling reality. Drabant clerk Norsbergh speaks of the 'weighty bomb-throwing and flying grenades as though a heavy hail from heaven'. Squadron Chaplain Johannes Siöman, of the Småland cavalry regiment, says the fire was wholly terrible and 'unhearable' and that 'hairs stood on end from the thunder of cannon and grape-shot and the volleying'. Another of those who witnessed it, David Nathanael Siltmann, a Prussian lieutenant-colonel and councillor who followed the Swedish army as an observer, wrote home, notably shaken, saying that the Russian fire was so heavy it was almost impossible to describe. He too likened it to a hail-storm.

The Swedes took very heavy losses before offering any reply to the rain of metal. The Kalmar battalion suffered especially badly. Its command-ing officer, Gustaf Ranck, was shot down with a large portion of his men. 'In one volley as good as half the regiment were lost,' wrote one survivor. Another, Lieutenant Friedrich Christoph von Weihe, praised the Swed-ish foot: 'They ran forward with death before their eyes and were in large part mown down by the thunderous Russian cannon before they could find employment for their muskets.'

The thin line pushed forward through the smoke. Men and officers stumbled on through a seething, exploding chaos of powder-sparks and musket-balls. Not a shot was returned. In accordance with the iron drill of Swedish battle-tactics they waited until the very last moment. The nearer they came, the greater would be the effect of their volley. One volley would suffice: then came the moment for the charge with bayonet, pike and sword. The line advanced with its muskets silent. The dead and wounded were left lying in its wake.

There was a discernible movement in the wall ahead of them. The foremost Russian ranks knelt down. Muskets were raised to fire positions. The Swedish foot soldiers quickened their pace in the evil-smelling fog of smoke and powder. The last stretch was taken at a run, straight into eternity.

# 17 · 'As Grass Before a Scythe'

The volley came at a range of about 50 metres. All four ranks along the lengthy Russian front fired simultaneously. A thundering barrage cut through the ragged lines of charging men.

Many eye-witness accounts down the years have attempted to describe the effect of concentrated volley-fire on a battlefield. Some say the sound bears a resemblance, immensely amplified, to a piece of coarse cloth being ripped apart. Others liken it to the rattle caused by a large quantity of marbles being rapidly poured over tin sheeting; with brief pauses, when only a few single shots are heard. Various similes are used to describe the visual effect of the volleys on long rows of upright soldiers. Some say the lines sway like corn; others that they stagger and waver, like a slack rope shaken at one end.

A Swedish participant's account of this battle relates that the Russian artillery 'laid our men low, as grass before a scythe.' The familiar simile says it all: a massed sheaf of missiles, like an invisible cutting edge, suddenly slashes into the line. The men, all in almost the same instant, fall to the ground together like stalks of bunched grass. A battlefield could sometimes offer a remarkable sight: dead men lying in neat, regular rows, removed from this life and strictly arranged in a well-ordered military formation. We would probably associate the scene with a formal mass execution by firing squad.

Seconds after the deafening salvo came the returning echo of its terrible effect on the Swedish line. This was the thud of countless falling bodies, and the clatter of weapons dropping from the hands of those hit. A Russian wrote that it sounded like a house collapsing.

Lewenhaupt rode almost precisely in the centre of the line. The fire at this stage of the attack, when the musket volley combined with the artillery, was so strong, he says, that 'it were impossible, humanly to believe, that any man of all our sorely exposed infantry could emerge from it with his life.' Even now he would not reply to the fire. The thought of the spoilt powder ached in his mind and he wanted to advance as close as possible, for maximum effect from the delayed Swedish volley. He was no longer in touch with the full extent of his line; the billowing fog of gunpowder prevented him seeing what was happening out on the right. He still had some control over the single Skaraborg battalion, the badly mauled Kalmar battalion, the 2nd and 3rd battalions of the Life Guard and the two battalions of Upplanders. This central section of the line continued to close with the wall of Russian men and cannon, which was still firing with the implacability of a force of Nature.

Out on the right, the remaining two battalions of Life Guards were also well up with the centre. On the far left wing, however, the poor initial alignment of the Östgöta battalion and the 2nd battalion of the Närke-Värmland regiment was making them lag behind.

The Swedish right and centre, in spite of the murderous volley, maintained their steady advance. What happened now was familiar to them from previous similar situations. The Russian line buckled and began to fold. Still shooting, but dragging their pikes, the enemy foot started to pull back. Some abandoned their three-pounder cannon. Lewenhaupt shouted: 'Fire!' The Swedes rapidly doubled their tattered ranks; the two rear ranks stepped forward and ranged themselves level with the two forward ranks. The distance to the retiring Russians was very short, in places only 30 metres. The muskets flew up, the salvo roared. The collected broadside worked to good effect in some quarters, cutting the Russians down as they fled. Elsewhere, the faulty powder merely fizzled in the touch-hole. Where it did explode, the thin pops were later compared by Lewenhaupt to the dry sound of a pair of gloves being slapped together.

Everything now started to disintegrate into the chaotic confusion of a shattered anthill. There was the same blind tearing to and fro, the same frenzied rushing and apparent absence of purpose other than a constant advance to kill and kill again. The Russians fell back before the attacking Swedes. The Kasan, Pskov, Siberian, Moscow, Butir and Novgorod regiments all began to falter. The foremost Russian line made a complete about turn and marched straight back into the second line, which had so far been waiting behind them without taking part in the battle.

This was a critical moment for the Russians. The second line functioned as silent support for the first, and provided replacements and re-inforcement. But if the first target were beaten it would often draw the second with it in defeat. The second line became incapable of repulsing an enemy which had broken through the battle-order. Incredible confusion arose when a retreating first line crashed into the stationary second; large groups of terrified soldiers would draw hitherto unaffected men with them in their flight and create a contagious general panic. A shouting, terror-stricken crush could develop, helplessly driven before a sharp hedge of bayonets, to be trampled underfoot or scattered to the winds. Should the Swedes succeed at only one single point it might be possible for them to shatter the whole broad front. The deep Russian array of two lines, and their great numerical superiority, could become an impediment rather than an advantage for them.

After the rattle of their volley the Swedish battalions pressed forward in eager pursuit of their faltering opponents. The Russians were not yet routed. They withdrew in a more or less orderly manner, but too slowly to escape their pursuers. The second line hampered the retreat of the first. After a short chase of about 100 metres the Swedes caught up with them and began driving pike-points and bayonets into their backs.

In the centre of the line the 2nd and 3rd battalions of the Life Guard pushed forward side by side. Mannersvärd's 2nd battalion burst through the Russian front line and captured four cannon. The 3rd battalion quickly took a couple of Russian guns, passed them and continued to drive the enemy back. Out on the right edge the 1st battalion also stormed forward. Under command of battle-happy Captain Gadde they broke into the Russian lines, capturing four banners and six cannon, the greatest success of any battalion. Gadde rushed forward to one of the captured pieces, swung it round to point the muzzle at the retreating Russians and fired a few rounds after them. Alongside Gadde's men the Grenadier battalion, Corporal Smepust's unit, also went forward well, and captured some enemy cannon.

The long row of Russians swayed and wavered. A large section of the speckled green wall was on the verge of being crushed inwards upon itself. If one portion were to collapse then surely the rest would soon follow. No matter how improbable, nor how crazy the odds might have seemed at the start of the attack, victory was now within reach. The Russian lines needed pushing back perhaps only a very little farther. If a great bough is to be broken, assiduous bending and pulling will suddenly snap it with a crack. Release the branch before it breaks, however, and it will recoil with violence.

Massive cavalry shock action by the Swedes would now provide the additional weight needed to turn the enemy retreat into a real rout, completing the Russian defeat already scented. The horse would have to be launched out on the far right, extending the line, to cover the overlapping Russian front. But this was a day when almost nothing went to plan for Swedish arms. The cavalry failed to arrive.

The cavalry were also wanted out on the left, which still lagged behind the right. The extreme ends of both wings, faced with the long, outflanking Russian front, had probably more or less instinctively been drawn outwards, to minimize the overlap. The more central battalions would then have adjusted accordingly. The whole line would have stretched out, expanding the already large gaps between the battalions even farther, in places up to 150 metres. The thin blue line had ceased to be a line at all. And the extreme left had still not made battle contact with the Russian front.

With the battalions on the right forcefully pushing back their opponents, their distance from the dragging left increased even more. The central gap grew into an abyss. When the Russian foot opposite the Swedish left began to press forward in turn, a kind of revolving-door effect took place. The infantry on the Russian right wing were their élite: the Brigade of Guards; the Astrakhan, Ingrian, Semyonovski and Preobrazhenski regiments. The adolescent tsar had founded the famous Preobrazhenski regiment as his personal plaything, manning it with anyone from young boyars to stable-lads. With the years it had developed into the Russian army's finest unit. The battalions on the right wings of both armies pushed forward strongly, while their comrades on the left were falling back. The Russians still threatened to enfold the Swedish line on both wings, however, and at the same time to force their way through its widening gaps.

Gyllenkrok, positioned behind the forward-storming battalions of the Swedish Guard, saw that the left wing had fallen behind. He galloped towards it. Colonel Appelgren, commanding officer of the single Östgöta battalion, stood with his men on the extreme left, facing the mighty Russian brigade. Gyllenkrok shouted out that 'the Guard are already at strike' and urged him to 'make haste'. Appelgren was hemmed in. Indicating the extended Russian line, now quite close, he replied: 'Ye see, I am altogether encircled by this long line of enemy standing here.' He implored Gyllenkrok to fetch cavalry in support. 'I will do my best,' Gyllenkrok replied, and spurred away. He rode west to find some cavalry before it was too late.

Most of the cavalry's right wing was still in a disorganized state. Any prompt, concerted support from them could not be expected. The only mobile portion were the squadrons under Creutz, who, late in the day, had formed up and were now riding to the Swedish right. The Russians on this wing, seeing the flood-tide of horses, fluttering standards and cold steel surging towards them, acted with well-drilled precision. The four battalions of the Nizhni-Novgorod regiment and the Busch Grenadiers swiftly formed a large *carré*, or square. This, the standard formation for meeting cavalry, created a minor fortress of cannon, muskets and splayed pikes. As Creutz approached, the Russians opened fire with cannon, sending shell-splinters whistling into the wedge-shaped squadrons as they charged.

The left wing of the cavalry was split in two. The section north of the small marshy patch was to provide flank cover against Bauer's and Volkonski's squadrons, located round Pobivanka and Tachtaulova. The Swedes here were drawn up and ready for battle. The rest of the horse on the left were still in disarray, far behind their foot, as inactive as their compatriots on the right.

Galloping westwards, Gyllenkrok finally sighted some organized, mobile cavalry. He ordered them to move in support of the infantry on the left, adding, with urgency, 'for God's sake, quickly.'

The horsemen wheeled half-right to position themselves for a charge. As they completed their manoeuvre their eyes were greeted by a hair-raising sight. The Swedish infantry nearest them threw down their weapons, and turned. The foot soldiers had started to flee.

# 18 · *'The Devil Couldn't Make Them'*

Creutz's section of the Swedish cavalry was fully engaged in battle with the Russian square, when it was attacked from the rear. Squadrons from the Russian left wing under Menshikov had swept forward in an arc out on the plain and arrived at a position from where they could fall on the Swedes from behind. The Swedish troopers had already lost several standards in their contest with the square. They extricated themselves, made a complete about turn, reorganized and charged against the new threat. Their opponents retreated at full speed. This was the moment when the first Swedish foot soldiers threw down their muskets and started to run.

Their panic is understandable. The stress of great losses in a very short space of time, particularly severe among the officers, the supervising, combat-leading and cohesive force, and the menacing threat of encirclement had broken the men's will to fight. War is a brutal game with incalculable psychological factors: the more hard-pressed, the more volatile and unreliable the soldiers' psyche. Danger is diluted when shared by six hundred, but each is only as brave as the man beside him. Behind their panic lay war-weariness, fatigue and despair. Who can tell what trivial, minor incident – perhaps an unclear order, a misunderstood movement – might finally have strained their shaking nerves beyond endurance?

In *Battle-Terror Speaks*, Georg Stiernhielm creates a perceptive, forceful personification of panic on the battlefield:

> My dam is the dark and fearsome night
> and I myself am pale and hateful.
> The chill of fear, the beating heart
> and icy, trembling terror
> create my might and bring me triumph.
> Few arms or armour do I need
> to fetch an army down:
> a shadow or a dream, or an alarm,
> a voice, or sudden sound, a cry,
> strange sights, a fleeting thought,

> a slip of deed or word, my weapons are,
> my armour and my harness
> whereby I vanquish many thousand men
> and harry hosts unnumbered.

Lewenhaupt also noticed that as the left wing began to retreat, the right pressed forward all the more. It happened very quickly. The battalions split at the seams in a matter of moments. The point where the line had broken was swiftly transformed into a chaotic jumble of dead bodies and fleeing men, scattering across the plain like rivulets of water. Lewenhaupt turned his horse and rode towards them with utmost speed. Both the Närke-Värmland and the Östgöta battalions were collapsing into headlong flight. The men simply had to be brought to stand firm.

Lewenhaupt rode first into the swirling, streaming chaos of the Östgöta regiment. In the middle of his men stood their wounded commanding officer, Appelgren, desperately shouting to them to stand. Lewenhaupt rode up him, saying: 'Colonel, I beg you for God's sake to get your soldiers to stand again, do ye not see how we drive back the enemy on our right?' 'I cannot get them to stand, for I am wounded,' said Appelgren. 'May God help you, General, to make them stand.' Lewenhaupt made the attempt: riding about in front of the fleeing men, he implored, threatened, struck out and swore.

An army is no more than a rigidly organized crowd of men. Under stress it obeys the same laws as any other crowd. The mass of fleeing men all pull each other along in the same direction. Each finds security in the herd, none thinking that he personally will fall victim in the mindless stampede. To get them to stand and turn to face the very threat which was lending their feet wings was no easy task.

> When I seize hold the matter ends.
> No order is obeyed.
> None heed and none hear 'Stand!'
> None cares for any other.
> Wit, courage, might, and sense are fled;
> and foremost he whose legs are best.
>
> G. STIERNHIELM

All Lewenhaupt's curses, shouts and blows were fruitless. The flight went on, as if the terror-stricken soldiers were both deaf and blind.

Now, at last, the desperately needed cavalry began to enter the action. The confused conglomeration of squadrons in the meadows by the woods and round the little morass had still not been disentangled by Hamilton, Creutz and Rehnsköld, the general officers responsible for the cavalry. Creutz, commander of the entire right wing, had removed part of it in his attempt to support the infantry. The remainder weltered in chaos behind him. No one gathered the squadrons together for concerted action.

Perhaps only ten or 15 minutes had passed since the thin blue line had set out on its death-march over the dusty plain. To organize a scattered or impacted squadron was a time-consuming business. There was no room to deploy all of them into their elaborate plough-shaped formations. Moreover, the senior commanders depended in part on aides, but mainly on their personal presence, to communicate orders and see they were executed. Rehnsköld in particular had hurtled about issuing orders in person; this ensured that the orders actually arrived, but it took inordinate time, and time was of the absolute essence just at present.

Field commanders of this era generally had very poor control over their troops. In the heat of battle they almost inevitably began to lose their grip on their forces. The battlefields filled with dust, smoke and noise. Visibility became extremely limited. The few available methods of communication, repetition of commands and sound signals, broke down. Mounted aides were frequently killed, or rode astray in the *mêlée*, before they had time to deliver their messages. All hope of executing complicated master plans would disappear. Even the simplest plans tended to crumble in the smoke. Battles would often degenerate into uncontrolled, noisy, chaotic affairs where even a battle commander of genius could do little more than stand and watch. Neither commander of these two armies was any longer steering the course of events. The battle had taken on a life of its own. It was no longer a game played between human opponents, but an uncontrollable natural phenomenon, an earthquake where men ran dizzily to and fro, blindly pulling and pushing.

The lack of cohesion in the Swedish cavalry was fatal. When the squadrons now charged through the fire and fog of powder there was no longer a massively centralized thunderbolt of steel blades and hoofs, but a weakened series of isolated punches to the vast body of the monster, aimed at random.

A group of 50 troopers galloped past the cursing Lewenhaupt. With drawn swords, they rode straight towards the battalions surging forward in the footsteps of the fleeing Swedes. In face of this foolhardy charge part of the Russian line came to a halt, hesitated and pulled back. But the effort was doomed from the start because of the enemy's overwhelming numerical superiority. The little troop was ground down, and its badly mauled remnants forced to retire.

Two squadrons of the Nyland cavalry regiment launched an equally gallant and desperate charge. At the head of his own squadron, the Life Squadron, rode the regiment's highly regarded commanding officer, Colonel Anders Torstensson, grandson of the legendary field marshal of the Thirty Years' War, Lennart Torstensson. The other squadron was led

## Map 6 · The Final Battle

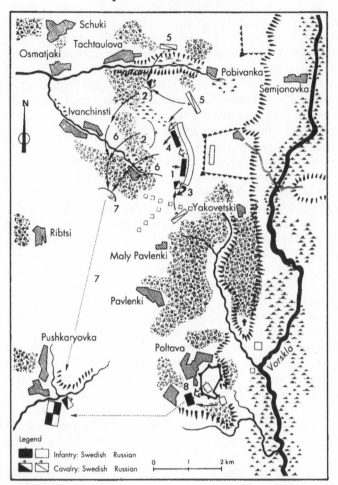

1. The Swedish foot attack. The right wing advances, the left lags: a gap appears between the wings.
2. Most of the Swedish cavalry are in disorder, powerless to assist.
3. Creutz's squadrons charge, but are attacked from behind by Russian cavalry.
4. The Swedish foot on the left begin to flee. The Russians advance into the gap between the Swedish wings.
5. Russian cavalry attack.
6. General panic breaks out. Most of the Swedish units flee the battlefield.
7. An attempt is made to steady the fleeing cavalry, but fails, and the retreat continues towards the baggage-train.
8. The Swedes near Poltava hold off a series of Russian attacks, and gradually they too move back to the baggage-train.

by a Captain Naltaker. The two squadrons, totalling about 150 men, cut their way straight into the Russian masses and a hand-to-hand *mêlée* ensued. They could only very slightly delay the enemy battalions. The outcome was predictable. They were soon swallowed up. Only 50-odd returned. Nearly all these were wounded, among them a captain, a cornet and the regimental chaplain Croel, who always followed his unit into battle. Thirty-two-year-old Lieutenant Johan Gyllenbögel, from Kimito near Åbo, had both cheek-bones drilled through and was captured. Anders Torstensson, aged 33, unmarried, fell with his men. The charge was a sacrifice. Offering their own and their troopers' lives, these officers won a short respite for the foot soldiers.

The troop ordered by Gyllenkrok to relieve the infantry at the moment they first started to flee also charged. They failed to break into the enemy ranks. As they rode in they were met by a violent volley from muskets and cannon, and fell back before it. When cavalry launched a shock charge at infantry the steadiness of the defenders was crucial. If panic seized them at the sight of the forward-rushing wall of horses, they would disintegrate, and be easily ridden down. If they kept their nerve, and delayed their musket-fire until the very last moment, the cavalry would succumb, and the charge would be repulsed.

The horses were trained to endure the frightening sights and sounds they would be exposed to: fire, drums, shots and waving flags. But it was impossible to train them to remain steady in face of a thundering volley at close range. The animals would rear back from the muzzles, the roar and the smoke, leaving the rider powerless. Mediocre troopers on broken and well-trained horses had a better chance of success than the best riders on raw animals. If the infantry fired their salvo at a range of around 100 metres, the horseman might regain control of his mount, and perhaps reach the foot before they had time to reload. But if they held their fire until the last ten metres, the best cavalry would have to give way: the horses would crash into each other, stop or veer off to one side in terror.

Gyllenkrok failed to find any more squadrons as he rode on to the left. He turned and galloped back, hoping to find cavalry out on the other wing. Meanwhile the collapse of the foot on the left was spreading. He came across a fairly large group of men wandering aimlessly without trace of order or formation. Gyllenkrok called out to them: 'Pull yourselves together, lads', and asked: 'Is there no officer here?' As earnest of the hard fighting they had just endured the weary men replied: 'We are wounded and all our officers are dead.'

The revolving door began to lose its momentum. The advance of the Swedish right slowed down. The solid wall stopped wavering, steadied and began, slowly, irresistibly, like a tidal wave, to push back against the thin blue line. The Russians pressed forward under their own weight, flooded into the widening gaps and began to beat round the flanks of the Swedish battalions. Farthest out on the left the Russians facing the fleeing Östgöta and Närke regiments advanced rapidly and pursued them.

The Uppland regiment was in desperate straits. The two fleeing battalions had completely exposed their left flank, round which the advancing enemy now swept. On their right was only the yawning fissure between the two wings. The Upplanders stood stubbornly firm but the Russians streamed in through the gap and broke the Swedish line once and for all into two parts.

The left of the line had been cut off at the shoulder. The foot to both right and left were out-flanked. Those nearest the central gap, the Upplanders to the left and the 2nd and 3rd battalions of the Life Guard to the right, would soon be completely surrounded. Every unit in the line, which clung to the position it had reached, was in danger of being encircled. The enemy pushed forward into the gaps between the battalions, gripped their flanks and edged round them, snapping at their backs. Each Swedish battalion was a wounded animal, bleeding from a hundred cuts, struck at again and again, but still biting and scratching with tooth and claw, hitting out wildly, blind with pain and mad with anger. There was little hand-to-hand fighting. The Russians seem to have contented themselves with pumping whistling sheaves of bullets from short range into the stumbling Swedish troops. It was an execution. The fire was concentrated, continuous and murderous. Men, in hundreds, were lacerated by ball and splinter, fell to the ground, crawled in pain, and died.

It was turning into a bizarre variation of the battle at Cannae in 216 BC, where initial retreat made the opponent's flanks vulnerable to encirclement. Here it was not a deliberate manoeuvre, however, but an unforeseen consequence of pressures arising when against all odds the Swedish foot succeeded with their attack.

The officers could not halt the flight out on the left. Lewenhaupt caught sight of Major-General Sparre, commander of the Västmanlanders, who had attempted to extricate Roos. He was fully engaged in vain efforts to stop the fleeing men. Lewenhaupt cried out to him: 'My dear brother, let us for God's sake get them to stand again: on our right we are driving the enemy back.' Sparre answered, in total despair: 'The Devil couldn't make them stand,' and asked, rhetorically: 'Can you get them to stand? It's impossible.' Their efforts were hopeless. The men's will to fight had drowned in a flood of fear.

Lewenhaupt gave up. He thought of returning to the units still fighting, but by now this was too late. The battalions were almost completely swallowed up by the surging Russians. With their thick ranks blocking his way, it was impossible for him to get back.

The heat was intense. Dust and the fog of spent powder covered the lines. Troops rode down and trampled over the wounded and the dead. The Swedes fought for their lives in the suffocating smoke, caught in a vice of pikes and flashing musket muzzles. They struggled to hold the Russians back, to escape and stay alive.

Out on the far right the Russian threat to out-flank the line had been temporarily checked. Creutz's cavalry were prevented from pressing home their charge, but had nevertheless forced the Russians to halt and form a square. This made it easier for the two Guards battalions under Gadde and Rosenstierna to make their chastened escape from the trap. Gadde's battalion had been completely surrounded and attacked in the rear. Gadde was wounded in the right arm, left hand and thigh, but kept command over his men. Carrying the four banners they had captured, the whole battalion cut their way through the Russian lines and withdrew from the field. The Grenadier battalion also succeeded in making their retreat. Their commander, Rosenstierna, gravely wounded in arm and chest, was captured.

Both battalions set off towards the protective foliage of the Budyschenski woods, beckoning about a kilometre behind them. As best they could, they dragged their wounded with them. The Kalmar and Skaraborg battalions were worse pressed. Ranck had been killed in the artillery fire, and the Skaraborg men also quickly lost their commander, Ulfsparre. He fell with the greater part of his regiment. The central 2nd and 3rd battalions of the Guards were in an equally desperate situation. The men of the 2nd took to their heels after most of their officers, with Mannersvärd at their head, had been killed. The 3rd battalion also lost their commanding officer, Lewenhaupt's nephew Gyllenstierna. Most of the officers and other ranks fell with him. The Russian lines closed round the rapidly dissolving battalions, attacked on all sides and wrapped them round in a glowing cloak of fire and smoke. The dead began to form heaps. The heaps grew into mountains.

The toll of slaughter is witness to the battle's heat. Of the ten battalion commanders who led their men into this attack, seven were killed within half an hour, and the remaining three were wounded. The flank commander, Carl Magnus Posse, was also wounded. A meat-mincer had ground the Swedish infantry to nothing. It had only been a matter of time.

Now the cavalry began to flee as well. A number of squadrons nearest the fighting turned about and crashed into those behind them. These, too, spun round in confusion, rode back in turn into those behind, and so on: a chain reaction of terrified disintegration spread through the horse. One squadron after another fled from the field.

In his hunt for the king, Prime Minister Piper encountered nothing but disordered cavalry. The crush was so great he could not make his way through. When he saw the units begin to fall back, colliding into each other, locked together in immense jams, he decided to look for the king among the infantry. He trotted out on the field, in the direction where the right wing ought to have been. Straining to see ahead, he spied a large square of foot soldiers. Assuming them to be Swedes he rode towards them, only to be quickly prevented by an officer informing him they were Russians. The two Guards battalions had already withdrawn well back from their original position. The Swedish cavalry under Creutz, however, had clearly persuaded their opponents to remain in the security of their square formation. Piper turned his horse, found his way again blocked by fleeing cavalry, and was sucked back with them.

What had started as a small trickle of fleeing men had swollen into a mill-race of chaos and fear. More and more were being drawn involuntarily into the welling flood of panic. Lewenhaupt rode along downstream with it, through a grove of trees, in the direction of a little village. There he hoped to bring them to stand. The running foot soldiers were swelled out by retreating cavalry, which lent yet more force to the stream of headlong flight.

Lewenhaupt drew his sword, stood in their path, and called out in commanding tones for them to stand. Many repeated his words as they fled. 'Stand, stand,' they shouted, making no effort of their own to comply. Shreds of military discipline still lingered in their fear-dimmed brains. This, and their respect for authority, made them render lip-service to Lewenhaupt's furious commands. But they were all intoxicated by the same frenzied terror, and the maelström was stronger than they. In spite of their shouts of 'stand', they ran, away from the battle and away from the war. Seeing that he would not be able to arrest this torrent of fear, Lewenhaupt began to slash and thrust at the fleeing men. It was hopeless. He gave up again and steered his horse back to what they were fleeing from. Perhaps something could yet be saved.

# 19 · 'It Goes Ill!'

Not all the cavalry fled. On the right wing, Hielm's dragoons launched a fresh counter-charge and managed to penetrate the Russian wall. Three squadrons of Taube's dragoons, a relatively newly raised regiment, wheeled up in battle formation to ride into an attack. When they looked around they saw no other squadrons in formation: they would be charging on their own. Commander of the first squadron was Captain Didrik Celestin von Sternbach, a 30-year-old German born in Stettin. Head of the second was 26-year-old Marcus Tungelfelt, from Stockholm. His brother Anders, the elder by a year, wounded 20 times in the course of the war, had served with the same regiment until 1707. At this precise moment he was out on the plain, somewhere among the sorely pressed battalions of Life Guards. The third squadron was commanded by Carl Magnus De Laval, a 28-year-old captain born at Foxerna in Västergötland. His troop, which at the beginning had been held in reserve behind the Life company, numbered roughly 60 dragoons in the line.

The three compact wedge-shaped groups of men and horses, with standards fluttering, sped towards the Russian line. Two thundering salvos greeted them. When De Laval, at the head of his squadron, tried to break though he was met with such powerful volleys 'on the nose', as he put it, that he failed. The ineffectiveness of cavalry against steady infantry and judicious fire was again made all too apparent. The squadron scattered in the haze of powder. De Laval collected them together fairly quickly however. They and the other two squadrons gave up their attempts to dent the enemy infantry.

A new menace, in the form of Russian cavalry, was beginning to sweep over the field. It had passively bided its time until now. A massacre could be expected if it reached the fleeing men. The Russian infantry, constrained by its strict line, was unable to keep pace with the running Swedes. But the Russian cavalry would easily catch them, and ride them down in droves with minimal effort. On the right, the three squadrons of Taube's dragoons did what they could to hold up the advance. They met with some success.

The Russian cavalry was in action on the Swedish left as well. Command on this wing was held by Major-General Hamilton, also colonel of the Östgöta cavalry. One of his aides was an 18-year-old lieutenant, Wilhelm Ludvig Taube, from Örebro. With the Östgöta regiment, to protect the army's flank farthest out on the wing, were the Skåne dragoons and the Åbo cavalry. This substantial force of about 2,000 blades had received the order to aid the foot, but the Russian horse, probably both Bauer's and Volkonski's detachments, threatened to attack them in the rear.

Volkonski's cavalry was stationed round the village of Tachtaulova, from where they could easily out-flank the Swedes. The manoeuvre they carried out was similar to that on the right, when Creutz was attacked in the rear, deflecting his attack on the Russian line. As the Russians now rode towards the Swedish left the cavalry had to concentrate their efforts on saving their own skins.

The Skåne dragoons held the most vulnerable position. Their left flank was completely exposed, and they were in difficulties from the first Russian advance. They were quickly surrounded. In the *mêlée* the Russians seized one of their guidons. Their commanding officer was Prince Maximilian, the man who had rebuffed the Cossack who offered to change sides earlier in the day. The loss of the regimental standard immediately prompted him to order a counter-charge.

Banners and standards were important in several ways. They provided direction for the troops and kept them collected in battle. As a rule, every infantry company had a banner, and every cavalry squadron a standard, or guidon. The banners were often the size of sheets, but the standards were much smaller and easier to handle. They identified and aided the recognition of units at long distance. However, they functioned more significantly as symbols. Men fought stubbornly around them. The capture of one of these beautifully embroidered pieces of silk cloth was a feat of glory and a token of success. It could also mean an award of chinking coin or promotion for the daredevil who had achieved it. The thought could spur a man on to great deeds. Gory struggles round flags were commonplace.

It had been customary in the Middle Ages for church dignitaries to bless the army's colours. The persistence of this religious association helps to explain much of the great meaning they still held for the combatants. In times of peace the flags would be kept in the church of their district. The presentation of new colours and standards was an occasion for heavy ceremonial, loaded with emotion. The regiments would swear solemn, blood-filled oaths. The standard-bearers, the ensign and the cornet, had to promise to defend the colours with their lives. Swearing on the colours was highly significant: some held that a soldier was not bound by military law until he had been sworn in. Problems could arise before newly raised units received their colours.

It was also part of the ritual for every soldier to help knock in the many rivets attaching the flag to its pole. The loss of a company banner was a disgrace and a disaster: often the cloth would be ripped from the pole to stop it being taken by the enemy. Besides making manoeuvres in battle much more difficult, such a loss could also lead to severe punishment for those responsible, and even to the dissolution of the company. The colours symbolized victory or defeat. They, and the cannon, were the trophies most desired, and always included in final accounts of the battle. These patches of cloth offered something palpable to fight for, when the actual aims of the struggle might be somewhat obscure and empty of meaning for the individual man.

The Skåne dragoons rode resolutely into renewed attack and broke through the Russian line. The men reached a cornet and tore the standard from his grasp. Thus they were quits for their own recent loss. The episode exemplifies the duelling element in the battle, somewhat reminiscent of a game or sporting contest. The Russians capture a standard, the Swedes counter and take one back: a draw. The hand-to-hand bout continued. In a short spell the dragoons captured another four Russian flags. Maximilian claimed to have taken one of them single-handed. However, the regiment's situation was still critical. They were surrounded by Russian horse which, as one of the survivors, Lieutenant Joachim Lyth, relates in his journal, 'fell upon us on all sides like a frothing river'.

The Östgöta cavalry fought next to the Scanians. They fought desperately but suffered great losses. The two units repulsed repeated Russian attacks, and their dogged resistance succeeded in impeding effective Russian pursuit of the men fleeing on this wing. Their situation grew worse as the casualties mounted. Lieutenant Hans Litner, an Östgöta officer, tumbled dead off his horse. Sergeant Erich Björck, a friend who had met him the previous day, spirited and merry, commented a little cynically that 'thereby all his moneys loaned out by friends and acquaintances were come to nought'.

The Russians around them steadily increased in number. Cossacks and artillery united with the horse already engaged. The situation became truly desperate. The vice of cavalry and cannon firing at close range would shortly crush the two regiments flat. Maximilian conferred with his officers, and decided they should cut their way out and try to rejoin the main force. They smashed a hole through the surrounding Russians and galloped through, pursued by six dragoon regiments and a large number of 'Cossacks, Kalmucks and Tartars': an estimated strength of 2,000 horsemen.

Only a small number actually succeeded in fighting their way out of the bag. The young aide, Wilhelm Ludvig Taube, relates that they 'became surrounded on all sides, so rather few escaped, that were not either felled or captured'. He himself was taken prisoner, together with Major-General Hamilton, the flank commander. The Östgöta regiment was almost totally wiped out, and later had to be re-recruited from scratch. Would the fragment now fleeing across the field escape or would both units be completely annihilated?

An ominous rumour that the king had been killed added to the general demoralization. The word spread like quicksilver through the cavalry, whose already low morale sank further. Captain Peter Schönström, a Västmanlander serving with the Swedish Adelsfana, one of the units guarding the baggage, later commented on the cavalry's poor performance. It had not, he said, 'everywhere thrust home so zealously, as perhaps it would, had the king been well'. The health and well-being of the Swedish king undoubtedly had an effect on battle morale.

The king was not dead: not yet. The royal entourage, with its substantial escort, stood on their knoll a little behind the right wing of the line of foot. Enemy troops advanced towards the prominent group, but were repulsed with little difficulty. Rehnsköld galloped up to the king and reported: 'It goes ill, Your Grace, it goes ill! Our foot are running away!' In disbelief, the king replied: 'Our foot? *Running?*' With no time for further explanation, the field marshal turned his light grey horse about, flung the words: 'Preserve your master well, dear lads!' over his shoulder, and disappeared at a gallop. The defeat was a fact.

Major organized fighting was now only raging round the Swedish infantry trapped out on the field. The battalions were in their death-throes, crushed and milled down by the weight of overwhelming numbers. A mighty flood of musket muzzles, bayonets and pikes welled in over the bleeding, incarcerated groups of men. Like a row of sand-castles eroded by a rising tide they crumbled and fell to pieces.

The two battalions of Upplanders suffered worst. Corralled by the Russian counter-surge, they were ruthlessly massacred. Massive numerical superiority pounded the regiment into the dust. The commanding officer, Gustaf Stiernhöök, was slaughtered. So were Lieutenant-Colonel Arendt von Post, the major, the regimental quartermaster, the adjutant, nearly all the company commanders and almost the entire rank and file. In the Life Company and the Lieutenant-Colonel's Company ten of the 12 officers were killed. The two survivors were both wounded. Half the total number of officers taken prisoner were wounded, many of them gravely. They included the commander of Rasbo Company, Nils Fehman; Lieutenant Fredrik Hanck in Sigtuna Company, whose brother was killed, and Lieutenant Jakob Sneckenberg, of Bälinge Company, who was dying. Another severely wounded prisoner was Lars Forsman of Sigtuna Company. Forsman was a veteran who had been with the army since the landing in Denmark in 1700. Like many others, he was stripped of everything he had. Even his blood-soaked shirt was coaxed off his badly mangled body.

There could only be one outcome for the Upplanders caught in this suffocating grip: men died in their hundreds in a hundred different ways. Only a handful, by pure chance, escaped the scythe. The soldiers saw their comrades fall, and must have known that soon it would be their turn. One by one, the faded banners with the orb of the realm toppled and vanished from the air.

Georg Planting was one of the few survivors. A 26-year-old captain, he had studied at Uppsala University. After joining the army, he had been commissioned ensign by Charles XII personally, on the battlefield by the Dvina in 1701. He had seen many battles and been wounded many times: a badly cut and damaged hand, a smashed shoulder and a shell-splinter in one leg. After the life had been knocked out of Georg Zacharias Grissbach, commander of Hundra Parish Company, Planting took command of one of the remaining pockets of men and led a final hopeless stand. The inevitable end came when a musket-ball drilled his right thigh, and he fell into Russian hands. The flood of steel washed over those still standing. Georg Planting wrote that the regiment, down to 'non-commissioned officers, musicians, corporals and other ranks, *in toto*, fell where they stood'.

A small group escaped this holocaust. Roughly 70 men had been detailed to the baggage-train the day before. Apart from these, extremely few cheated death. The Uppland regiment, which had gone into battle almost 700 men strong, no longer existed. Two days later, when the survivors were called to muster, only 14 could be found.

After the fighting came the slaughtering. A 37-year-old captain of the Guard, Lars Tiesensten from Västergötland, lay with one leg shot off not far from where the Upplanders had fought their last. He saw the Russians let themselves go on the remnants of the regiment with their naked weapons. In a frenzied rage they lunged with blade and bayonet at every Swedish soldier, dead or living. A forest of pike and sword was raised and lowered. Tiesensten could see a hideous, heaving, twitching mountain of bodies, a hundred men or more on top of each other. Into this monstrous monument of dead and living the Russian soldiers indiscriminately thrust their gory weapons.

The phenomenon is known from other battles. A group of human beings in extreme fear of death crush together and clamber over each other in a last desperate attempt to find protection. It is as if, in the last pulse-beats of their death-throes, they are carried back to their infancy, crying for their mothers and huddling under other bodies for security. Tiesensten saw the Upplanders lying 'in a heap and as if fallen upon each other or thrown up on the pile, wherein the enemy with pike, sword and bayonet eagerly slaughtered and massacred as much as he was able, despite not recognizing what was living and what dead'. Many had come through the hurricane of fire merely to meet another base and bestial death.

The trapped battalions to the right of the Upplanders met a similar fate. A few small sections managed to fight their way free in the tumult and slip away, but only very few. Most of the 500 men of the Skaraborg battalion were transformed into corpses, kneaded out and levelled with the sandy soil. Forty men returned alive: a major, two captains, five lieutenants, five ensigns and 27 soldiers. Most of these were wounded.

One by one the battalions were overcome. In due course, the remaining soldiers in the 3rd battalion of Life Guards found themselves alone, the Swedes to their right and left all fallen. The grip tightened harder round fewer and fewer; a few guardsmen stood together in final defiance. Then each man stood alone, without escape, without hope, without comfort. The living stumbled for a few moments over the corpses of their comrades. Then they too were dead. The sheep had been sacrificed.

# 20 · 'He Tramples Down'

Paradoxically, a soldier in battle is at gravest risk when he attempts to leave the field. Most are killed in flight, when they turn their backs to the enemy and are unable to defend themselves. To kill running opponents is easy and safe, and the casualties of routed troops are often uncannily high. The losses of the defeated are in any case always great, and disintegration and wholesale massacre is the constant threat hanging over them.

At this moment the great majority of the Swedish soldiers had no thought but escape. Most of them had to find their way to one of the four narrow crossings over the Ivanchintsi brook and the patches of marshland, and thence through the Budyschenski wood. At first the flight led west, away from battle and the whining hail of grapeshot sweeping clean the plain. Stiernhielm's nightmare vision of 'battle-terror' now possessed the Swedes.

> Here comes the enemy, he sets about
> the one whom victory I begrudge.
> He shoots, stabs, slashes, tramples down,
> all he can overcome,
> so none remain to tell the tale:
> and all the honour will be mine.

In the woods the defiles were already teeming with panic-stricken men and horses attempting to make their way through. On the battlefield many of the fleeing were either killed or captured – or both: captured first, then killed. The men on the left wing, the first to run, were the most vulnerable. They had the greatest distance to cover before they could disappear into the deceptive security of the woodland. Most of the men the Russians caught up with seem to have been killed on the spot. Few prisoners were taken at this stage of the battle. An official Russian account says the Swedes were pursued with swords, bayonets and pikes. It notes with satisfaction that they were put down 'like animals'.

The pursuing Russians were careful not to attack larger, more united groups. Those Swedes with the best chance were soldiers belonging to organized units that kept together, or joined up with larger ones. Thirty-odd men, probably from the 1st battalion of the Västmanland regiment, led by Lieutenant-Colonel Carl Anders Sinclair, 34, from Göteborg, took up a position behind one of the many farm fences. Ensconced behind it, they managed to negotiate their way into captivity, thereby escaping massacre.

One after another, the more senior officers, who dashed about in vain attempts to stop the rout, fell into the hands of the pursuers. These officers were desirable trophies. No hands were lifted against them. The first to be captured was Major-General Berndt Otto Stackelberg, 47, from Estonia. A member of the general staff, he had commanded the third column of the infantry, which had included the Upplanders and the Östgöta regiment. Appelgren, the wounded Östgöta commander, who had so desperately entreated Lewenhaupt to help halt his fleeing men, was taken at the same time. Josias Cederhielm never managed to deliver his report on the road round the village. He was wounded and taken prisoner while trying to stem the flight.

It must have been a common fate to be sabred down from behind in flight. During the 1950s the skeletal remains of four unknown soldiers, probably Swedes, were sent home for forensic examination. These fragments provide a blurred glimpse of four deaths on the smoke-dimmed field of battle. The first was a man aged about 30. He had been cut down from behind and above by repeated blows from a sword or sabre. The cuts were not fatal. His *coup de grâce* was a shot through the head. The probable course of events was that a Russian trooper caught up with him, slashed him about the head until he fell, then pulled out a pistol and fired into his already severely lacerated skull. Or perhaps someone found him wounded, then killed him.

The next was a man aged about 35. He had also been hacked down by a mounted enemy. A powerful, traumatic blow to the back of the head had cut in deeply. The wound would not have been directly fatal and he would either have bled to death, or received other wounds. The third, a man between 35 and 40, had taken a similar blow on the left from above, not forceful enough to end his life. Death had been caused by two or three thrusts through his left temple. Perhaps he too was killed as he lay helpless on the ground. Lastly, the fourth: 25–30 years old, he would have seen the man who took his life. He was struck in the forehead by a point which penetrated his brain. He would have turned towards his adversary, to surrender or defend himself, when the lance was driven in. His killer was mounted, presumably a Cossack.

The volleys began to diminish. Firing continued, but the uninterrupted roar was slowly dying down. On the battlefield the fog began to disperse. During the hottest moments of the battle gunpowder smoke and dust had billowed so thickly that the king and his company had not seen the rout.

They now remained virtually alone, not realizing until the dust began to settle that they were among the last Swedes still on the battlefield. Their situation had at once become extremely serious. Almost unopposed, Russian troops were spreading out over the field in their hunt, and the king of Sweden was now among the prey.

With Russians all around them, delivering intermittent reminders of their presence in the form of an occasional cannonball, it was a matter of urgency for Charles and his escort to depart. A Drabant corporal, Christer Henrik d'Albedyhl, was sent to reconnoitre. He was quick to confirm that all troops in the immediate area were hostile. The king ordered retreat, and the whole entourage turned, like most of the other Swedes, to make for the woods. More Drabants were dispatched to look for Swedish units and lead them to the retinue, for additional protection. Besides the court officials, Drabants, Life Dragoons and a variety of other unattached persons, sections of the Mounted Life regiment began to gather round the white litter. The escort was already strong, but needed maximum reinforcement.

Creutz's pursuit of the cavalry which had fallen on his rear, while engaging the large Russian square, had taken his squadrons some distance. The pursuit had been quite successful: the enemy had been scattered and chased off until they disappeared between the small mud houses in Maly Budyschi. Creutz would have been better employed at the main infantry battle, however. It was too late now. A Drabant, quickly followed by another, rode off to him, and ordered him immediately to break off the pursuit and take his men to the king. The units had dispersed in the frantic chase. Only the North Skåne cavalry were close. A few squadrons of Hielm's dragoons were located a little farther on, near the village occupied by the Russians. The terrain round the village was fairly rugged, and the Russians were still plentiful. An orderly was sent from the Scanians to direct the dragoons to retreat. The scattered squadrons were difficult to control: Creutz only managed to collect part of the original force. They rode back north, towards the battlefield, where the Russian infantry were now on the march, blocking their route to the king. They took the risk and rode straight through, with no reaction from the enemy foot, who must have supposed them to be Russian cavalry.

Out on the plain the Russian infantry had moved on. People from the encampment were now picking their way across it, through the bodies of the Swedes spreadeagled in the burning sun. The dead, dying and wounded were being plundered. Clothes were ripped off the living and the dead. The scattered weapons were rapaciously raked in.

Banners and standards were collected as trophies and carried off in triumph. Hallart's infantry division, on the extreme left of the Russian front, came away with 22 banners, six of them the white banners of the Life Guard; and two cavalry standards, a white one from the Mounted Life regiment and another belonging to Hielm's dragoons. Both units had been part of Creutz's cavalry.

The Russians were busy killing as well as plundering. A number of surviving Swedes were killed as soon as found. But prisoners were also being rounded up. There is no evidence of consistency in the treatment of survivors. During this phase the killing of prisoners seems to have been a matter of individual Russian whim. Some wounded Swedes escaped. A 37-year-old major from the Skaraborg regiment, Sven Lagerberg, born at Stora Kärr in Västergötland, was one. During the final phase of the fighting he took a musket-ball clean through his body and remained prostrate. The advancing Russian battle line tramped over him. His salvation was a wounded dragoon, who helped him up on his horse and carried him towards the baggage-train.

Svante Horn, a 34-year-old premier captain, was also saved from the corpses piled high on the field. His regiment, the Skåne dragoons, had fought on the extreme Swedish left and been severely mauled when surrounded by Russian cavalry. During the conflict Horn's right leg had been shattered and he had remained where he was. This was not the first wound for this soldier of misfortune. In the war's first year he had received a musket-ball in the thigh. In 1703 he had his horse shot under him, was stabbed in the left arm, and badly trampled on. Later, in Poland, he had been in a wood with 24 men collecting firewood, when attacked by a troop of several hundred Poles. After a battle lasting seven hours, during which 23 of his men were killed, he had escaped. In 1706 14 pieces of bone had been removed from his skull after a head wound. The following year he had been caught in an ambush in Lithuania. Kalmucks had 'hit him round the head with a club, so blood spurted from his nose, mouth and ears'. Horn had been left for dead, a sword-wound in his chest, his stomach punctured by a pike and 13 more minor wounds about his body. He would have died had his servant, a man called Daniel Lidbom, not stumbled over his master's body and noticed faint signs of life. For the next few days the man had kept him alive by squirting a mixture of milk and wine through a straw inserted in the gap left by a tooth knocked out of his swollen mouth. These wounds had left him paralysed down one side, which had not prevented him joining the army's march to Moscow.

Again Lidbom scoured the field of battle, turning over mangled corpses, looking for his master's face among the pain-contorted, powder-blackened visages. Again he found him. They were soon both taken prisoner, but Horn's life had been saved.

A stream of prisoners were herded into the Russian camp. Many had been plundered stark naked, and were now exposed to mockery and humiliation. One of the naked prisoners obliged to listen to the scoffing Russian soldiery was Alexander Magnus Dahlberg, a 24-year-old sergeant from Holta parish in Bohuslän. He had followed his two elder brothers into the army at the age of 18, been present at Fraustadt and witnessed the mass execution of Russian prisoners. He was a pious, mild and compassionate young man. These qualities had earned him the nickname of 'old Polish farmwife'. During the previous year's campaign he had taken pity on a peasant woman in labour, thrown out of her cottage by other soldiers annoyed by her groans. Dahlberg had helped the woman give birth to her child in the cold porch.

Dahlberg and the other prisoners were given to hear they were 'wretches and weaklings, unable for thirst and famine to subsist on their Russian rations: it was too much for them, affected their limbs and made them dizzy in the head. But they could put their minds at rest. When they came to Moscow, which they had been yearning for, everything would be so well arranged for them that they need not worry in the slightest about their sustenance in Russia; there they would find hacks, picks, spades, crowbars, hods and barrows, all set up for the health of the Swedes, so when they used them, they would have no occasion to complain about lack of food or sleep.' This garbled mockery mapped out the future for many of the prisoners.

A few senior officers still rode over the field, attempting to save whatever could be saved. Gyllenkrok headed out to the right, guided by the dull sound of rattling drum-rolls. He assumed the infantry formed in a square in the distance were Swedes until he got close enough to see that they were Russian. Piper had made the same mistake. Gyllenkrok turned back. In front of him he saw some Swedish cavalry still lingering on the plain. As he rode in their direction he passed a group of foot soldiers at the corner of a small field, and called to them to 'pull yourselves together and form up'. They replied that they were wounded.

Gyllenstierna's dragoons, their blue standards flapping in the wind and their commanding officer, Nils Gyllenstierna, mounted at their head, stood drawn up in good order. Nils was blue-blooded, a count from a family of Danish origin. He was 38. Badly wounded at Kalisz in 1706, he had now recovered. Portraits show a man with intense eyes under handsomely arched eyebrows, a long nose and a small chaste mouth. Gyllenkrok left the wounded soldiers and rode on up to the dragoons.

A battalion of Russian infantry marched past quite near them, moving west towards the wood. Gyllenkrok urged the dragoon colonel to 'take that lot in the rear.' Gyllenstierna shouted 'Forward!' The Russians must at first have mistaken the nationality of the dragoons, but were now fully alive to it. The order to attack had hardly been uttered before a stinging salvo cracked out from the left of the battalion, a mere 50 metres from the colonel. It was enough for the dragoons.

Gyllenstierna's men turned tail and rode away. A few other cavalry units were drawn into the disorganized retreat. Gyllenkrok was swept along with them.

The stream of horsemen fled over one of the marsh crossings. The crush increased. Retreat shaded into panic as their fear mounted. The reassurance provided by larger numbers as the fragments reunited was dispelled by the panic of flight. In a fleeing crowd other people are no protection: all struggle against all. Ferocious pushing, butting and shoving took place across a narrow bridge. Gyllenkrok was jostled off it into the marsh, where his horse stuck fast. With a great effort the middle-aged quartermaster-general worked his animal free and swung back up into the saddle. The next moment he almost fell off again. A man on foot, wanting a horse and determined to get one by force if necessary, gripped Gyllenkrok's sword-belt and pulled hard at it. The quartermaster-general felt himself slide from the saddle, but before he finally fell the belt broke and slipped off him. Leaving sword-belt and scabbard behind, Gyllenkrok rode rapidly away, sword in hand. The cramped passage reaped its victims. Not all those who fell were able to struggle up again.

Russian dragoons began to reach the crossing, and made efforts to block it, adding to the chaotic desperation. The Småland cavalry had joined the retreat. A squadron chaplain, Johannes Siöman, who had been with them in the battle, said there was 'plainly nothing for it but to pull back through the woods', after the infantry had been defeated. Pastor Siöman was terrified. He recounted later that 'no man knew where to turn, but musket and cannon balls flew like hail round our ears.' He was sure he was going to die in this Hades of rattling missiles: 'The best counsel was to commend one's soul into the hands of the Creator, for to all human appearance there was no hope of survival.'

The retreat was more of a disorderly rout. The Småland regiment split into fragments, each seeking its own way out. One splinter of 19 men from the Life squadron included two officers, Cornet Samuel Lindberg and the quartermaster, Frans Hager. Frans had been inches from death shortly before, saving the regiment's commanding officer, Major-General Dahldorf, from falling into enemy hands. This may have been when Dahldorf's entrails fell out, his stomach ripped open by a Cossack. Frans escaped unhurt, but a cannonball blew his hat off and he had two horses shot under him.

The little troop of Smålanders moved off south and fell in with Östra parish squadron, from their own regiment. Captain Johan Gyllenpamp, 40, from Skåne, took command of the combined group. Shortly afterwards they were in action again. Russian dragoons attempted to barricade a crossing over a morass near one of the redoubts. The Smålanders managed to beat them off and rode through. For Frans, however, it ended badly. As the retreat continued he fell into Russian hands and was stripped of everything he owned.

Meanwhile the king and his retinue were on their way to the verge of the wood, about 800 metres north-east of the church in Maly Budyschi. Suddenly their progress was checked by a Russian battalion emerging from a grove of trees to their right. Creutz's thinning detachment, which had just joined them, was ordered to charge. The squadrons formed up and faced the Russians. The battalion shortened pace, but quickly regained their courage, perhaps realizing just how weak the threat actually was. They continued to advance cautiously, rolled their regimental cannon into place and opened fire. Fresh salvos of canister rubble scorched the air and tore holes in the Swedish ranks. If Creutz's charge was ever launched into this fire it seems to have had little effect.

One of the members of the king's entourage was Colonel Conrad von Wangersheim. He had expected to command the Österbotten regiment but the appointment had never materialized. He claimed he had been passed over, for failing to pay Piper a sweetener for the favour. Colonel von Wangersheim turned to the king and called for the advance towards the enemy to be halted. He was concerned that the slightly craven behaviour of the Russian battalion was only a feint to coax the Swedes in their direction. The king was deaf in that ear, and asserted that they had to get into the wood. The order was unambiguous. They were to cut their way through at any cost.

The Drabants, headed by Lieutenant Hierta, took the lead with a squadron of North Skåne cavalry. The remarkable procession of cavalry, Drabants, civilians, courtiers, staff officers, stragglers, wounded and, somewhere in the middle, Charles on his litter, moved forward. They swung in between the wood and the enemy battalion. The Russians turned right, to face them. Muskets flew up to the ready, and were aimed. A blaring volley crackled from the green line. Grapeshot and musket-balls cut men and horses to the ground. Missiles slashed the foliage. Severed branches rained from the trees. There was no hand-to-hand fighting: the Russians stood to one side, emptying lead ball into the Swedes as they marched past, as though on a shooting range.

The Life regiment suffered a humiliating loss in the musket-ball storm. As reward for the unit's exemplary conduct at the battle of Lund in 1676 Charles XI had donated a pair of large silver drums. These were carried on a special horse in the battle, and played on by the regimental kettle-drummer, Falk. In the passage between the battalion and the wood both Falk and his horse were killed. In the rout the silver drums were left lying beside the horse's carcase and the kettle-drummer's riddled corpse.

Somewhat reduced in numbers, the king's detachment carried on past the battalion, into the wood. The Russians followed close behind, eager for the rich prize. The Swedes marched towards a morass. It was a matter of urgency to get out of firing range. But they were still exposed to powerful fire. When they had gone some way across the marshy patch further disaster struck. The royal equipage got stuck.

The Russians had time to find their range. A cannonball hit the litter, striking just in front of the king's wounded foot, killing the leading horse. One of the stable-masters was standing next to the litter. He had already been wounded in his right arm, which was now paralysed. When the cannonball smashed into the litter a cloud of wood splinters whirled through the air, many striking the stable-master in the side and severely wounding him. The rear horse also collapsed and the white litter was shattered. The situation was extremely dangerous for the king and for everyone round the litter. Russian soldiers advanced at the double. Halting by the edge of the marsh they poured random fire into the group clustered together halfway across it.

A hurricane of iron blasted unremittingly into the men and horses. The king was lifted out of the useless litter. Only three of the 24 guardsmen were still alive. With great difficulty the remaining soldiers helped the king up on a horse belonging to Trooper Bass of the Life regiment. At the same instant a musket-ball grazed the head of one of the bodyguard, Nils Frisk. The king's new mount had only taken three steps when it, too, was hit: a cannonball sheared off one of its legs. Hultman, the steward, had just swung up into the saddle of his second horse of the day when another cannonball removed its hind quarters. Hultman was showered with blood. Still holding the silver beaker and the king's medicaments, he extricated himself from the twisted, mutilated carcase, and looked round for another mount.

The flight was degenerating into massacre. Round the litter dead and wounded men fell on top of each other. The steward was among those who later maintained that 'assuredly it was God, who protected our blessed King from the numerous bullets, which flew around His Majesty'. Those deserving the greater credit were the many cavalrymen, Drabants, officers and courtiers who crowded round the king, and received the missiles intended for him. There was a living shield of faithful subjects round Charles the whole time. About 20 of the Drabants fell, and many others were wounded and captured. Johannes Fredrik Rühl, a corporal aged about 30 from Pernau, was badly wounded in the head and taken prisoner.

Many of the civilians attached to the court and the chancellery also perished. The registrar, Stephan Hirschenstjerna, and the king's chamberlain and historiographer, Gustaf Adlerfelt, were both killed. A cannonball struck 38-year-old Adlerfelt as he stood next to the litter. His great life's work, a record of the deeds of Charles XII, had come to a drastic full stop. The physician appointed to tend the king's foot also suffered: Professor Jacob Fredrik Belau was taken prisoner.

The North Skåne cavalry regiment lost between 70 and 80 men in the fracas. Among those shot dead were Johan Galle, an unmarried middle-aged man; and Major Magnus Johan Wolffelt, who had started his career in Saxon service but returned to Sweden at the beginning of the war.

The tightly packed crowd was showered with gore at every hit. Hultman writes that 'I and my clothes were sprayed all over with blood from the dying'. Bloody pieces of humanity were hurled in every direction. In this grotesque chaos the overriding objective was to save the king. His new mount useless after the shot which removed its leg, the king needed another horse, quickly. He turned to Johan Hierta, of the Drabants, with a curt command: 'Hierta: your horse.' Hierta, gravely wounded, was lifted to the ground from his saddle. His place was taken by the monarch. Charles, dressed in a blue cloak and waistcoat, his long sword in his hand, his right leg booted and spurred and the left wrapped in a tattered bandage dripping blood, was helped to the reins. The blood-drenched company immediately made off from the miry death-trap. Hierta was so badly wounded he could hardly walk. He was left supporting himself against a fence. Nordberg, the tall court preacher, who survived the rain of lead, wrote that the bleeding lieutenant 'to all appearances could expect to meet his final doom' by that fence. Hierta was quickly surrounded by Russians, while the king withdrew on his horse.

The need to secure a new mount was a problem for many at this stage of events. It was a common experience for a cavalryman to have his horse shot under him. The large area presented by the animal, much easier to hit than its rider, was a preferred target: and a fallen horse weakened a cavalry charge far more than a fallen trooper. Well-disciplined riderless mounts would stay in formation, as a rule, but a horseless rider was little danger, even if unhurt. In flight, a man on foot was lost if pursued by cavalry. Pursuing infantry, advancing in line, would be slow, and a running man might well escape. Cavalry in the strictest formation would catch a man on foot.

So there were quite a number who suffered the loss of their chargers in the battle, some repeatedly. The more well-heeled officers often had several horses. Regulations stipulated that a cavalry major should be equipped with five horses, a captain four, a cornet three and so on down to the ordinary trooper who only had one. Obviously, a common trooper never had the same chance as an officer. Horseless, he would be stranded on the field.

At the head of his squadron of Mounted Life troopers, Johan Blum, a captain from Livonia, lost three horses during the day. A Drabant, Lance-Corporal Nils Christer von Baumgarten, born in Kalmar, had two horses shot under him, apart from receiving a severe impact wound in the shoulder from a cannonball.

Desperate to escape capture or being trampled down, many resorted to violence in their efforts to seize a new mount. Others, like the king, would acquire one by unashamed requisition from a subordinate, willing or unwilling. Lewenhaupt encountered Major-General Axel Sparre, doggedly attempting to stop the panic. His horse shot, he needed another immediately. Ensign Bengt Salstéen, 30, born in Västmanland, dismounted and gave Sparre his horse. He asserts he did this 'voluntarily': perhaps because Sparre was his regimental commander. The major-general swung into the saddle and rode off, leaving the ensign 'at hazard'.

Nils Bonde and Carl Roland, who had met by chance shortly before the battle, had very similar experiences. Bonde, the aide-de-camp, lost a variety of horses and servants, and had one horse shot under him. He was almost trampled down, escaped by the skin of his teeth and found another mount. Roland had joined Hielm's dragoons, one of the units in Creutz's charge on the Russian square. At the end of this engagement he suddenly found himself grounded. Presumably having just received their order to close up round the king, his comrades all galloped off, leaving him alone, on foot.

He could now curse his omission to bring his reserve mounts. An enemy squadron bore down straight towards him. A faint chance to save himself presented itself. Ahead of the Russians, a large riderless horse came bolting. Roland managed to leap alongside it, fumbled his foot into the stirrup, hauled himself into the saddle, and dug in his spurs. With the many-legged monster, on hammering hoofs, breathing down his neck, Roland guided his charger towards a small marsh and out over its spongy surface. His pursuers galloped eagerly after him. Unlike their mounts, however, they were large and heavily-built, and their over-loaded horses sank, one after another. It was a matter of chance that the horse which Providence had delivered into the young Stockholmer's hands was strong enough to work its way across the bog in spite of its load. The Russians failed to make the crossing, and Roland escaped.

But he was still in danger. With the Russians floundering in the marsh behind him, he began looking for Swedish troops and his own regiment. He caught sight of a mounted unit and rode nearer. Dust and smoke gummed up his eyes, and Roland found it difficult to make out which side they belonged to. He was very close to the unknown horsemen when he realized they were Russian. He whirled round and galloped off. After further aimless riding he eventually fell in with a troop which proved to be Swedes. The perils were over for the time being and Roland rejoined his unit.

Another way of acquiring a new horse was by confiscating someone else's reserve mount. Major-General Lagercrona, who had ridden his steed completely into the ground, provides an instance of this. As a soldier, Lagercrona was not a great success. In the past year he had managed a few really thundering blunders. During the campaign, in command of an army detachment, he had first got lost, then bungled a golden opportunity to capture the strategically important stronghold of Starodub. His talents were more of an administrative-economic nature. He enjoyed a measure of the king's confidence by virtue of his ability to drum up working capital for the army at short notice. His brusque manner and love of litigation in matters great and small had made him many enemies. He now needed a replacement horse. When a servant came riding past with a well-accoutred chestnut horse, equipped with pistols and other trappings, he seized it.

The chestnut belonged to Carl Strokirch, a 30-year-old captain from Nässelsta in Södermanland, serving with the Life dragoons, one of the units now attached to the king's group. Lagercrona felt quite justified in taking the horse, since he was a highly placed officer and, as he saw it, required it in the service of the king. A Drabant, Bror Rålamb, was witness to the whole incident. Strokirch was later captured, while Lagercrona escaped. In 1731, 22 years after the battle, Strokirch sued Lagercrona in a county court south of Stockholm, for horse theft. He finally received justice in the form of 700 copper and 10 silver daler coins in damages.

Carl Gustaf Hård from Fogelås, commanding the cadre of Drabants, left the king's entourage to try to stop the rout and rally even more protective support for the monarch. He came across Lewenhaupt, and asked him to help. 'My Lord General, I cannot get the men to make a stand. They are completely abandoning the King.' Lewenhaupt replied resignedly 'I have done my best: it is impossible;' but added: 'Where is His Majesty?' 'Just here, near by,' said Hård. The general determined to make a last attempt. Plunging back into the stream of fleeing men, he again exhorted them: 'Stand! In the name of Jesus! Do not desert the King: he is here.' Mention of the monarch struck a chord with some of the foot. Someone shouted: 'If the King is here, we will stand.' A few of them stopped. It was sufficient to stem the mindless panic. Round Lewenhaupt, the pace abated. The soldiers and troopers slowed down, and finally halted.

## 21 · 'All is Lost'

Lewenhaupt followed Hård back to the king, now mounted on Hierta's horse, his bandaged foot thrown up across the animal's withers. The wound was bleeding copiously. Charles greeted Lewenhaupt with a friendly expression, saying: 'Still alive then, are ye?' 'Yes, Your Majesty,' replied Lewenhaupt, 'God best knows how things stand.' The two of them conferred. Lewenhaupt maintained there was nothing more they could do on the battlefield. He suggested they should try to collect as many of the men as possible and make for the baggage-train. There was some doubt whether they could find their way to Pushkaryovka. Asked directly by Charles if he knew the way, Lewenhaupt replied he did not. In response to general query a couple of soldiers from the Vallack regiment came forward, saying they knew.

The sight of a large stationary group had a remarkable effect. A kind of quiet eye of the whirlwind began to form round the king. Groups of fleeing men were persuaded to slow down. Stragglers and wounded joined the group. It was apparent to the senior officers that most of the infantry gathering round them came from the left wing, but there were few or none from the right. Lewenhaupt remarked that most of them 'must be biting the grass'. A young officer from the Life Guards led a fragment out of the closed inferno on the right, and found his way to the king's group. His band of survivors was not impressive: it consisted of a few hundred men, most of them wounded. The young Life Guardsman was its sole remaining officer, the rest of them were reported killed.

Numerous squadrons of cavalry also united with the king's entourage. Many had been in no conflict at all. They claimed to have received no orders of any kind, and had merely been swept along in the surge of panic. Not all of them joined up voluntarily with the growing group. Count Poniatowski, King Stanislaus' Polish envoy at the king's head-quarters, caught sight of two Swedish squadrons wandering about, apparently aimlessly. Riding after them, the count urged the officer in command to collect his men and return with him to the king. He was met with outright refusal. Poniatowski drew his sword and set its point at the man's breast. Overwhelmed by the Slavonic élan of this persuasive argument, the squadron's commander and his troops followed the count back.

The king became conscious of the ever-increasing number of troops milling about him. Dizzy with heat, exhaustion and loss of blood, the monarch started to assert that he considered himself fit for renewed battle. He was mounted, after all, and had both infantry and cavalry. But the oration was no more than empty rhetoric from the hero's befogged mind. The retreat soon resumed, in a somewhat more orderly manner. The objective, if they could only manage to reach it, was the baggage-train.

Although the bulk of the Swedish army were now in retreat through and around the sultry Budyschenski wood, out on the field fighting continued. Those fleeing could still hear the rattle of musket volleys behind them. With the support of two other squadrons, Carl Magnus De Laval and his men were successfully conducting a rearguard delaying action against the advancing Russian cavalry. From a position behind a steep gorge they rebuffed successive attacks. The Russians were prevented from reaching the passage behind them, still thick with fleeing men, which the king's group had just filtered through. De Laval's cavalry had no option but to fight: the defile was choked and they were forced to wait their turn.

They were few, and hard pressed. A squadron of Hielm's dragoons was a welcome sight as they rode in to join them. The menacing Russian horse constantly offered to attack; but whenever the Swedes lifted their carbines to the ready, across their knees, the Russians turned aside. This quadrille of alternating Russian advance and recoil, as the Swedes raised their weapons, continued for about a quarter of an hour, which passed in a state of restless waiting.

The passage cleared at the eleventh hour. The dragoons shouted a warning to De Laval: 'Capitaine! Their foot are coming up behind the horse.' The ranks of enemy cavalry divided, Russian infantry emerged from concealment behind them and marched towards the Swedes. The infantry's musket-barrels pointed in their direction, and a crashing salvo rent the air. De Laval realized he would soon be surrounded. There was no reason to stay where they were: the passage was free. First the squadron of Hielm's dragoons left, followed by Sternbach's and Tungelfelt's companies. De Laval's troopers, impatient and afraid, shouted: 'Capitaine, we who are last will fare badly.' He attempted to calm them. The situation was pressing. The most highly prized objects had to go first: the standard, carried by a 25-year-old German, Cornet Johan Jakob Schultz from Stettin, led off. The rest of the troop whirled after him in column.

A rearguard was formed to protect their retreat, consisting of De Laval himself, a Finnish sergeant-major called Johan Henrik Seréen and eight dragoons. The measure was necessary. A Russian squadron advanced rapidly, threatening to attack the retreating Swedes in the back. But there was little the ten men could do against a whole squadron. The troop fled, and De Laval turned tail with them. On a good horse, he had reasonable hopes of getting clear. He was forced out across the same bog the king's litter had stuck in, however, and the horse went down. When he raised his head again, he could no longer see a single man of his rearguard. Its precipitate retreat seems to have given the Russians an opportunity to attack the Swedish squadron as they left: both Schultz, the standard-bearer, and the Finnish sergeant-major were captured.

De Laval was stuck in the morass, with his men gone and Russians swarming around him. Shamming dead, he dropped back down into the mire. The Russians were fooled. They began to plunder the corpses, tore the clothes off them, and collected up the banners and musical instruments lying scattered among the lifeless bodies. They also found a real treasure: next to the shot carcase of the Life regiment's drum-horse, and the mortal remains of the drummer, Falk, they came across the two great silver kettle-drums.

De Laval lay low for a while; but eventually worked himself loose, freed his animal and started to pick his way carefully through the morass. Finally, near a pond, he gained firm ground. He re-mounted and rode slowly away from the sticky, naked bodies in the defile.

Piper followed the routed men through the wood and, out in the open on the other side, began vainly looking for his master. He met Rehn-sköld, trotting through the summer heat at a rapid pace, followed by a regiment of dragoons. Pleased to have made contact with anyone of high authority in this chaos, Piper approached him and asked where the king was. Rehnsköld replied brusquely in German: 'I don't know.' The fat man beside him went on: 'For God's sake, let us not desert our King, lying sick and helpless on a litter.' The taciturn field marshal's dejected reply was merely: 'All is lost.' 'God forbid,' said Piper mechanically. 'An army may be driven back, but can re-form, and oppose the enemy.' The conversation continued as they followed the verge of the wood, farther and farther away from the battlefield.

Gyllenkrok was also lucky enough to extricate himself from the turmoil in the wood. Out on the plain he met up with a Swedish squadron led by a large-limbed commander he had not seen before. He urged him to help collect the men: 'Do your best to get more of them to make a stand.' 'Certainly, Colonel, I will do my utmost,' was the officer's obliging reply. As other squadrons approached, they were halted and ranged to the right of the first. Slowly a new line of battle began to form. Gyllenkrok was about to ride off to the right when an officer came up and pointed out to the field: 'Colonel, look, there is the field marshal.' Gyllenkrok turned and saw Rehnsköld, surrounded by cavalrymen, deep in conversation with Piper.

Piper continued to heap self-evident truths upon the morose field marshal as they rode on. He wanted Rehnsköld to try to get the fleeing men to stand, adding 'where ye are unable to persuade them, ye should show them where they must go, so that as they ride off, being so scattered, they may not all be cut down by the enemy.' Rehnsköld said nothing. He must have had something similar in mind. The field marshal clearly hoped to lead some of the cavalry back to the battle area, in an attempt to relieve those units still fighting.

They paused briefly to exchange words with Dücker and Taube, both commanders of their own dragoon regiments. Perhaps the two colonels provided information of importance, for before Piper noticed it, Rehnsköld was gone. They pointed him out on the field, presumably riding off to reconnoitre something on his own. The minister caught up with him and stubbornly continued to harp on about getting the men to stand, or 'at least, if this was impossible, that he would tell them they had to make their way to the baggage.' The two of them returned to the waiting company, where the light-footed field marshal again disappeared and the process was repeated a third time. The two most powerful men with the army after the king, familiar enemies, facing each other with irreconcilable rancour, rode back together.

Before long the field marshal was off again, riding towards the battlefield. He was now caught up by Gyllenkrok, who said: 'God save us: everything here is going badly. Does Your Excellency hear the volleys continuing to our left?' Then he added: 'Here are a heap of squadrons that have rallied. Will Your Excellency command they should go somewhere?' 'Everything is going wrong,' answered Rehnsköld numbly. He rode on, towards the field round the system of redoubts.

Dull reports of cannon fire rolled towards them from the forts nearest the wood. Gyllenkrok warned: 'Do not ride in that direction. Those are enemy *troupes* before us.' Rehnsköld brushed the warning aside, asserting the troops were 'our people'. Some of those with him agreed they were men from the Swedish right. They still had not grasped the catastrophe that had struck the right wing. The quartermaster-general was sure of his case: 'I do not believe it. I am riding back to where I know our own men to be.' The others continued stubbornly on, although they were approaching the bastion's fire.

On his way back to the waiting cavalry Gyllenkrok met Piper, who was riding south with his escort across the plain. He tried to warn him as well and called out: 'Do not ride yonder for the enemy are there.' Piper may not even have heard the words of warning for he made no answer, and continued unmoved on his way with his entire group. He had decided to try to leave the battlefield and had got hold of a 36-year-old major from Östergötland serving with the Närke-Värmland regiment, Johan Behr, who said he knew the way to the baggage-train at Pushkaryovka. Under Behr's guidance the group bumped along over the billowing plain, the sun burning down upon them. The expedition promised to be hazardous. Multitudes of irregular Russian cavalry were already infesting the field.

Gyllenkrok rode straight back to the waiting squadrons of Swedish horse and was gratified to note that their number had increased during his absence.

Another three Russian squadrons approached. In battle order, their carbines resting at the ready on their thighs, they rode towards the stationary Swedes. Just as they were passing Gyllenkrok's men, at a distance of less than 50 metres, he ordered the nearest squadrons to attack. As the Swedes prepared to charge the Russians fired a salvo, turned aside and peeled away to the right, spurring hard.

The enemy infantry's pursuit began to tail off as one after another of the Russian battalions reached the glades of the Budyschenski woods. Swedish prisoners, many fully equipped with weapons and horses, were herded together in large flocks. As the battle on the plain progressed, the massive wall of Russian foot had broken up into smaller fragments pressing forward at random in their efforts to catch up with the retreating Swedes. The Russians were already starting to seize booty, which further disrupted their line of battle.

A general halt was ordered at the verge of the wood. Battalions in line formation were patently unsuitable in wooded terrain. The units were disordered in any case, and the Russian command were reluctant to risk letting them be drawn into skirmishes, difficult to control in the woodland undergrowth. The ranks were re-formed and made ready for any possible renewed action.

The Russian artillery fell silent. The heavier pieces, 40-pounder howitzers and mortars, and 20-pounder mortars, had on average delivered 17 or 18 rounds apiece. The average of the eight-pounder cannon was 12. In spite of their lower rate of fire, the long-distance 12-pounders had fired off an average of between 36 and 37 rounds. They had kept up a constant bombardment until the retreating Swedes disappeared into the Budyschenski woods. The most numerous pieces were the three-pounder regimental cannon. Because the fighting had been at its hottest on the left of the Russian line, where Hallart's division was stationed, the regiments there had fired more than double the amount used elsewhere: an average of over 42 rounds per barrel. In all, the total complement of Russian three-pounders had fired 1,110 rounds: 70 per cent ball, 30 per cent canister. The Russian artillery as a whole had delivered at least 1,470 rounds, a good third of which had been canister. These dry statistics give little indication of the guns' terrible impact in terms of the piles of shredded human flesh.

Some of the Russian foot – presumably those not reached in the confusion by the order to halt – pushed on into the wood. They took up positions in hedges and ditches, to shoot those Swedes still wandering among the trees. Creutz, one of the last on the spot, led his squadrons through the woods. Russian infantry fire forced them to fall back towards Maly Budyschi, which they passed through with further losses. Men went down in the churned-up marshes. To the left of Creutz rode the North Skåne cavalry. Their commander, Gustaf Horn, stuck fast in the mire and was taken prisoner. Left of the Scanians was a section of Hielm's dragoons. The whole detachment finally emerged from the cool foliage of the woods, on to the hot plain.

Contact between the two armies gradually decreased. The floods of routed men on the footpaths through the woods petered out, turned into trickles and finally to droplets. The great organized conflict ceased, and battle dwindled to opportunistic, haphazard engagements between units, sections, small handfuls of men or single individuals.

After the halt of the Russian foot, only their regular cavalry continued a sporadic pursuit, generally in improvised formations. They were aided by Cossacks, roving everywhere in clusters large and small. The Cossacks were particularly given to attacking isolated stragglers. The fleeing Swedes were either absorbed by the larger groups of foot and horse forming round some enterprising senior officer, or units that had kept their nerve; or else they carried on over the plain by themselves, south to the supply-train at Pushkaryovka.

Five kilometres to the south, round the scarred palisades of Poltava, there had been a pause in the fighting. A Russian spokesman found his way over to the Swedish trenches. The atmosphere became a little less tense, the formations relaxed somewhat and the combatants approached each other tentatively. The Russian was met by Captain Christoffer Adolf Wendel, a 50-year-old German born in Mark Brandenburg who had a chequered but not untypical past. Having first served a number of different masters on German soil, he entered the Danish service. He fought against the Swedes in the Scanian war, and was captured at Halmstad in 1676, whereupon he promptly changed sides and enlisted in the Swedish army. He had been with the Södermanland regiment since 1678.

History does not give a precise account of what happened next. Perhaps Wendel surmised the time had come to switch flags and master again. He began to negotiate terms of surrender. No doubt he considered he had a mandate for this, since his superior had just been killed. The Swedish troops in the trenches were of a different opinion. They had suffered relatively minor losses and their battle morale was fairly well intact. Their disinclination to surrender was sufficient for them to raise their muskets and shoot Wendel dead.

The volley that felled him was an immediate signal for renewed battle. Both sides instantly withdrew to their former positions and made ready.

But, instead of a Russian assault, the same spokesman reappeared, visibly shaken by Wendel's fate, this time to open discussions with Colonel Cronman. The Russian announced the defeat of the entire Swedish army, and invited the Swedes to give up. Cronman voiced his disbelief of this news, adding that 'any accord was out of the question'. Rebuffed, the Russian asked for permission to return to his men: the Swedish soldiers were already clamouring to shoot. He was given this assurance and ran back for his life. Both sides reopened fire, the volleys rolled and the killing began again.

On the plain to the north, Rehnsköld was still doing what he could to repair the defeat. Although it was now far too late, and the forces at the dejected field marshal's disposal far too few, he did not flinch from leading his troopers straight into the jaws of the Russians. Perhaps he hoped to dissuade further enemy cavalry from attacking the scattered units welling out of the wood. Perhaps, burdened and broken by his monumental failure, he was merely seeking a grandiose and fitting death.

Rehnsköld's cavalry engaged the enemy round the redoubts. Claes Planting, a captain related to the Georg Planting captured at the last stand of the Upplanders, pointed out to him the danger of being surrounded by large Russian forces. Some of the Swedish horse began to flee, and as Planting was deprecating their flight Rehnsköld sped off in a personal attempt to stop them. He failed. Instead, the trusted right hand of King Charles XII, Commander-in-Chief of the Swedish army, Field Marshal Count Carl Gustaf Rehnsköld, was taken prisoner. A very fine fish had landed in the Russian net.

By this stage of the battle, however, the capture was of very little significance. Rehnsköld had little overview of what was going on, and negligible control over the Swedish forces. He was virtually helpless, with no hope of playing the field commander, and saving the day with some stroke of genius. The army's collapse was too far gone, the rot too deep. The diligent field marshal had finally ended by functioning as any ordinary officer, zealously riding to and fro across the meadows, attempting to collect the scattered bands and lead them into action.

The remnants of the Östgöta and Skåne dragoons, from the far left of the original battle-line, had a long ride to safety. The section which fought its way out of the surrounding cage of steel was vigorously pursued, and constantly attacked by Russian dragoons and irregular cavalry. Only about 100 men on winded horses were finally left. The commander of the Scanians, Prince Maximilian, leapt from the saddle: either he saw it was hopeless to continue and meant to surrender, or else he expected to make a gallant last stand. He is said to have shouted: 'Brave men stand with me!' and a wounded lieutenant-colonel in his regiment, 28-year-old Carl Henrik Wrangel, is said to have followed his example.

Dragoons had some training for battle on foot, but before they had time to form up the pursuers were on them. They all surrendered. The young regimental commander roused curiosity among the Russians. An officer asked Wrangel if it were not the king of Sweden who had been captured, but was told it was the Prince of Württemberg. Prince Maximilian was greeted with extreme civility and courtesy. The precious captive was immediately taken to one of the senior Russian commanders near by, Brigadier Gröppendorff, thence to be politely conveyed to the tsar himself. We do not know how his men were treated, but if the handling of other Swedish prisoners is any guide it would not have been with kid gloves.

Isolated refugees continued to hobble out of the woods. Hultman, drenched in blood, managed to find his way to the plain on foot, still burdened with medicines, and still carrying the king's silver beaker. Cossacks and Kalmucks, roaming the fields around him, came fairly close but left him unharmed. He secured a horse, and somehow managed to dodge the perils of his surroundings, eventually to rejoin the king's retinue. He found his king among the crowd and very obligingly at once dismounted, lifted up the bandages 'then dragging in the mire', dried the blood with his already blood-spattered sleeve, and re-bandaged the wound. The doctors appointed to tend the royal foot were by this time either dead or taken prisoner.

Another who managed to cheat death was the badly wounded Johan Hierta, whose horse was now carrying Charles. His brothers Adam and Christian, proving blood thicker than water, in battle as elsewhere, rode back to look for Johan. They took a horse with them. The Russians seem to have ignored the bleeding man by the fence. The brothers found him, helped him on the horse and galloped away. Johan survived, with a fair portion of honour in his baggage. He and his two brothers were ennobled about six months after the battle. Johan Hierta's patent of nobility states, somewhat disingenuously, that he 'at the battle of Poltava gave notable proof of a loyal and irreproachable subject in that he when Our horse was shot immediately dismounted from his own and gave it to Us, on an occasion where he could neither obtain another nor hope for escape, and thus for sheer love of Us, great-heartedly offered up his life to the enemy.' It may be recalled that Charles *ordered* Hierta off the horse.

The time was past eleven. Gyllenkrok and others intensified their efforts to collect the remaining cavalry. Lagercrona, on his new chestnut horse, joined in. It was a difficult task. Agitation, fear and confusion filled the air; and the men had almost no ammunition left after the many hours of battle. However, the officers did what they could to bring the squadrons to order again. They managed to organize most of them, in spite of the tension.

Undoubtedly this temporary calm was because the pursuit seemed to have tailed off. Russians were soon sighted again, however. The three squadrons recently driven off had somehow ridden round the Swedes and now reappeared behind them, near Maly Budyschi. They made for the rickety little bridge used by so many of the fleeing men, and turned towards the backs of the reordered cavalry. In this way they completely blocked the crossing, and also threatened the rear of the Swedes, facing outwards over the field. To chase the persistent intruders away again, Gyllenkrok rode over to the squadrons on the left, intending to order them to turn about and charge.

Before they had time to make their move, there was a disastrous mistake. Lagercrona shouted 'Forward! Forward!' He probably meant the right wing to advance in line with the left. The command was ambiguous. Lagercrona was an infantry major-general, with minimal experience of cavalry drill and tactical commands. A few squadrons who had lost most of their officers misunderstood, or chose to misunderstand, the order and rode away, not in the direction of the enemy, but southwards over the plain.

In the prevailing tension this was enough for one troop after another to join the flight. The avalanche resumed its flow. Gyllenkrok shouted despairingly at them to 'Halt, in the name of God.' Others cried: 'Halt! Halt!' but to no avail. The reassembled cavalry melted away and scattered over the dusty billows of the plain. Pastor Siöman's thoughts on seeing this disintegration were: 'So long as fury and conflict are at hand, the Swedes are good soldiers. But if they begin to retreat or flee, nothing can hold them.' This is no more than a generally valid comment on the incredible difficulty of restoring morale to troops who have lost the will to fight, or succumbed to panic.

The distance from the cavalry rallying-point to the baggage-train at Pushkaryovka was about five kilometres. The disorganized mass of squadrons now moved more or less instinctively in that direction. They covered the billowing fields through oppressive heat and dust. It was nearing noon and the day was getting very hot. Gyllenkrok rode resignedly with them. He came across Carl Hård of the Drabants, and voiced his complaints to him about 'how badly our cavalry are behaving'. Hård agreed 'it was impossible to get them to stand'. Hård had been sent ahead from the king's company to ride down to Pushkaryovka and tell the regiments there to make ready for battle. He had run into some Russians, however; and received a wound which was slowing him down. He asked Gyllenkrok to complete the task for him. Gyllenkrok struck spurs into his horse and disappeared at a gallop.

The king's group straggled on behind. When through the wood they hesitated, unsure of the way to Pushkaryovka. A captain of fortifications, Carl Balthasar von Dalheim, came forward. He had been seconded to Lewenhaupt, probably as an aide, earlier in the day, and had accompanied the grenadier battalion in the assault. Shot through the right leg, he had retreated with them through clumps of trees, and past the marsh where the king's litter lay abandoned. Finally he had joined the group round the king. He had reconnoitred this terrain for Rehnsköld some time prior to the battle. The route forked three ways. The road to the right led to Maly Budyschi, the left to Poltava. Dalheim directed them down the middle road to Pushkaryovka.

By now there were a couple of thousand men surrounding the king. They formed up in one large square. This living fortress marched along quite sedately, musket muzzles pointing outwards. Fortunately for them, the pursuit was fairly slack. The Russian cavalry roving the broad fields from the Budyschenski wood to Pushkaryovka were mainly Cossacks and Kalmucks. They generally behaved warily and showed little inclination to attack.

The squadrons under Creutz also moved slowly, with the thought of giving stragglers a chance to join them, but the results were meagre. Creutz was exchanging regrets with another senior officer on how badly the battle had gone, when Charles himself rode up, clapped him on the shoulder and said: 'All our foot are defeated.' He then asked: 'May something not be done to save them?' Creutz explained why their progress was slow. The king contented himself with this.

As Creutz and the king were conversing, a couple of Russian squadrons charged, but were seen off with little trouble. Immediately after this a large swarm of irregular cavalry rode towards them at full gallop. Amazingly, they buzzed through the gaps between the squadrons and were gone, having done no damage at all. A few Swedes made as if to give chase, but knew from experience it would be fruitless. The king's company and Creutz's men continued their sluggish procession across the level plain.

Some time after one o'clock they came within sight of the baggage wagons. The regiments and artillery were drawn up and deployed in front of them. The king ordered the soldiers and Drabants to guard their rear with muskets and march swiftly on. He struck his mount with his right spur and disappeared full pelt in the direction of the baggage-train, a number of his escort close on his heels. Quite soon they met a small barouche rolling towards them. It contained Major-General Johan August Meijerfelt, a native of Finland, and Carl Hård, the Drabant. Both men had been wounded, had their injuries treated, and were now returning to look for Charles. The barouche drew up sharply as soon as they sighted his Majesty.

The king said: 'Help me off the horse to those in the wagon,' laid his arm across Hultman's shoulders, and hopped over to the carriage on his undamaged foot. When seated inside, he turned and told Hultman to mount his horse and follow on. The barouche spun round and rolled away over the glowing sun-baked dust, down to the safe haven of the baggage-train.

## 22 · 'To Gather in Retreat'

At Pushkaryovka the multiple thousands of wagons and carts, sick and wounded, labourers, minions, civil servants, women and children had barely been affected by the battle. The contingent left to protect them, three regiments of cavalry and four of dragoons, was rather weak, numbering little more than 2,000 blades. Added to this force was most of the Swedish artillery: 31 pieces of ordnance of various calibre ranging from small three-pounders to big 16-pounder howitzers. They were manned by a total complement of 150 gunners. Most of the Ukrainian and Zaporozhian Cossacks were also here. Their duties included manning a breastwork of cannon mounted to defend the baggage.

Initially it seemed that these troops would have nothing to do. The sounds of firing drifted down to them on the wind. The sounds grew gradually weaker: a favourable sign. Then they started to hear renewed volleying, closer, of 'relentless duration'. A little later, Russian cavalry materialized up on the plain, showing signs of wanting to attack. The cavalry and Zaporozhian foot were ordered forward and told to form up for battle. After the cannon had fired a few missiles at them, the Russians appear to have judged the resistance a little too strong. They departed in the direction of the Budyschenski wood.

Then the first refugees arrived. Out of them bubbled confused accounts of massacre and defeat.

Axel Gyllenkrok was one of the first of the officers. He burst in among the covering troops at a gallop. The maximum strength had to be mustered to relieve the fleeing. He asked Anders Wennerstedt, commanding the Uppland dragoons, to have his regiment of 300 men mount immediately, and ride out to aid the men approaching. Wennerstedt, 59, son of a parson from Gristad in Östergötland, responded promptly and was soon on his way, leaving the quartermaster-general calling the officers round him to 'pull all their men together and form up'.

Although some of the cannon were well deployed, most were on flat ground, unprotected by frontal defences or infantry cover. At Gyllenkrok's behest the artillery commander, Colonel Niklas Rappe, had wagons hauled forward to construct a small fort round them. A few more foot soldiers were shaken out, presumably by combining small sections from different regiments sent to Pushkaryovka the previous day. About 300 men tramped off to give the batteries further cover.

The fleeing soldiers now began arriving in greater and greater numbers. Some still bore the trophies they had managed to take in the battle. The remnants of the 1st battalion of Life Guards carried their four captured banners. The Skåne Dragoons had a few Russian standards. Disorganized squadrons poured forth over the plain. At times the edgy infantry covering the baggage found it difficult to make out if the approaching horse were Swedish or Russian. Mistakes were inevitable. A few nervous Zaporozhians manning the cannon opened fire. Two rounds were discharged before it was noticed that their targets were Swedes.

Most of the soldiers reaching the baggage were in a pitiful state. Shock and fear were dominant, and panic only a breath away. They were marked by the anguish of defeat: their spirit was broken, crushed by the heaped weight of their own dead. When these men welled past the defenders the aura of fear spread to those who had not been in battle: morale disintegrated even further. The supply-train was soon in great disorder. The atmosphere seethed with rumour, and at times it was difficult to get the men to obey orders.

For the Swedes to draw breath now, just because most survivors had reached the wagons, was out of the question. The sense of security was illusory; the situation was still critical. The Russians would be certain to start a more purposeful pursuit, reach Pushkaryovka and attack. A powerful onslaught striking at the Swedish troops, in their present confused and disconsolate state, would end in disaster. The defensive covering force was weak. The men had been infected by the atmosphere of defeat. Sven Agrell, a battalion chaplain, was despondent: if the Russians were to storm them, 'not a pin' would survive, in his view.

It was imperative for the Swedish command to gain control of their troops. Every available force had to be summoned up to meet the anticipated Russian pursuit. The barouche containing the king rolled into the baggage area shortly before two o'clock. His arrival seems to have infused some spirit into the diminished Swedish will to fight.

When the barouche halted, near one of the royal household tents, the king was exhausted by loss of blood and the oppressive heat. Despite this he at once set to work on the next phase of operations. The higher officers were called to him and the monarch inquired time and again after his nearest advisers, Rehnsköld and Piper. There was a prevailing ignorance of their fate. The officers gradually began to collect round the barouche. The atmosphere was gloomy, and no one knew exactly what to say. A few pregnant moments passed in shocked, taut silence. Defeat was a new sensation for these warriors, cogs in a victory machine which time and again had stunned the whole of Europe with astonishment. Now they saw themselves smashed to pieces by the army of a nation they thought of as semi-barbaric.

The silence was first broken by the 27-year-old monarch himself. He gave a short laugh and remarked, in a transparent effort to restore heart to himself and those round him, that the day's events need be of no consequence. It is unlikely anyone believed him.

As many as possible of the disordered cavalry were pulled together and drawn up in front of the baggage. Sentries were posted out on the plain to give warning of Russian attack.

It was necessary to collect the troops before making the next move. The only major detachments near by were the regiments at the siege-works, now fighting for their lives against a superior Russian force. Gyllenkrok went up to the king, who asked him 'What have ye to say?' The quartermaster-general offered his commiserations and said he did not know if he had done right, but he had sent to tell the forces at Poltava to withdraw to the baggage-train. The king said: 'That is well done. I have issued the same order.'

They were not entirely sure where the Poltava detachment actually was at this time. Gyllenkrok had just questioned an officer of dragoons, who had commanded an outpost near the town. All he knew was that they had not arrived at the baggage. Ignorant of the king's similar order, Gyllenkrok had then sent his message that they were all 'to gather in retreat at the baggage-train'.

They were now faced with the problem of what to do next. It was obviously impossible to remain where they were. The king had a rough plan in mind. First the army would move south-east, to Starie Senzhary by the Vorskla; then follow the course of the river, down past Novie Senzhary to Bjeliki, a distance of about 40 kilometres. By taking this route they would gather up the Swedish detachments dispersed along the Vorskla. These were Meijerfelt's Dragoons, about 1,000 blades, at Novie Senzhary, and a merged section of 300 men under Lieutenant-Colonel Thomas Funck, at Bjeliki. A third contingent of around 500 men, under Silfverhielm, was at Kobelyaki, another 20 kilometres down the river.

The next question concerned the army's ultimate objective. There were three distinct possibilities: they could make for the friendly Tartars in the Crimea, go to Turkey, or march right back to Poland. The last option was the hardest. They would have to fight their way through Russian, and hostile Polish, forces in south Poland, with pursuing Russians constantly at their rear. Turkey and the Crimea were preferable. The routes would be relatively clear. They would not have to fight to get there, and new alliances could be formed. Turkey was first choice. Communications to Poland from Turkish territories were good.

A direct retreat to Turkey meant that the army would have to cross the Dnieper. This would be a significantly shorter route than first crossing the Vorskla from west to east, then following the Dnieper on its eastern bank down to the Crimea.

But the final choice of route depended on whether there were any suitable crossings. If the army could not cross the Dnieper it would have to go via the Crimea. The king delayed his decision until they contacted Funck's and Silfverhielm's detachments by the lower reaches of the Vorskla. They ought to know of any suitable crossings. When asked by Gyllenkrok about the army's march objective, Charles answered: 'First get to Funck, then look around.'

Gyllenkrok was detailed to plan the departure. He advised heading the march with the valuable and slow-moving artillery, escorted by 300 men. The king approved. The quartermaster-general rode off to set preparations in motion.

Round the siege works at Poltava battle restarted as soon as Colonel Cronman rejected the Russian invitation to surrender. The conflict fluctuated. The Russians repeatedly changed their assault troops, launching one attack after another. They would make minor progress, only to be driven back by a Swedish counter-attack. For about half an hour the assault waves washed back and forth over the powder-dimmed trenches until Russian efforts ended. Calm again descended. Another lull in the fighting allowed the soldiers on both sides to relax and peer curiously across at each other.

At some point during the afternoon the Swedes broke off the struggle. On Cronman's orders the troops withdrew into the ravine behind which they had their camp. Not all were reached by the order to retreat. At the farthest forward point, in the trench running alongside the palisade, a section from the Kronoberg regiment remained isolated. The 32 men and two non-commissioned officers were commanded by 22-year-old Lieutenant Paul Eggertz, replacing the previous commander, Major Pistol, who had been killed. They were now surrounded by enemies occupying the trenches round them.

The Russians urged them to give up. Eggertz conferred with his men. Deciding not to parley, but fight their way out, they managed to reach a section of Södermanlanders. The combined band shot and cut its way back to the ravine. Men died right and left. The party was sparser by the time it finally broke free of the trenches. At the end of the 200-metre dash Eggertz was hit by Russian fire. He fell with two musket-balls in his body. One entered his right leg and he remained on the ground, unable to rise. The ravine was close, however. He pulled himself forward on his arms and rolled down the bank. At the bottom he was picked up and carried to safety.

Down in the wooded ravine the collected troops were met by a 24-year-old dragoon, Captain Carl Gustaf von Trautwetter, who burst through with orders from the king. At a specified farm, they were to link up with 200 Life Guards who had been posted about three kilometres south of Poltava, at Nizhnyi-Mlini. The combined group was then to march to the baggage at Pushkaryovka. By now Cronman and his men must have known the nervous Russian's account of the Swedish army's defeat was not a cunning lie but an inescapable truth.

When they left they were not pursued. Of the two regiments bearing the brunt of the trench fighting, the Södermanlanders had suffered worst, but the Kronoberg regiment had also lost many officers and men. Their dead included their regimental chaplain, Abraham Imberg. A number of Swedes taken prisoner during the struggle had been massacred. About 160 Swedish dead were left in the trenches, sprawled in the cherry orchards and below the palisades of Poltava.

Next to report to the king was Lewenhaupt. He had arrived at about the same time, probably in company with the large group of foot which had followed Charles across the plain. Having checked his baggage-wagons, swallowed a morsel of bread and drunk some water, he sought out his Majesty. The king, still sitting in the barouche, continued to ask anxiously for Piper and Rehnsköld. Numerous rumours were current concerning their fate. People claiming they knew what had happened were sent for and questioned. A cavalry captain knew enough to say that Rehnsköld had been taken prisoner, but there was no clear news of Piper. The consensus of opinion was that he had been either captured or killed.

Piper's company consisted of the army's Procurator Fiscal Kaspar Lampa, Chancellor Dittmar, Court Preacher Jöran Nordberg, Secretary von Düben and a few officers and servants. Under guidance of Major Behr, they had an adventurous ride after setting off for the baggage-train. Possibly Behr led them astray. In any case, when they rode up from a small depression overgrown with bushes they found the field before them teeming with irregular Russian cavalry. Their nerve failed them. To reach Pushkaryovka they would have to fight their way through clouds of horsemen. Rather than fall into the hands of the Kalmucks, they opted to make for Poltava, to give themselves up. They were well received by the fortress commandant, Kelen, who greeted them with all the courteous ceremony befitting the capture of a count and a prime minister.

Another highly placed missing official was State Secretary Olof Hermelin. Hermelin was gone, never to be seen again. Rumours of his fate were soon rife. His disappearance exercised the imagination of the survivors. Some would have it he had been captured in the battle. When taken before the tsar, Peter had exploded in furious denunciation of Hermelin, his insulting and defamatory pen, and his anti-Russian pamphlets and propaganda. Then, in a fit of the oriental despotic rage which constantly simmered within him, the tsar was said to have had him cut down where he stood, right under his marquee.

Others later claimed he had been transported to a monastery in Astrakhan, and confined there. The theory of capture gained credence because Tsar Peter named him a prisoner in letters he sent on the day of the battle. Probably this was the result of a misunderstanding. The likelihood is that Hermelin had been killed in the fighting. There were people who positively asserted this, and priests who claimed to have attended the burial of his corpse on the battlefield.

Those who had gone were gone. What mattered now was the rest of the army, and what to do next. Lewenhaupt had fixed ideas on this. They were to do what he had done after his defeat at Lesnaya the year before: destroy all slow-moving baggage, mount the infantry, then share out as much ammunition and as many provisions as a horse could carry. This was to make the retreat from the Russians, whom they knew to be coming, as rapid as possible. It was a radical solution, to which the king raised objections: 'What will become of the cannon?' The artillery could be taken as far as possible, in Lewenhaupt's opinion, but if necessary it too would have to be destroyed.

The king sat quietly for a while, reflecting on this advice. In principle, however, he had made his decision. Gyllenkrok was already fully engaged in preparing for the army's departure, with the baggage intact. Presumably wanting to be rid of the contentious and prolix general, Charles sent him off to collect the treasure-wagons and conduct them to the artillery.

Lewenhaupt's proposals had not left the king completely cold, however. The gigantic train of baggage was indeed the overriding problem. Past experience had shown that the thousands upon thousands of wagons, many drawn by sedate oxen, would drastically slow the rate of march. Speed was now of the essence for the army's salvation.

There were reasons for keeping as much as possible of the baggage intact. Many, especially the senior officers, travelled with quantities of war-plunder and personal possessions loaded on their own wagons. To jettison all this would not be popular. Another reason was purely the matter of practical maintenance. Whether their final destination were Poland, Turkey or the Crimea, the march would take them across immense tracts of desert wasteland, where supplies would be badly needed, and virtually unobtainable. Without transport, most of the provisions stored in the service corps would have to be left.

A compromise solution ordered patently useless vehicles to be winnowed out and destroyed. This mainly affected wagons belonging to the dead. However, it is very uncertain whether the order was obeyed to the letter. Not surprisingly, some units appear to have tried to take as much as possible with them on departure.

The hours slipped by in feverish preparation. For security reasons it was decided to remove all regimental treasure-wagons from the rest of the baggage, and locate them with the cannon, the ammunition and equipment wagons, and craftsmen's carts. They would thus be well in the van, as far as possible from the pursuing enemy, protected and supervised by the artillery escort. The afternoon grew late. As the Swedish command gained some control over the situation the sense of panic and fear was somewhat allayed. Enough time was found to provide a main meal for the famished men, most of whom had hardly eaten for the last 24 hours.

In front of the jumble of wagons, tents, animals and scurrying people, the covering troops and artillery still stood out on the dusty plain, awaiting the Russian pursuit; the attack which, if struck home with purpose, would give the riven Swedish army its *coup de grâce*. For the Russians, too, the hours slipped away. Small scattered bands of enemy cavalry showed in the distance, but turned back when they saw the well-ordered Swedish lines. The Russian onslaught, so anxiously expected, was slow to arrive.

# 23 · 'Bodies Mountain-High'

The battle was over. The Russian army had won an overwhelming victory. But they seemed to be missing their chance of totally annihilating their harrowed opponents. Consolidation of the remnants of the Swedish army at Pushkaryovka was being allowed to take place almost undisturbed. This failure of their enemy to seize their opportunity was a great relief for the Swedes. It gave them faint hopes of escape.

There are many indications that the Russians had been surprised by the magnitude of their triumph. Their rough-hewn battle-plan appears to have consisted of nothing but their massive attack: pursuit does not seem to have been prepared for. The Russian infantry had fallen into considerable disorder during the main engagement. It never got beyond the verge of the Budyschenski wood. Continued pursuit was left to the cavalry, but was carried out with no co-ordination, and patently with no very exact directions from higher authority. The squadrons merely roved aimlessly about, attacking small groups of fleeing Swedes. By this late stage the Russian command had probably lost control of their horse, so it was impossible for them to improvise effective pursuit, at short notice, in the smoke-dimmed chaos of victory.

In fact, the Russian command were more interested in celebrating the victory than completing it. While the rattle of muskets could still be heard from the Budyschenski wood, their foot were being mustered where they had stood before the battle. Lengthy and ceremonious parading, orating and saluting now began. The tsar rode along the lines of infantry with his hat in his hand, saluting the warriors and thanking them for their contribution. He and the generals embraced and kissed, exchanged congratulations, rejoiced to high heaven.

Directly in front of the lines, in the centre of the corpse-strewn battlefield, a field chapel and two large and richly decorated tents were erected. As a superb celebratory meal was being concocted in one of the tents, a thanksgiving mass, *Te Deum laudamus*, was held in the field chapel. It ended with a thundrous triple salute from cannon and muskets. The tsar rode from the mass, the soldiers presented arms, and banners were dipped in salute to the sound of martial music.

After the parade, the tsar held an audience in one of the tents. Streams of officers surged forward between its ornate walls to congratulate him. The highest-ranking Swedish prisoners were not forgotten. They were also allowed to add their congratulations. Field Marshal Rehnsköld, Major-Generals Schlippenbach, Stackelberg, Hamilton, and Prince Maximilian Emanuel were led into the tent between hedgerows of parading grenadiers and cavalry. In an elaborate and emotional ceremony, conducted by Prince Menshikov, the Swedish captives tendered their swords to the tsar on their knees.

When this scene was ended, and the Swedes had ritually acknowledged their defeat, the tsar invited them and the Russian generals to join in the celebration banquet. They all moved to another magnificent tent, sewn of costly fabrics from China and Persia. The blood-soaked soil of the plain was concealed by carpets. Hands were courteously kissed, and the tsar poured out the vodka himself. The dinner began. Toasts were drunk to the health of the tsar, his family, his fortune in war, and so on. The cannon thundered in salute, Swedes and Russians conversed politely, compliments were exchanged over lavish dishes. It was a refined and chivalrous occasion.

Only Lieutenant-General Ludvig Nikolaus von Hallart managed to disturb its harmony and polish. He grew somewhat the worse for vodka and began hurling obscenities at Piper, who had now also joined the festivities. Hallart was enraged by the hard treatment he had received when imprisoned in Sweden, after the battle of Narva, and in his cups irately accused Piper of having ignored his written supplications. It all became embarrassing. Menshikov intervened diplomatically and told Piper to pay no attention to Hallart's tirades. The lieutenant-general was drunk, after all. The banquet in the tent on the battlefield continued peacefully, as all around it shredded human beings lay dying.

The field presented an atrocious sight. About 9,000 dead and dying, countless wounded – certainly more than 4,000 and very probably at least 10,000 – as well as innumerable slain horses lay spread over a fairly restricted area. Bodies sprawled on pastures, in groves, among the trees of the woods, down the ravines, everywhere. The redoubts were burial mounds, the gullies coffins filled with corpses. In places where the struggle had raged most fiercely the corpses lay thick, making a carpet of bodies. Round the third redoubt there must have been approximately 1,000 dead bodies packed into an area of 250 square metres.

Anyone observing this lamentable scene would have seen and heard what others on similar battlefields have seen and heard. At a distance the earth seemed to move as though alive: the numberless wounded in the tattered carpet of human flesh shifting in their agony and pain. The air was filled with ugly pulsating, plaintive sounds, unceasingly rising and falling:

the wails of many thousands of wounded and dying men. Where the apocalyptic main battle had taken place the dead and dying lay stacked in grotesquely twitching mounds. Other shot-shredded heaps lay further afield, or else the ground was coated with human remains. A verse chronicle written immediately after the battle by a man named Pyotr Bolesta records that 'blood streamed in rivulets down to the Vorskla, and bodies mountain-high were piled'. The stiffening corpses were surrounded by litter:

> There lie the drums and kettledrums, the banners and standards,
> Musket and carbine and flintlock, pikes, pistols and steel blades.
>
> HARALD OXE

It was all one bizarre, enormous midden of dead and living matter, a ghastly conjunction of order and disorder, the shattered and the whole: a picture of perfect chaos. The quantities of abandoned weapons, equipment, clothes and anything of any value of any kind would have vanished from the battlefield very quickly. Much had already been pillaged during the fighting. Only what was totally worthless would finally be left: the butchered horses and, of course, the human beings, dead, dying or merely wounded. Useless to anyone, they were the longest remaining detritus of war.

The battle was catastrophic in terms of human life. The combined total of dead in regular troops for both sides was fully 8,300 men. The unknown numbers of irregular forces dead on both sides must have brought the figure up to more than 9,000. Many of the dead would have been killed by their own side. Some calculations estimate that up to 25 per cent of all infantry losses arose when the rear lines accidentally shot their comrades standing further forward. This indicates both the inaccuracy of their aim and the extent of the confusion and chaos which reigned during the battle.

Swedish losses were horrendous. About 6,900 dead and dying Swedes were left on the field in the afternoon. A number vanished in the turmoil never to be seen again. Some fled to the woods round Poltava where they were tracked down by local peasants and beaten to death. If, dulled by the fantastic casualty figures of later wars, these totals do not seem remarkable, it is salutary to reflect on the ratio of deaths to total combatants. Of the 19,700 Swedes engaged in the fighting, 6,900 fell. More than one in three of the soldiers who had gone out to battle at dawn this morning had been killed.

In terms of total casualties, the proportion is even more striking. Added to the 6,900 dead, there were 2,800 prisoners of war. The number of wounded who escaped the battlefield and followed the army in retreat to the Dnieper is not known, but estimates suggest about 1,500. Even disregarding these, total Swedish casualties amounted to 9,700 men, a proportional loss of 49 per cent. With the uncertain figure of 1,500 wounded included, the ratio becomes 57 per cent. Half the Swedish fighting force were either killed or captured.

Russian losses were much lower. There were 1,345 Russian killed. The number rises if the subsequent deaths of the wounded, and the casualties of the irregular forces, are taken into account. There were five dead Swedes for every dead Russian. The disproportionate figure suggests that the massacres of wounded or captured during the battle's last phase, for which there is ample evidence, were probably more widespread than has so far been realized. A further strong indication is that on the Russian side there were about 2.4 wounded for every soldier killed. The same ratio applied to the Swedish side would mean more than 16,500 wounded. This figure exceeds the number of the entire remaining Swedish army.

The sun-baked field was coated with naked, twisted, mutilated, charred human bodies mixed with gory rags and horse carcases. The very warm weather quickly took effect, and the corpses started to rot. An unmistakable, nauseating odour soon permeated the area. Down the ages many have described the bizarre changes undergone by unburied corpses on a battlefield. The bodies alter hue, and a practised eye can usually tell by its colour how long the cadaver has been dead. The sequence runs from white, through yellow, to yellow-green or grey; then finally to black as the flesh begins to resemble tar. The corpses grow in volume, expand and stretch their uniforms. This chemical process was in operation on the soggy pastures by Poltava. The heat would help to speed the metamorphosis. The exposed bodies of the dead began to ferment and swell grotesquely. Soon their features were unrecognizable. The soldiers were transformed into a vast, stinking, anonymous mass of blackening bundles which once had names.

It was an urgent problem to get the dead under the soil. Steps were taken to start rapidly clearing the battlefield the following day, Tuesday, 29 June. Six Russian officers were given the unpleasant task of counting the dead. Orders went out to gather up and bury the bodies. The Swedish command was also concerned with this detail: Major-General Meijerfelt was sent over to the Russians the same day with instructions to raise the question of burial of the fallen Swedes, among other matters. The Swedish prisoners of war were allowed to carry out the whole of this repugnant labour.

They began by earthing over the dead Russians. Two enormous mass graves were dug about 500 metres south-west of the fortified camp, halfway between the camp's ramparts and the system of redoubts. There had to be two graves. In complete accordance with hierarchical ideas, it was not thought fitting for officers and other ranks to share the same grave: inequality persisted after death. The dead Russians were collected and transported to this place. Round them stood a guard of honour. Regimental padres from every unit were summoned to hold a mass for the souls of the departed. The tsar gave a speech beside the brimming graves, bowed three times and then cast the first shovels of soil over the bodies of his subjects. The infantry fired a salute of three rounds. A large mound of earth was thrown up over the graves. (The mound is now called the Swedish grave, despite the fact that no Swede rests there.)

Orders also went out to bury the Swedish fallen. They were not treated with equal piety. Up by the little morass their tattered bodies were chucked into the bog, where they merged with the sludge. The mire barely covered them. There was no common mass grave for the Swedes. Their remains were stuffed into the earth here and there as they happened to be found. The body of Erich Måne, an Upplander with Hundra Parish Company, was stumbled on by his comrades where he had fallen, near the second redoubt. He was buried on the spot. Captured Swedish army chaplains were permitted to participate. They included Nicolaus Vennman, born in Umeå, of the Mounted Life regiment; Laurentius Sandmark, padre with the Västerbotten regiment and Petrus Fluur, seconded to the same unit, ordained a preacher in the diocese of Härnösand in 1694. Prayers were read over the numerous graves. The bodies vanished into oblivion. Their anonymous burial-places, unmarked by crosses, were soon gone without trace. Very few Swedish graves are known today.

The countless horse carcases posed a problem. The soldiers probably drew the line at these. The citizens of Poltava and the local populace were ordered to attend to this matter. The dead animals were collected and buried, occasionally mingled with human remains.

The chore was completed fairly quickly. In spite of the fact that most of the corpses and carcases were under ground by the Wednesday night, the stink of rotting flesh still polluted the summer air for a long time to come. The soil seethed with worms scavenging through the decomposing bodies. The odour finally made it impossible for the Russian army to remain at Poltava, and they had to move on. The powerful perfume which follows a magnificent military triumph finally drove them into retreat: the dead defeated the living.

What happened to the wounded? A precise figure is given for Russian wounded: 3,290. The corresponding figure for the Swedish army will never be known, but it can be taken for granted that many of the almost 2,800 prisoners belonged in this category. As stated, an estimated 1,500 wounded accompanied the retreating army.

Wounded Russians had recourse to their own minimal sick-care facility. Except for those captured with Roos at the bastion by the Vorskla, where part of the terms of surrender required the wounded to be cared for, wounded Swedes appear to have received no treatment whatsoever from their conquerors. Instead, many were killed when the Russians came across them. Swedish resources for treatment on the spot were almost non-existent. Care of the wounded was in the hands of four field surgeons and four orderlies, captured during the battle: eight men for the treatment of wounded among 2,800 prisoners.

Hardly any proper collection of wounded from the field seems to have been organized. Men languished under the burning sun for days after the battle. Lieutenant-Captain Niklas Norin, abandoned by his regiment near the redoubts with seven wounds in his body, spent three days there. He finally managed to drag himself up to the Russian camp to surrender.

One of Norin's regimental comrades, Giovanni Battista Pinello, suffered much the same fate. An Italian born in Genoa in 1682, he had first studied in his native town, then completed his education at Leiden and Paris. In Schleswig he met two Swedish clerics, and accompanied them to Sweden, where he converted to Protestantism and changed his name to Johan. In 1702 he joined the Swedish army in Courland. He had served with the Västmanlanders since 1705, and seen much action. He had received several wounds in the fiasco at Veprik, the year before. Now he was again severely wounded and remained among the corpses for 48 hours before being discovered and taken prisoner.

Many in Pinello's and Norin's situation would have died of shock, loss of blood and dehydration. Survival would depend on the type of wound suffered. Those with relatively superficial stab-wounds from pikes, bayonets or swords probably had the best prospects, if they did not succumb to an infection. Deep stab-wounds would seriously damage inner organs, and a stab in the chest or stomach could be very dangerous. Because these wounds were usually badly polluted, complications were likely. Victims of cuts or slashes from swords or Cossack sabres had reasonable chances of surviving if the wound had not damaged ligaments, muscles, major blood-vessels or bones. There would have been a number of fractures, often caused by falls from horseback. Broken arms and legs could mend, but cracked vertebrae would generally be fatal.

The experience of Jakob Lärka, from Kalmar, must have been fairly typical. Lying on the battlefield, he was ridden over and lost an eye. There must have been many whose bones were crushed and fractured as they lay wounded on the ground and were trampled on by men and horses' hoofs. Some, like Göran Öller, 28, from Stockholm, were totally blinded. The wounds of many others would have made them invalids for life.

There can be no doubt that more wounds resulted from shot than anything else. Shot-wounds, especially those causing loss of limb, would also generally have the worst prognosis. There was a plentiful supply of mutilated, limbless bundles, men who had lost feet, legs, arms or hands. Anders Forbes lost both his feet and three fingers from his left hand.

Anders Leijonhielm's left leg was blown away by a cannonball. Lars Tiesensten, the Life Guard officer, also had a leg shot off. Cannonball was the worst. If a cannonball did not merely remove a limb, it would almost always prove fatal.

Grapeshot and ordinary musket-ball were also lethal. The kinetic energy of the ball was low, and men could take potentially fatal hits without being knocked over. Balls which penetrated deeply into the body and punctured inner organs were fatal. Soldiers whose intestines spilled from their stomachs could expect little but death. Projectiles were likely to tear dirty fragments of cloth, bits of button or the contents of uniform pockets into the wound, and badly contaminate it. Often the balls would create secondary projectiles, splinters of wood, stone, gravel or shattered pieces of bone or teeth, which travelled further into the body. The difference between being hit by musket-ball or grape-shot, and a rusty old nail or a shard from a grenade, was that the nail or shard caused nasty lacerations in the flesh. The location of any wound, regardless of type, was critical. Even a minor lesion at a place where nerves and large blood vessels were near the surface would cause a quick death from loss of blood.

Seriously contaminated wounds were extremely common. Much depended on whether the various infections could be kept in check. Wounds had to be washed and cut clean, to prevent tetanus, wound diphtheria, gangrene and gas gangrene. These infections were barely understood, and medical science was even less competent to treat them. The season was the worst possible. The heat provided perfect conditions for bacteria to flourish. Apart from being ludicrously inadequate in numbers, the Swedish medical personnel were extremely short of medicaments. Future prospects for the wounded, especially the Swedish wounded, were grim.

The wounded would be dying for a long time to come. In the Närke-Värmland regiment mortality was high during July. A sergeant, a drummer and 22 other ranks died, very probably all men who had been wounded, and suffered from lack of treatment, starvation and complications. Many would survive deformed, or as lifelong invalids. Gustaf Pistolsköld, a recently commissioned premier cornet with the Mounted Life regiment, born in Närke, was badly wounded in the left shoulder, and lived on with a severely shortened arm. The primitive state of army medicine meant that many wounds of good prognosis healed badly, if at all. Georg Kihlman, a 34-year-old Smålander, had one of his knees shattered. Twenty years after the battle his wound was still open and unhealed.

Unsurprisingly in these gruesome circumstances there were bound to be mercy killings of the most grievously wounded. There are accounts of Swedish wounded being killed by their own side after the battle. On the evening of June 28 there must have been many mangled and mutilated human fragments who, in the delirium of their agony, envied the dead and prayed to God to grant them death.

Towards evening Tsar Peter sat down in his tent to broadcast the news of his great victory to the world. His mistress Catherine received a brief letter:

> Little Mother, good day. I wish to tell you that God today in his great mercy has granted us a matchless victory over the enemy. In short, their entire force has been defeated, and you shall hear more of this from us anon.
>     Peter
> P.S. Come here and congratulate us.

Peter also sent out 14 more or less similarly phrased letters, addressed to a variety of Russian potentates and members of his family. He wrote joyfully that 'I, with God's blessing and thanks to the bravery of my troops, have just won a complete and unparalleled victory with little loss of blood.' After a short account of the battle the tsar promised more news later. He likened the fate of Charles and the Swedish army to that of Phaethon. (To prove his divinity, this character from Greek mythology had tried to drive the chariot of the sun. Unable to manage it, he set heaven and earth alight. A thunderbolt from Zeus cast him down into the river Eridanos, where he drowned.) 'In short,' wrote Peter, 'the enemy has suffered the fate of Phaethon. I can give no account of the king. I do not know if he is to be found among the living, or whether he has joined his ancestors.'

In his letter to Count Apraxin the tsar added a short footnote which breathed a sense of relief, and showed he had already realized that the day's events marked a turning-point in the war: 'With God's help the last foundation-stone of St Petersburg has now been laid.'

At about this time, Count Carl Piper, the Prime Minister, was pleasantly engaged at dinner with Field Marshal Boris Petrovitch Sheremetev. Here, too, the drunken Hallart created a painful scene by swearing and glaring at the honoured Swedish guest and prisoner. The host made excuses for his inebriated colleague. At the end of the meal Sheremetev most courteously offered Piper his sleeping tent and bed. He also advanced him a small loan of a thousand ducats for his pocket. Chubby Piper then retired to sleep in the field marshal's bed. It had been an exhausting day.

Out on the field of battle, under the starry vault of heaven, the first night of agony began for seven times wounded Niklas Norin, and for thousands more. Many others, Swedes and Russians alike, slipped out of this life into merciful oblivion.

The sharp summer light turned dull. Down at the rallying-place by Pushkaryovka, waiting ended for the Swedes. March preparations were complete. The stream of battlefield survivors had dried up. At about seven o'clock they broke station. Division followed division. Column after column pulled away, on tired tramping feet, clattering hoofs, creaking wheels and rattling carts. To the proud music of drum and trumpet the army filed off as the sun went down: men converging from one side, wagons from the other.

The march led off with the artillery and treasure-wagons, the cadre of 300 foot in escort. Then followed the whole unwieldy train of baggage. The infantry wagons, headed by those of the Life Guards, rolled in strict order of regimental seniority. Next came the cavalry baggage, not in seniority, but in the order they had camped. The cavalry and the tattered regiments of infantry brought up the rear. Last came a rearguard, probably made up of the mounted Uppland Tremänning regiment, the Karelian cavalry and perhaps one or two other units. They were led by Karl Gustaf Kruse, commanding officer of the mounted Upplanders.

The king, seated in his carriage, remained with the rearguard until the lengthy convoy was on its way. Minor problems arose at departure. The cavalry were held up when the plodding baggage attached to the infantry jammed at a gorge. At last, as the first stars of the June night began to emerge, even the cavalry's long lines disappeared into the dusk. At dawn they had launched their attack. As the sun went down, they rode away: those still alive. Their weightless shadows soon merged with the night.

# THE RETREAT

Reflect, there's nothing stable in the world: all is in flux;
And as a fire, a stream, a glass; and flowers, and the grass
Blaze, flow and gleam, and bloom and flourish at the fall of night,
But cold are found, still, broken, dried and withered on the morn:
So are the lives of men dissolved like smoke before the wind.

GEORG STIERNHIELM, from *Hercules* (1658)

# 24 · '100,000 Roubles'

Preparations for the Swedish army's retreat were allowed to proceed unimpeded, with no sign of enemy pursuit. The Swedes were greatly relieved that the Russians failed to follow up their advantage, as it much improved their situation. If their departure were not too delayed the Russian foot would never catch them up. A pursuer without infantry would be handicapped if it came to battle, since unsupported Russian cavalry would not willingly charge enemy foot. The army had been given a respite. It would not last long.

The Swedes aimed to get as far as possible before darkness set in. The first objective was Novie Senzhary, 35 kilometres to the south, where the plan was to take up night quarters. This meant marching as rapidly as possible: orders were issued to roll along. Halts, to allow laggards to catch up or repair wagons that broke down, were forbidden. Detachments were sent ahead to clear the way.

Initial progress was quite good, but it was late, and march discipline grew ragged in the dusk. Gustaf Abraham Piper, the crippled young ensign travelling with the baggage, noted that 'none obeyed the other, and each marched according to his inclinations, God favouring whoever came first'. At the village of Federki an awkward bottle-neck arose at a clogging morass, which could only be crossed by one ramshackle bridge. Here the men overtook the jumbled wagons: now they marched in front of them. Kruse's guard still brought up the rear. After another fitful, spasmodic five kilometres, the march stuttered to a halt. The convoy had progressed no further than Starie Senzhary, 20 kilometres south of Poltava.

This was disappointing. To prevent a complete standstill the Swedish command ordered the artillery, the treasure-wagons and the troops to continue south towards Novie Senzhary. The baggage-wagons were allowed to stop until dawn, under protection of the rear-guard. As the artillery and its escort left Starie Senzhary they were provided with stronger support. A detachment from Meijerfelt's Dragoons joined the 300 foot soldiers.

For the rest of the night the march went more or less to plan. They pressed on at a very hard pace. The artillery reached Novie Senzhary some time after midnight, the troops nearer dawn. The king arrived before the troops, at around half past one. He was exhausted. Carried into a cottage, he soon fell asleep, surrounded by a few senior officers, who lay down on the bare boards in comatose slumber.

The pause for rest did not last long. At dawn, reports were received that the Russians were approaching. The previous evening the tsar had sent the Semyonovski infantry regiment under Prince Golitzine and ten dragoon regiments under Bauer in pursuit of the Swedes. Their pursuit was rapid. The tsar had exhorted his men to 'use the greatest zeal in tracking down the Swedish king'. Anyone capturing Charles XII was promised 'the rank of general and a reward of 100,000 roubles'.

The artillery left Novie Senzhary early in the morning of 29 June, several hours before the troops. As before, the guns were followed by the treasure-chests, and now also by the wagons of the chancellery, the court and the Drabants. The soldiers did not sleep long at Novie Senzhary. The baggage was collected, the horses unharnessed from the least necessary carts and transferred to pull wagons containing sick and wounded. All infantry was now mounted, and any baggage left went up in smoke. Between six and seven o'clock the march resumed. The immediate objective was now Bjeliki. Meijerfelt's Dragoons, who had been stationed there, moved out to link up. The Swedish command took two precaution-ary measures as the army moved on. Meijerfelt was sent back north to seek contact with the tsar. Gyllenkrok rode ahead, to locate a crossing over the Dnieper.

Meijerfelt's primary mission was to detain the pursuers. He also took with him important instructions empowering the captured Piper to start negotiations, on peace terms and exchange of prisoners, with Tsar Peter. This was merely a feint, however, to persuade the Russians, if only temporarily, to break off their pursuit. The king also gambled on Meijerfelt being able to return to the army by the following night with news of the Russians' strength and plans.

Having covered little more than five kilometres on his way north, Meijerfelt ran into a force of about 8,000 Russians led by Bauer, closely followed by Golitzine's troops. He informed them of his directives, and the Russians halted to await new instructions from the tsar. The tsar, however, was not to be deceived. Meijerfelt was detained at Russian headquarters. The tsar's command refused point-blank to drop their pursuit. Neverthe-less, the purpose of Meijerfelt's mission was partly achieved: the pursuing troops were delayed for a useful couple of hours. Bauer's and Golitzine's forces did not resume their pursuit until the afternoon. The Swedes gained a modicum of priceless time.

Gyllenkrok, meanwhile, was riding south with a posse of quarter-masters. His mission to find a crossing was an improvised plan compelled by the rapid Russian pursuit. In point of fact the commander of the detachment in Bjeliki, Lieutenant-Colonel Funck, ought to have been supplying the life-saving information on where a crossing might be found. Funck had been summoned to the king in Novie Senzhary on the evening of the 28th. The message reached him far too late, and he never had time to report.

A potential crossing-point was already known to Gyllenkrok. One of Mazeppa's men had told him earlier, at Poltava, that near Koleberda, a place about 30 kilometres upstream from the ravaged small town of Perovolochna, there was a ford where at low water it was possible to drive wagons across the Dnieper. Unfortunately, he had lost contact with his informant. When he reached Bjeliki, 15 kilometres from Novie Senzhary, Funck met him outside the town gate. Gyllenkrok wanted to seek help from the townspeople. If anyone was found who knew about the Koleberda ford, 'or any other passage, offer purse upon purse, as high as ye like', he told Funck desperately. 'I'll stand for its payment.' Funck felt there was little hope of extracting any information of this sort from the sullen burghers of Bjeliki. He had already tried, in vain. Thwarted, Gyllenkrok decided to ride on another 20 kilometres, to Kobelyaki, where Silfverhielm's detachment was located. Silfverhielm might know of a crossing.

The slow-moving baggage and artillery gained the greatest respite from Meijerfelt's little ruse. On June 29 the infantry and cavalry baggage marched independently, ahead of the cannon and troops for most of the day. The army still followed the course of the Vorskla. Uncertainties about the possibility of crossing the Dnieper probably made it desirable to have the option of a passage across the Vorskla, towards the Crimea, near at hand.

That morning, the Russians had been only five kilometres away. The Swedes were being hunted. Panic lurked among them. The columns trundled southwards with all possible speed through the summer heat. The horses tired. Wagons collapsed, and were constantly being abandoned, smashed or set ablaze. Before the eyes of the half-starved men, piles of provisions went to waste. All the time the rearguard kept urging them on. Repeated exhortations to make haste ran through the rolling columns, 'for the enemy are closing hard'. Although the rearguard were not in direct battle contact, the Russians were far too close for comfort. This was a flight, not a retreat.

Two and a half kilometres outside Kobelyaki Gyllenkrok met Lieutenant-Colonel Silfverhielm. The post commander spoke the words Gyllenkrok must have been longing to hear. When asked about a passage over the Dnieper he replied 'he had been down there daily, knew every bush', and assured the quartermaster 'he would get the army across'. The place was called Tashtayka. It lay a short way upstream of the river, west of the town of Perovolochna. The water level there was admittedly rather high, and a crossing would need pontoon bridges or boats – or both. But Silfverhielm promised he 'would be able to produce as many boats' as Gyllenkrok wanted. All this was confirmed by a non-commissioned officer on the post commander's staff. Perfect.

The convoy pushed on. It linked up with Silfverhielm's 500 men at Kobelyaki. Everything now pointed to a crossing of the Dnieper, but Gyllenkrok wanted the king's approval. If the entire army was to cross the river, a bridge would have to be built. Gyllenkrok wrote a dispatch to Lewenhaupt containing two requests. First he needed the king's final decision on the matter: were they to cross the Dnieper? Second, he required carpenters and gunners (the artillery was responsible for engineering work) sent to him immediately, with materials for pontoon construction: ropes, nails and anchors. These men were to march to Perovolochna, where there was access to timber, and construct boats and barges, for further transportation to Tashtayka. Gyllenkrok then went to Kishenka, on the Vorskla. Eight big barges were found there, which were moved downstream to Perovolochna.

The columns reached Kobelyaki in the late afternoon, June 29. The king halted briefly, ate a light meal and pressed on to Sokolki, about 20 kilometres further south. A good 40 kilometres remained to cover before the Dnieper was reached. During the afternoon and evening the long columns of the baggage-train inched past Kobelyaki. The troops were stationed on a large meadow a little way outside the village, to stay there until first light. The horses needed proper grazing, and the men afforded guard against the approaching Russians.

Gyllenkrok received no answer from his superiors. Fourteen carpenters arrived, however, in the evening, indicating that his message had reached its destination. The men were equipped only with axes and lacked nails and anchors. By now Gyllenkrok was becoming very apprehensive. He had inspected the recommended crossing-place, and realized that it was going to be much more complicated to achieve a crossing than he had bargained for. The river was good and wide.

To construct a pontoon crossing he would need a large number of boats. Silfverhielm's positive assurance that he could produce as many as were wanted seemed to have been rather over-optimistic. So far, only a small number had been secured. To build new boats in the twinkling of an eye when there was a shortage of material was not easy. There was in fact very little forestation between Perovolochna and Tashtayka. The terrain was flat and steppe-like. Only a few bushes and clumps of trees grew by the small marshes scattered here and there. Now that the work-force turned out to be extremely small and ill-equipped, Gyllenkrok began to doubt the possibility of effecting a passage across the water.

## Map 7 · The Retreat

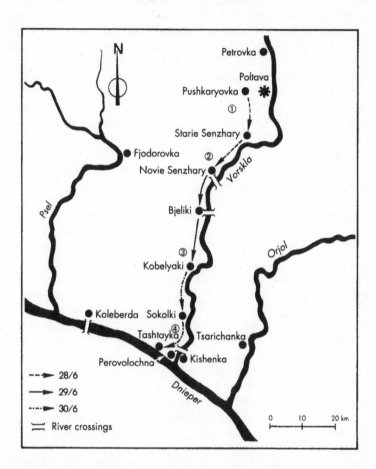

1. The Swedish army leaves Pushkaryovka on the evening of 28 June.
2. The vanguard reaches Novie Senzhary late at night. On the morning of 29 June Meijerfelt is sent to negotiate.
3. The same day, in Kobelyaki, Gyllenkrok is told of a crossing over the Dnieper. On the morning of 30 June, Swedish rearguard troops are in battle contact with pursuing Russian forces. The retreat continues.
4. Towards afternoon on 30 June, the Swedish army begins to reach the crossing at Tashtayka. There are only a few boats, and no bridge.

He sent an officer and thirty men to Kishenka, just north of Perovolochna, where there was a ford across the Vorskla. Their instructions were to halt the army and the king when they arrived, and stop them proceeding to the Dnieper before Gyllenkrok got there himself and could confer with the king. He obviously wanted to explain the difficulties, and leave Charles to decide whether to pursue the attempt to cross the Dnieper, or cross the Vorskla at the ford and make for the Crimea. If the troops arrived before his Majesty, they were at once to be set to pull down all wooden buildings at Kishenka, and start building rafts.

In order not to lose any time, should the king still decide to risk the Dnieper, Gyllenkrok purposefully carried on preparing for a crossing, in spite of his doubts. The carpenters were set to work on making rafts from the timber at Perovolochna and 150 men from Silfverhielm's contingent were seconded to assist. The rest marched off to Tashtayka. When they arrived they saw the water level had risen. Swimmers were sent into the river to mark the shallows with rods. A search was made for the river's narrowest point. The hectic work continued in the darkness.

On the morning of June 30 the pursuers had closed in further. At Kobelyaki, Creutz mustered the troops at dawn. Changes were made in the order of march. The weak regiment of Life Dragoons bringing up the rear was replaced by some of the Mounted Life regiment. The troops were also ranged in *ordre de bataille* in case of action. Creutz must have known that the Russians were close.

The long columns of men and horses moved off the large meadow where they had camped the night, and worked their way up over a rise. After a while a message ran down the line: the enemy had been sighted. The Russians were already at the recently vacated camp-site. Between Perovolochna and the present position of the Swedes there were reports of at least three narrow passes. They were just about to enter one of these, and the situation was tricky. If the Russians attacked as they squeezed their way through a bottle-neck it would be very difficult to deploy the troops for counter-action.

Dismounted infantry took up fire positions behind a hedge not far from the village. Sections of the Småland cavalry regiment covered the exits from Kobelyaki, and the columns fell back. A minor Cossack sally was beaten off by volleys from the infantry. The second pass, through a deep valley near a marsh, was negotiated in the same way. There was some exchange of fire, but no great damage was done. The Russians kept their distance and showed little inclination to attack. Encouraged by this, no doubt, and to lend the wagons further respite, Creutz allowed the troops to halt, dismount and let the horses graze. Behind them, the Swedes saw great clouds of dust hanging in the sky, a sign that a large Russian force was on its way.

The baggage and artillery continued on ahead towards the Dnieper. The wagons had substantial problems in the passes on the road. Much time was lost as the long, disorganized columns of rolling stock muddled along. At times the rate of progress was very low. As before, many wagons and their loads remained on the route because of breakdown or terminally exhausted draught-animals. Again the wagons were smashed or set alight.

The route was punctuated by smoking, soot-blackened wrecks of shattered wagons, spilled supplies and ruined goods, abandoned oxen and broken horses, the dead bodies of wounded men who succumbed in the heat and were heaved out of the carts, and quantities of things simply thrown away to lighten the loads and improve chances of escape. 'A very lamentable march,' was one man's description. There was little food. Many had been famished for days. The march led across wasted, arid fields, in a 'dreadful heat and thirst, so that one would fain have pined away', recounts young Piper.

Early on June 30 Gyllenkrok sent men to Perovolochna and Kishenka to report any sign of the army. They returned from both places with negative news. Work on preparing a crossing continued. An old church was pulled down, to be used for the pontoon. They tried to transport the timber up-river, but the current snapped the ropes and swept the logs away. With no news of the army, Gyllenkrok grew worried, but at about nine o'clock a little boy came across the fields to say 'the army was on the march'. To safeguard the crossing thirty-odd soldiers were sent over to the opposite bank and deployed there by Gyllenkrok. He was just siting a couple of sentries on a rise by the bank, when, in the far distance on the river's eastern side, he saw horsemen riding towards him. The army was approaching.

There was still some time to go before they made contact. The halt ordered by Creutz at Kobelyaki had lasted a good two hours before the troops resumed their march. Irregular Russian cavalry made a few more sporadic attempts to attack the rear. These were also beaten off, and the horsemen then contained themselves at a respectful distance of a couple of kilometres, level with the Swedes.

The army suffered few casualties from action on the march, but one or two stragglers fell into Russian hands. Some were captured when venturing back along the route to retrieve objects from abandoned wagons. As the march now rumbled along it was spurred by rumours that a crossing over the Dnieper had already been completed. The wagons did not follow the Vorskla right down to Perovolochna, but cut west, slightly north of the town's burnt-out ruins, and rolled straight on to Tashtayka. When Creutz drew near the area, reports confirmed that the crossing was secured. He and his men also sped on to Tashtayka.

Gyllenkrok caught sight of the first horsemen spurring towards him at about noon. A torrent of wagons and carts soon followed. Gyldenklou, an aide, galloped up to the quartermaster-general and told him to attend the king, who would soon be there. Dismayed, Gyllenkrok asked 'whether the army were not halting at Kishenka?' The aide did not know. Gyllenkrok further enquired whether the officer he had sent to Kishenka had spoken with the king. Gyldenklou replied that he certainly had, but his Majesty wanted to talk to Gyllenkrok personally. At this moment the king himself approached. The army had continued mindlessly headlong for Tashtayka, towards the crossing they imagined to be ready. It was doubtful if it ever would be.

# 25 · 'Fight at My Command!'

Gyllenkrok gave an account of his problems with the work-force and materials to explain why he thought the army should have halted at Kishenka. The king's only reaction was to mutter: 'Well, well, I'll turn back then.' He did ride back, but only a short distance, and remained on the field by the river. More and more baggage-wagons, artillery and soldiers began to congregate there, in the warm breeze.

Lewenhaupt had also found his way down to the Dnieper. He did not like the lie of the land nor the place Gyllenkrok had chosen. It seemed like a dead end, a trap. Worried, he rode back to his hand-horses and found Schlippenbach's Dragoons dismounted at the same place. Tired, tormented by diarrhoea and the heat, he looked for a shaded spot where he could rest. Major Rosenkamp put up a shield from the sun, next to the cart of a *cantinière*, and Lewenhaupt lay down. As he lay there, he was surprised to discover a stoat, hiding in his hat, and caught it. Rosenkamp and one or two other officers ran up to take a look at the captive animal. It struck Lewenhaupt that, like the stoat, the army was 'in a place, where we had taken ourselves prisoner'. He set the creature free, 'praying to God that we, too, might manage to depart this place unscathed'.

The troops descended from the plateau to the low-lying fields beside the river. The baggage and regiments merged, and a chaotic welter of men and wagons resulted. The whole army began to form into one elongated shapeless mass, stretching all the way from Tashtayka to beyond Perovolochna. It was perfectly apparent that the site was fraught with problems. In front of the army flowed the broad river. The fields were overlooked and encircled by higher terrain. These bluffs, referred to as the sandhills, cut by the fast-flowing Dnieper, were the end of the steppe plateau.

Between the sandhills and the fields were many small marshes and swampy patches. By the river, half-way between Perovolochna and Tashtayka, another extensive morass obstructed access to the bank. The place was open. The limited vegetation consisted mainly of bushes and saplings, round the marshes, near buildings and along parts of the river-bank. Otherwise the soil was sandy and dry and offered little grazing for the horses. An approaching enemy could easily block the road the army had come down, which led to the ford across the Vorskla, at Kishenka.

And if this enemy were to deploy artillery along the extended heights, the Swedes down on the river meadow would be completely exposed to their guns. One small consolation was that the marshes at the foot of the sandhills would hamper a direct Russian attack. At the same time they also restricted Swedish mobility. This constriction was the principal feature of the place. The only other way out was over the Dnieper, and failure now to cross the river would mean the Swedes had ended up in a real cul-de-sac.

Shipping across the river on whatever floating transport was available had already started. Silfverhielm and 300 horsemen were making the crossing. Mazeppa went with them, taking his entourage, stepson, women, baggage, a number of Zaporozhians and Cossacks, and the Swedish company of one-horse carriages.

There were two small islands out in the flood-stream at the crossing-place. The Dnieper was a good 'cannon-shot wide'. Boats were loaded with saddles. The horses were driven into the water to swim across. The problems soon became evident: the river was broad and swift, and a strong wind forced many of the swimming horses to turn back. Mazeppa's group had use of several boats, but the crossing was risky, none the less. Money, gold and silver vessels were lost in the torrent.

Cossack followers of the hetman were told to make their own way across. Most of them attempted to swim. The horses were coupled together and led down to the river bank. One Cossack would guide the leading horse and the others laid their heads on the hind-quarters of those in front. The men would hang on to the horses' tails or manes. But even experienced Cossacks had problems making the crossing. Some drowned.

The Swedish command seems to have gradually realized that the problem of the crossing was becoming unsurmountable. By now, however, evening on June 30, it would be an extremely complicated operation to turn the whole army round, go back the way they had come, and attempt to ford the Vorskla at Kishenka. They clung to the idea of constructing a pontoon, or of somehow making a crossing from their present position, a little longer. The whole of the general staff gathered in one of the king's tents. Charles instructed Creutz to try to find a better place. Night was about to fall. Somewhat irresponsibly, if understandably, Creutz decided to postpone the search until the dawn. The evening darkness deepened as the Swedish command deliberated, conferred and furrowed their brows over maps and plans.

Apart from the difficulty of manoeuvring the cumbrous and chaotic mass of baggage, artillery and troops, there must have been strong psychological barriers against turning back. The march had rolled south with a will: away from the enemy, towards the mirage of salvation. To turn north again, back towards the Russians, had to feel wrong. The army was in a dreadful condition. The mood, especially among the first-hand survivors of the slaughter at Poltava, was one of fear and dejection. Pike Corporal Erik Larsson Smepust describes the men marching for the Dnieper with 'sorrowing hearts'.

The Swedish army had sunk into a paralysing despondency. Since leaving Pushkaryovka feeding arrangements for the troops had been haphazard. Separated from their wagons on the move, the regiments would have had difficulty getting access to supplies. Some soldiers had not eaten a single piece of bread for the last three days. For them, the threat of famine hovering before the battle was now a reality. The headlong forced march had left few moments for real rest, and the general staff, as well as the men, were weighed down by a deep and numbing sense of exhaustion. Officers and men alike were utterly worn out.

No doubt it was thought little would be lost if the army remained in place for the night. A break for rest and food was desirable. The risk of the Russians arriving in the next 12 hours was deemed to be slight. Opinion was divided, but some of the general staff took the view it would be days before enemy troops would catch them up. Those that did would be exhausted and therefore more or less harmless. The king, in optimistic vein, opined that 'if the enemy meant to pursue, he would have been here long ago'. Creutz, it was true, had clashed with Russian units earlier in the day, but they were only irregular light cavalry of little consequence in battle. There was no need to fear them.

Meanwhile, as the high command were brooding over the best course of action, large sections of the army had already made their decision, and were working hectically to pursue it. The Dnieper would be crossed at any price.

As though mesmerized, bewitched by the rumours of salvation, the marching columns had been irresistibly drawn to Tashtayka, and then down to the river bank. All the troops and wagon-drivers must have been totally convinced that the army really was going to cross the Dnieper. This conviction would have been very strongly reinforced when they arrived, and saw Silfverhielm's men, the one-horse carriages, Mazeppa and all his company being transported across. Hardly any could have imagined the possibility of escape by fording the Vorskla and heading for the Crimea.

The sense of fear and bewilderment was strong. People became frantic to get across by any means they could. But the boats and rafts, such as they were, would never suffice for everyone. Whatever wretched floats were at hand suddenly acquired immeasurable value. In a disintegrating, demoralized and panic-stricken fever of *sauve qui peut*, the rafts built by Gyllenkrok's work-force were forcibly seized by the crowds streaming down to the river-bank.

Those who failed to secure vessels in this drastic manner immediately began to build their own. Even colonels and other senior officers left their units to construct their own floats. The panic was contagious. A desperate search for wood began. The snowball became an avalanche. Buildings were razed, wagons smashed to pieces. Personal baggage was gone through, and possessions of value, or thought worth saving, picked out. The most pathetic craft were pushed out into the waters. Attempts were made to get across on wagon covers made of boxes or oilcloth, cart-wheels stripped of iron, frail rafts of young green saplings.

Horses were tied together and driven into the stream. Many men tried to swim across, some with floats, others without. The river was broad and swift, and a strong wind was blowing. Groups of up to 20 men entered the water. Few reached the other side: most drowned. Those on the bank became horrified witnesses as the river swallowed up one after another of the swimmers. Many horses also drowned.

For some it seemed as if these attempts were plain and simple suicide. Johannes Siöman, the squadron chaplain with the Småland cavalry, commented: 'When it was seen with what distress the crossing was made, then I resolved, and others with me, rather to remain with the crowd, it might turn out for me as fate willed, for it were better than to do away with myself in the water.'

The efforts to swim across diminished, but competition mounted for the few precious craft. People fought and hurled each other into the water. Those who had somehow managed to obtain some kind of floating vessel were offered huge sums to take others over. Desperate men outbid each other for a ticket to salvation. Prices rose rapidly. A place for one person cost anything from ten to 100 ducats. Enterprising individuals started running their small craft to and fro in a shuttle service. As evening shaded into night, the Swedish army, its soul eroded by defeat and anxiety, was falling apart.

Two matters of high priority were now concentrating the minds of the Swedish command. First, they had to decide where the army was to go. Second, they were making prolonged and determined efforts to persuade Charles to leave, and cross the river immediately.

By now it was virtually accepted that the army would not be able to cross the Dnieper. Gyllenkrok's view was that they had three options: go back into the Ukraine, make for the Tartars in the Crimea, or await the Russians and fight one last desperate battle.

Now that Cossack support could no longer be hoped for, the first option could be dismissed. The king toyed with the thought of fighting, but was met by alarmed opposition. Gyllenkrok was quick to express the opinion that 'consternation among the men is now so great that if they see the enemy, the majority will go over to them, and the rest will most likely

drown themselves in the river'. 'They shall fight at my command!' replied
the king adamantly.

Fearfully, the officers begged the king to save himself. Lewenhaupt
went down on his knees by the king's bed. Openly weeping, he began a
detailed description of the army's hopeless situation. The king impatiently pushed him away, and spluttered: 'General, ye never know what
ye say.' Ignoring the rebuff, Lewenhaupt persisted, blackly insisting
there was 'nothing for it but either be taken prisoners of war, or all be
massacred'. The thought of an apocalyptic last battle was still floating
through the king's mind. His only response was a reckless and heroic:
'Yes. Let it slam first.'

The king now became a target for concerted persuasion. A horde of
weeping and lamenting senior officers, courtiers and advisers wailed,
prayed and begged: his Majesty had to save himself; he must not risk the
possibility of capture. Apart from genuine concern for the king, this
obdurate counselling may have concealed a fear that if Charles were
allowed to stay he might realize the vague thoughts he harboured of
letting the army expire in one final thundering Ragnarök. At last the king
was persuaded. He would save himself across the Dnieper, but this
decision was firmly linked with another: the army was to make for the
Crimea.

Creutz was appointed overall army commander. When Lewenhaupt
heard this, and understood he was meant to follow the king across the
river, he took it, typically, as an implied criticism, and promptly volun-
teered to take over command. The king acceded.

The wounded Carolus, with a number of senior officers and a small
escort, would cross the river as soon as possible. He would thus be placed
beyond reach of the perils attending the army's further hazardous
progress. The royal entourage would move over the steppes towards
Turkey. Their first objective was Ochakov, on the Black Sea. The army
was to destroy all the baggage, for maximum mobility, then cross the
Vorskla and follow the Dnieper's east bank to the Crimea. From there it
would continue to Ochakov and rejoin the king.

Orders now went out that all baggage had to be burnt. The horses were
to be used to mount the foot soldiers and camp-followers. All victuals
collected up were to be rationed out. Each regiment was to parcel out as
much ammunition as each man could carry with him. The treasure-chests
were to be emptied and the money shared out. No regiments were to
attempt to cross the Dnieper: all were to make ready to march off at
dawn. Efforts were made to try to solve the problem of the shortage of
officers in the infantry. Field colours carried by irremediably weakened
companies were to be burnt. All officers with the rank of major were
called together and given these orders.

As these new directives were going out to senior officers throughout the army, the commanding officer of the Life Dragoons, Örnestedt, attended the king and said he could promise to get his men across the Dnieper before seven o'clock the following morning. Might he have permission to ship them over? Charles passed Örnestedt on to Creutz. After reflecting on the matter, Creutz agreed to the request and gave the Life Dragoons permission to cross the Dnieper. This was yet another mistake.

The new orders do not appear to have reduced the consternation to any noticeable extent. The instruction to burn the baggage caused considerable 'tumult and murmuring'. Many, the more senior officers in particular, had large stores of baggage bulging with war-plunder and personal possessions. Some regiments followed the order to the letter and burnt up everything, but in other quarters the business of destruction proceeded very sluggishly.

In this atmosphere of tension and uncertainty the sight of the Life Dragoon regiment's efforts to get across the river, sanctioned by highest authority, was sufficient yet again to induce many others to follow their example. Frantic construction of rafts continued into the thick of night. It was virtually impossible to hold the men back. A number of sick and wounded were ferried over the river. As expected, many of them vanished in the dark waters of the swirling Dnieper.

The king sat in his barouche and went over the plans for the march. A small company gathered round the carriage, which stood ready and harnessed. It was about ten o'clock. The time for the crossing was approaching.

Gyllenkrok, who had been appointed one of the party, took out a map pinned on a board, and gave it to Lewenhaupt. On it he indicated the places the army had passed through, and their present position. To further assist Lewenhaupt on his march for the Crimea the king left some Tartar guides. Then followed the farewells.

Lewenhaupt wished the king and his party good fortune and said he had a request. 'What would that be?' asked Charles. The general asked the king to ensure that 'my poor wife and children should not, for the sake of my loyal services, go begging after my death'. 'It shall be as ye request,' answered the king and extended his hand to Lewenhaupt, who kissed it. The carriage was jerked into motion, and lurched away in the dense night.

On the journey of about five kilometres to the river crossing by the little islands the carriage lost its way in the darkness but finally found its destination. The Drabants, now numbering only about 80 men after the bloodletting of the battle, were sent over first. Drabant Clerk Norsbergh, clad in the blue coat of his master, Corporal Jan Ehrensköld, and festooned with carbines and cartridge pouches, carried the Drabant Corps' cash and accounts in sacks as he was rowed over the Dnieper. On reaching the other side he remained sitting on the bank, while the boat returned to fetch a fresh load. The king's carriage was lifted into two longboats lashed together and rowed across by twelve Drabants. More mounted men, and 300 Södermanlanders led by Major Silfversparre, were shipped over as additional escort.

A few hundred baggage horses, to provide mounts for the infantrymen, were driven across in herds, or towed behind the boats containing the men. The limited number of boats shuttled back and forth. The passage was slow and hazardous. A number of wagons considered indispensable were dismantled and shipped across in pieces, to be reassembled on the other side.

Quite a number of wounded were also shipped over. These were almost all of officer rank, for, as one account bitterly puts it, there were no boats for 'more than were needed by the great and noble lords, who filled the places on the crossing'. During the night major-generals, colonels and lieutenant-colonels, adjutant-generals, two chancellery presidents, one court steward, one war councillor, one bishop, several secretaries and eighteen priests were rowed across the Dnieper. A number of the royal household were also freighted across: stable-grooms, master chefs, journeymen, servants, a deputy cupbearer and a butler, among others. The rats were leaving the ship.

One of those who made the passage was a 27-year-old oboist serving with the Life Guards. His name was Johann Jacob Bach. He had marched under Swedish colours since 1704. When he enlisted in the town of Arnstadt, five years before the battle, his brother, a promising young organist called Johann Sebastian Bach, had been very distressed. He had clearly tried to persuade Johann Jacob, three years his senior, to stay, and painted a picture of the horrors awaiting him in foreign lands. Johann Jacob was not to be dissuaded. As he prepared to join the Swedish army his 19-year-old brother Johann Sebastian had, in farewell, composed a melancholy little keyboard suite: 'Capriccio on the departure of a beloved brother'. A number of officers and men kept Johann Jacob company, defied orders, made their way over on their own and joined the king's entourage. The Dnieper was crossed by about 3,000 people in all: Swedes, Zaporozhians and other Cossacks.

Overwhelming weariness, a sort of mental paralysis in reaction to the appalling defeat and the long, hard march, can be sensed among those now shouldering the burden of responsibility for the army. After the king and his party disappeared down the road to the crossing, both Lewenhaupt and Creutz seem to have heaved great sighs of relief.

Three sentry outposts were sited up on the plateau edge and a fourth on a rise near the road running past Perovolochna. Late into the night reports were received that enemy Cossacks and Kalmucks had been sighted from the plateau bluffs. Neither Creutz nor Lewenhaupt seem to have been unduly concerned. The skirmishes with these horsemen earlier in the day suggested they were no great threat. Lewenhaupt ran about in search of the road guides, but fatigue and lack of sleep appear finally to have overcome him. He found his way into one of the tents left by the king, wrapped himself in his cloak, lay down on the ground and fell asleep. Later, Creutz also entered, and lay down to rest, as if the world held no fears whatever.

# 26 · 'Would They Defend Themselves'

When Lewenhaupt and Creutz went to rest they no doubt believed that under their command they still had the old Carolinian army, the matchlessly effective war machine. But the machine had suffered an unprecedented pounding; important parts were smashed or gone; the cogs did not fit as before. The war machine was cracked and broken.

Creutz did not sleep long. Lewenhaupt was lying beside him. He sat up and shook the general's arm. Lewenhaupt was dragged from the depths of sleep to hear Creutz asking him if he should not 'let the regiments stand to?' The general started up, and in a daze replied: 'Please do so, I'll be with ye right away.' Creutz left the tent. The darkness was starting to disperse; a thin sliver of light in the skies announced the arrival of a new day. Creutz called the aides together and ordered them to ride out to muster the units. He mounted his own horse, and rode along the regimental lines, commanding them to stand to. Lewenhaupt, still only half-awake, followed him, calling for his servants to bring him a horse. Neither servant nor horse appeared, so he continued on foot towards the nearest regiment, Meijerfelt's Dragoons, and shouted at them in German: 'To horse, to horse, mount, stand to!' It was about two o'clock.

The dawn light broke on an army verging on disintegration. The various orders issued late the previous night had only been partially implemented. Large numbers of soldiers were still at work on the river bank attempting to make their way over. Pathetic scenes were played out: craft constructed from carts or narrow staves tied together stood stranded at the water's edge. In some regiments half the rank and file were missing, persistently occupied with demented efforts to ship themselves across. Regiments and baggage had become increasingly jumbled in the darkness: chaos and confusion reigned.

The instructions to burn and destroy the wagons and baggage had only been half obeyed. Large numbers of wagons were still intact. The contents of the war-chests had not yet been distributed to the men, nor had the reserves of food and ammunition. The atmosphere throughout the night seems to have been a strange mixture of exhausted surrender, hopeless despair and distraught fear. Some had succumbed to total apathy and abandoned their duties to sleep, completely worn out. Others, still driven by fear, continued their feverish efforts to build rafts and persisted in foolhardy attempts to cross the river. Discipline, the iron fetters holding the army together, enabling it to function, had vanished. Senior officers tacitly consented to the men's forbidden efforts to cross the river, or else joined in themselves.

The stand-to was sluggish. Creutz called over a couple of colonels, rebuked them sharply and exhorted them to 'sit up and get a move on'. The only reaction from Meijerfelt's Dragoons to Lewenhaupt's vigorous order was sullen silence. He relates that 'not a man answered me a word, but looked at me, as if I were witless'. His shouts for officers met with the same numbing silence. The horsemen remained stationary and stared him straight in the face; stony figures with blazing eyes. Still unmounted, Lewenhaupt plunged on. He later found an officer who took responsibility for mustering the dragoons.

Soldiers could be seen lying in the grass behind their tethered horses reading little prayer-books. The men then gathered for regimental prayers. The small groups beneath the standards only slowly thickened into columns.

Quite apart from merely mustering the men, it was absolutely essential for the treasure-chests to be shared out. Creutz started to organize collection of all the chests next to the Mounted Life regiment, intending the regimental paymasters to divide the contents among the men. It was difficult work, for the wagons were scattered. Some were stuck in marshes and pools of water. Abraham Cederholm, who had lost his own treasure-laden horse escaping from Roos's martyred battalions, was the man given the task of ensuring that the regiments were each apportioned their fair share. As he stood conferring with Creutz, their discussion was interrupted by the sound of shots.

A cavalry captain approached Creutz to report that sentries had seen the enemy advancing. Russian cavalry were attacking the outlying Swedish posts on the plateau. The Swedes resisted briefly, then fled in the direction of the river. The Russians followed. Creutz sent a rapid dispatch to Lewenhaupt, then rode up the steep bank to the top of the sandhill. A group of Swedish horse was in full flight, pursued by a large number of Cossacks. The sight of a senior officer produced a modicum of oral heroism from some of the troopers. Still in full flight they began bawling at their cornet: 'Stand, you cobbler, you're not fit to be an officer, we'll stick our blades in you, stand if you're a real man.' Creutz succeeded in halting them. Reinforced by another outpost, they drove the Cossacks back. Fresh swarms rode up, but mostly made off round the Swedes' left flank, in the direction of the baggage down by the Dnieper.

The Swedes reined in their horses. Creutz, glancing back at the river, saw Meijerfelt's Dragoons in march formation and called up reinforcements. Two companies joined the group on the plateau, and they continued their forward push. The Russians were driven further back, and the Swedes rode up a couple of small hills. The plain opened out. The sight Creutz saw before him must have been a terrible shock.

The columns on the river meadow had already been ordered to move off when the rattle of gunfire was heard from the plateau. The foremost regiments started to work their way up the slope. The Swedish Adelsfana, a small unit of about 300 men led by Colonel Anders Ramsvärd, had been detailed to escort the artillery. The unit consisted of enlisted men financed by the Swedish nobility; its traditions stretched back to Erik of Pomerania and the early 15th century. Next to them came the Uppland Dragoons. Both units were repeatedly exposed to Cossack attacks. When they reached the summit, the significance of the firing they had been hearing became totally clear. An entire corps of regular troops was drawn up in crescent-shaped *ordre de bataille* before them. The Russians had caught up with the Swedish army.

Creutz, on his hillock, was taking in the same sight. The long, slightly curved battle-line extending over the plain was a combined force: mainly cavalry, but including infantry, artillery and irregular horse. It must have been an immense shock for the Swedes to see such a comprehensive array of arms. Command of the corps was held by Menshikov, and he now rode well forward to assess the Swedish dispositions. The Russian infantry had been mounted, two men to a horse in some cases, thus keeping pace with their cavalry on the march. This simple, genial piece of Russian improvisation had transported the Semyonovski Guard, the élite of the Russian brigade.

The foot soldiers were drawn up in the centre of the crescent. Their pack-horses were stationed in a long line slightly behind them. The wings consisted of ten dragoon regiments on each side. They were accompanied by artillery: probably the six three-pounder cannon attached to the Semyonovski Guard, and a number of two-pounders attached to the dragoons. These pieces were deployed to face the crest of the plateau bluffs, behind a thin shield of irregular horse and the advance detachments which had clashed with the Swedish outposts. The corps numbered about 9,000 men. Creutz sent back a report: Russians were heading straight for the rumpled army in the river vale.

The traumatic tidings that the Russians had caught up quickly became general property among the Swedes and new shock-waves of panic spread through their ranks. Renewed crowds hurled themselves into the Dnieper; some with horses, some without. Mounted on a horse by the river was battalion chaplain Sven Agrell. Born 1685 in Torup parish, Halland, he had started studying for the priesthood in 1702. The vocation lay near at hand, since his father was a vicar. He had only been ordained four months before the battle, however. The ordination had taken place in the presence of the king, which may have compensated for the delay.

Sven had packed his dearest possessions in a couple of bags and an oilcloth sack the previous day, in hopes of being able to take them across the river. Things had not gone smoothly: he had seen the hectic scenes by the river, the fights and the frenzied bidding for places. He had come to terms with two men on a raft who promised to take him over in due course. The evening had drawn on with no sign of them, and Sven had passed the night on the river bank, sleeping on his bags. The young preacher was now riding anxiously to and fro, looking for the men and their raft. He finally gave up, and decided to seek out his regiment to see what was happening there.

Returning from the river he saw a familiar face, a major from the same regiment, Sven Lagerberg. This was the man who had been shot in the battle's final phase, left wounded on the field, walked over by the Russian lines and finally rescued by a dragoon. Lagerberg was on his way to the river, lying on a camp bed slung between two horses. The wounded major told him that 'at the regiment nothing is being done' and asked Agrell to stay with him and 'bring him to the barge the king had used for his crossing'. This idea appealed to Agrell, and they made their way up to the ford by the islands, where wild disorder reigned. The major's bed was carried out into the water, to meet one of the boats. Once on board, the crew promptly threatened to eject him, saying they only had orders to ship over the king's own effects.

Faced with this prospect, the desperate major wrenched out his pistols and offered to 'shoot any man through the head who made a bid to throw him off'. This show of force allowed him and his clerical friend to stay on board, but they had to abandon most of their baggage. Agrell saved one bag, and Lagerberg clung on to a couple of field canteens. They were not out of danger. Frantic men continued to clamber aboard. The craft showed signs of foundering. Agrell tore off his clothes in order to get ready to swim. The crew began to heave objects and a few contemptible menials overboard, and soon the boat floated better. Cuts and blows rained over the unfortunate men attempting to cling on, as the vessel made way and steered across the Dnieper.

Hardly a tree-trunk was now left standing on the shore. Large numbers of swimmers continued to drown. With the Russian army closing in, some of those who had been saving their goods now began destroying them. Wagons were set on fire. Some consigned their possessions, such as furniture, to the river depths.

Back up on the plateau the hornet Cossack bands swept left, past the Swedish posts, and down to attack the disorderly crowds milling on the river bank. An orgy of plunder among the jumbled wagons now began. Several treasure-chests fell into Cossack hands.

Sven Agrell had hardly completed the crossing before he jumped into a small boat on its way back, in an attempt to fetch a horse and the rest of his own and the major's baggage. The arrival of the circling Cossacks made the return trip an even more hazardous venture. In extreme danger, he scrambled ashore and secured one of Lagerberg's valises. More was impossible: the Russian horsemen reached the water's edge and drove the Swedes out into the stream. The terrified people now fled in the only direction left to them: out to the motley collection of wretched craft bobbing about by the bank.

The little boat Agrell had returned in was almost swamped by the fleeing. The lucky few on board freed themselves with vicious blows. The unlucky many in the water were left to their fate. Shoving the boat before him, Agrell waded out until the water reached his neck, far enough so that 'no one could get at us'. Safely in the boat, he looked back to where he could now see the Cossacks and Kalmucks harrying at will. They snapped up anything they found, including Agrell's remaining bags. One of them contained his journal. In it he had carefully recorded the distance he had travelled since leaving his parents: 729 and three-quarter Swedish miles, up to the present day, 1 July, 1709.

The sun had now been up some time, but the army was still on the field below the sandhills. It was puzzling and very disturbing for the Swedes looking across from the opposite side of the Dnieper. They could hear the sound of cannon-fire, and saw the Russian irregular cavalry roving about on the other shore. The king decided that he had escort enough, and ordered the regiment of Life Dragoons, which had shipped over during the night, to return immediately. This must have been a great blow for the troopers and their commanding officer, Örnestedt, who had taken such pains to get across.

When the Russian battle-array was first discovered, it was still not completely blocking the Swedish army's route to Kishenka and the ford across the Vorskla. In a way, however, the unfortunate position of the Swedes made them automatic prisoners. It was unlikely they could evade their pursuers without an engagement. The question now was whether they would be able to hurry past the enemy forming up for battle. In the chaos and disorder they missed this slender chance.

The Russian battle-line moved forward slowly and deliberately, nearing the only exit available to the trapped Swedes. Their left wing finally occupied a position close to the road leading to Kishenka past Perovolochna. The Swedes were now effectively shut in. The army would have to fight its way out if it wanted to escape. The long sparse columns of march turned left to form a battle-front facing the sandhills and the

Russian army. What artillery there was fell into place. The muzzles of the Swedish cannon were aimed upwards at the Russians approaching the crest of the plateau.

Lewenhaupt was at a loss for what to do next. He was extremely reluctant to offer battle, with the Swedish army in its present disordered, ragged state. Probably in a hasty, panic-stricken attempt to gain time, collect his forces better and prepare for a formal battle or break-through, he decided to make contact with the Russians. The move invites comparison with the king's earlier temporizing ruse with Meijerfelt.

The obvious man for the task was the Prussian military attaché, von Siltmann. The night before, and again early that morning Lewenhaupt had been accosted by Siltmann, who wanted to go over to the Russians. Lewenhaupt now ordered Lieutenant-Colonel Trautwetter to provide the Prussian with a drummer, and sent him to the Russians with a mandate to start truce negotiations. Gathering up his baggage, the Prussian and the drummer set off for the Russian lines, in front of the entire array of mustered Swedish troops.

The outlying Swedish sentries had clearly not been told of this move for they opened fire on the small group as it passed them. The party ran the gauntlet through a shower of whining bullets, but reached the Russian lines unhurt. Von Siltmann was challenged by an aide who, on learning his identity, conveyed him swiftly to Menshikov. After the obligatory exchange of compliments, von Siltmann explained his mandate. Menshikov made it plain that the tsar's directive to him was that the Swedes were either to fight or surrender. All he could offer them was capitulation, on good terms. Armed with this ultimatum, the drummer returned alone.

The ultimatum reached Lewenhaupt via Creutz. The general had his hands full trying to collect the regiments and prepare them for battle. His efforts were not meeting with much success. Creutz rode up to him and reported the terms of capitulation. Their joint assessment of the situation was blackly pessimistic.

Lewenhaupt decided to address two matters of high priority. He first had to get the troops into a more favourable position. At this moment the army was packed together in the shadow of the plateau steep. The Russian artillery would be able to pour devastating fire upon the men standing directly below the muzzles of their cannon. The army at present was defenceless as a flock of sheep. The whole order of battle was instructed to pull off to the right, in the direction of a small field. But they needed more time. Their forces were still not properly collected for action. Secondly, the king and his company also needed time, to put the greatest distance possible between the Dnieper and themselves. Lewenhaupt's next instruction intended to gain this respite. Creutz was ordered to ride off to parley

*Map 8 · Perovolochna*

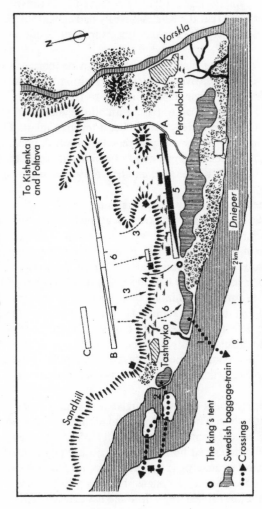

1. Swedish troops spontaneously start trying to cross the river.
2. The king is persuaded to cross at Tashtayka. Mazeppa's company, the royal household, the king's escort, and others cross at the same spot during the night of 30 June.
3. Early on 1 July Russian horse attack outposts at the plateau edge.
4. A Swedish counter-attack pushes them back temporarily. The Russian order of battle is discovered.
5. Swedish troops draw up for battle below the sandbank.
6. Russians deploy cannon on the brink of the plateau. Irregular horse circumvent the outposts and attack the baggage on the river bank.

⊙  The king's tent

�▯  Swedish baggage-train

•••▶  Crossings

with the Russians in person and 'there seek to draw out the time as much as he could'.

Disquiet mounted among the Swedes on the Dnieper's southern bank. It was now nine o'clock, and the army still had not moved from the spot. It became increasingly obvious that the Russians really had caught up. Soon the observers could also see regular Russian troops moving about on the other side.

At about a quarter to ten the king's company began its journey away from the river bank, southwards over the steppe. The king travelled in a wagon. The remainder made their way according to their abilities and situation. Many of the wounded had to ride, with all the additional pain implied. Others, like Chaplain Agrell, had no beast to carry them. They hung their boots about their necks and proceeded on foot. A good 350 kilometres of waste land, treeless steppe and hot sun lay ahead of them, before they were to see Ochakov. One after another, they disappeared into the tall grass.

The situation for the Swedish army was precarious. It was, admittedly, somewhat stronger than the Russian – 12,000 men against 9,000 – but only in numbers. The regiments were still very scattered. Lewenhaupt estimated that half the men were still down at the Dnieper, preoccupied with trying to get across. The Russians may have been tired after their forced pursuit, but their morale must have been sky high following their triumph at Poltava. The atmosphere among those Swedes who, in spite of everything, had gathered by their standards, was one of bewildered resentment and sullen defeatism. Faced with the prospect of yet another battle, of extremely doubtful outcome, they now began to go over to the Russians. Officers, non-commissioned officers, soldiers, servants, labourers, people of every category, found their way over in groups of five, ten and 20.

Taking Colonel Dücker and a Captain Douglas with him, Creutz rode over to the Russian battle-line. They were led up to Menshikov, posted on a high hill, from which he could observe the Swedish forces. In the ensuing conversation Menshikov described himself as a Christian who wanted to spare lives, and was therefore making 'a fair offer'. Creutz produced a few defiant phrases to the effect that the Russians should not think they were 'facing children'. Menshikov cajoled him a little and gave an assurance that if the Swedes surrendered then both officers and men could keep everything they had, baggage included. Creutz requested an hour's grace. Dücker, Douglas and a Russian went back to the Swedish lines with Menshikov's terms. Creutz remained.

Lewenhaupt now faced the ultimate question. Should they engage the enemy? Or surrender? The Swedish army was in a dreadful state, but their chance of fighting free was not utterly lost. The Russian troops were exhausted. In spite of everything, the Swedish cavalry was relatively strong; particularly those units which had been out of the battle, safely located with the baggage, or posted along the Vorskla. A flanking movement, followed by a resolute attack on the Russian left could possibly open the road to Kishenka. Many judged that an effort to break out should succeed. In a number of regiments preparations for battle were in full swing. Men were lightening their packs and getting rations ready in expectation of escape.

But many other factors argued against giving battle. The Swedish army was not collected. Disorder was still rife. Morale was very low. Attempts had been made to remedy this by capitalizing on the time gained, but with no very apparent success. Reserves of ammunition were extremely low in some quarters. Another grave concern was the rate of desertion. This really demonstrated that the Swedish will to fight was critically shaken.

Lewenhaupt was a very cautious soldier. He was also a thorough pessimist by nature. He could hardly fail to regard the Swedish army's present situation in terms of pitch dark, unremitting gloom without a glimmer of light. Under the pressures of the moment his deliberations must also have been highly affected by the excruciating experience he had just survived on the battlefield at Poltava. He had seen the unmanageable chaos produced by shattered morale. He had led the greater part of the Swedish infantry into extinction. Deeply shaken, he was to refer to the event as an offering of the innocent. His relationship with his men was overtly paternalistic. While their inferiority and subordinate status were taken for granted, they were deserving of his care. Lewenhaupt felt an emotional responsibility for the army and its people.

The Swedish soldier was not cannon-fodder pure and simple for Lewenhaupt and his colleagues on the general staff. They were too close to the army and, in particular, the battlefield, to be able to sustain a dehumanized, impersonal attitude. They rode into battle with their men, saw their orders result in death, and were frequently killed and crippled themselves. The armies were also fairly small, and the soldiers, often recruited at substantial cost, were too valuable, literally, to be merely thrown away. The cannon-fodder concept was a later product, born of industrialization and industrial wars, when people in vast conscripted armies became a raw material like any other, in an age when generals campaigned in self-imposed isolation, far from the reality of battle, and quite out of touch with the appalling consequences of their orders. Not that the ethics of military leadership in feudal wars stood on a noticeably higher plane – slaughter is butchery, whether watched or not – but they were different in character, with different consequences.

Battle, as Lewenhaupt well knew, could end in catastrophe. In his sensitive and gloomy mind 'could' had become 'would', and was on the point of becoming 'must'. He later asserted that any battle now would have been a massacre. He would have been driving 'the poor soldiers to the butcher's yard'. The language is patently overworked, but without doubt mirrors his honest, if ill-judged, opinion. For him, the imminent slaughter was pointless. He could not accept the burden of responsibility for such 'vain bravura'. Perhaps the deciding factor was his piety. Lewenhaupt believed in God, a living God to whom he was accountable. He was quite capable, of course, of launching an attack to save face before the king and his peers. Abject surrender was undeniably a dishonour. But, in his own words, 'I had greater fear of an omniscient God, who craves sore payment for intemperate acts of blood, than I regarded that dishonour'.

The impression he gives is of a soldier who has seen too much blood, no longer has the stomach for battle, and has lost heart. It is quite possible that he misread the situation, and made the battle much harder to win than it actually was. But it is difficult to censure him severely. The decision he came to may be queried from a military, but not humanitarian, standpoint.

Had the matter concerned him alone, Lewenhaupt would have accepted Menshikov's terms and surrendered as soon as he heard them.

To capitulate with the entire army was an immense responsibility, however. He would find the dishonour hard to live with. At about ten in the morning, in what has to be seen as a shameless and rather cowardly design to shed some of his burden, he summoned every regimental commander, and all other senior officers.

This was to be a meeting of singular note. It is unlikely Lewenhaupt told any of the assembled officers what orders the king had left, or what the alternatives open to them were. He simply asked them 'what they were minded to do, and whether they could assure him their men would fight?' He received equivocal answers. Many were secretly averse to breaking through the enemy lines since that would mean sacrificing their valuable baggage. They kept this to themselves, however. Most must have sensed which way the wind was blowing, and realized that Lewenhaupt was aiming to have them share the blame for an eventual surrender.

They promptly assured the general that they 'readily on behalf of their officers and men would fight in the service of the King'. Anders Ramsvärd, commanding officer of the Swedish Adelsfana, said he and his regiment had sworn their loyal oath to the king. He hoped none would fail to carry out that 'duty and devoir' to which he was bound and commanded. One colonel scornfully remarked that some officers were boldly promising to 'beat the whole Russian army', but that no attention should be paid to them. Otherwise they tended to project their own doubts on the rank and file. They said they could not promise their men would fight, 'for consternation and fear were spread among them all too greatly, so that, in this pass, they were ungovernable'. Some pointed out the shortage of ammunition. Others, with the scurrilous colonel of dragoons, Dücker, to the fore, swore that the rank and file would 'lay down their muskets, the moment they clapped eyes on any enemy advancing'.

These were not precisely the answers Lewenhaupt wanted to hear. Besides heaping coals on his already extremely defeatist view of the situation, they did not really offer *carte-blanche* support if he decided to surrender. Lewenhaupt patently shunned the responsibility of decision. The choice between battle and surrender was a choice between plague and cholera. But the officers were ducking his overtures, and responding with a plethora of evasive mumbles.

He concentrated on their comments about the men's loss of will to fight, and issued an order of a very strange kind: unique perhaps, for the commander of an army. The officers were instructed to go out and ask their men 'what they were minded to do, and would they defend themselves rather than be taken prisoner?'

After that they would vote on the matter and he would take his decision. The officers expressed doubts about taking a poll. They thought the men would declare themselves willing to fight, but refuse when the shooting started. Colonel Dücker asked what orders the king had given. Lewenhaupt's answer was misleading, not to say completely inaccurate. He failed to mention the march for the Crimea, or any other option, and replied: 'His Majesty cannot have given any order other than to defend ourselves for as long as we were able'.

The regimental commanding officers of the Swedish army rode away to their men to ask them if they wished to fight, or surrender.

# 27 · 'Not Without Tears'

High in the saddle on their horses, ready and prepared for battle, the regimental rank and file expectantly awaited their orders. Their commanding officers arrived. Riding from unit to unit they asked the men 'whether they thought they could overwhelm the enemy, which had surrounded them with a strong corps of infantry and artillery'. Those soldiers who, in spite of everything, had gathered round their battle standards and heard the question, were perplexed. 'How is it they ask us this now?' said some dragoons of Albedyhl's Life company, seasoned veterans who had fought in Hungary and elsewhere. 'They never asked us this before, the word was always: Forward!'

Beneath the banners and the standards, opinion was divided. It was difficult to get straight answers. Some considered it impossible to put up any successful resistance, because of the men's exhaustion and all the wounded and unarmed. 'Whereby a perfect desperation were to follow, which at length were to find an end by indefensible, nay, unchristian murder.' A number thought the enemy could certainly be defeated, but not much would be gained: for where would they go to after a battle? Others said they would accept whatever decision was taken. A number were set on battle, and getting ready to fight their way out, in spite of not knowing where to make for next.

'We cannot say we shall defeat them, but will do all that human strength may compass,' said Albedyhl's dragoons. Other units were also totally opposed to the thought of surrender. The Life Dragoons are said to have asserted they would 'rather fight to the last drop of blood than give themselves up to quarter'. Another regiment declaring its willingness to fight was the Åbo cavalry, led by a Livonian major, Erik Johan von Holden.

It is not to be wondered at that these men preferred battle to surrender. The treatment of prisoners of war was generally extremely inhumane. For a start, they were not often maintained in any way by the victor. Some felt that perhaps, after all, it was more merciful to do away with prisoners on the spot than expose them to captivity's long martyrdom of hard labour, starvation and sickness. There were no recognized rules giving prisoners protection or rights of any kind. Mortality was very high. It was worst for the men, which may have increased their reluctance to surrender; on the whole, officers were treated significantly better.

The officers returned. They came 'with an answer which was neither cut nor dried', as Lewenhaupt discovered. Privately he thought the opaque replies, none unambiguously for surrender, reflected the regimental commanders' reluctance to let their units appear in a bad light. Dissatisfied with the response, he decided to conduct yet another inquiry. What did the men want to do now? The commanders went back to their regiments with an exhortation to stress the extreme gravity of the situation.

The puzzled rank and file now showed increased opposition to the idea of fighting: understandably, when their supreme command led the van in defeatism. Some regiments admitted they were not about to let themselves be massacred. Others were silent, refusing to answer the question.

The cavalry were asked if they would be prepared to charge the Russian foot. The Swedish infantry, who should have shouldered this task, were so few. Not all were willing. The regiments showing the greatest readiness were those which had not seen battle three days earlier. Their ranks were undepleted. They had no fresh memories of slaughter. The foot, naturally enough, displayed the least inclination for further battle; they were unanimous for surrender.

Up on the bluffs, and on the plateau beyond them, the Russians stood waiting. They moved their cannon into place, and sighted them on the Swedes below. Time passed. Russian impatience grew. The artillery commander sent an officer to Menshikov, requesting permission to open fire. He was told to wait a little longer. An aide rode down to Lewenhaupt, and instructed him to hurry up with his decision.

Discipline in the Swedish army was still poor. To signal their unwillingness to fight, a number of soldiers fired their muskets in the air. Barking volleys echoed to the skies. Bands of defectors continued to find their way over to the motionless Russian lines. The demented attempts to escape across the river also persisted. The Cossacks allied to the Swedish army swelled the numbers filling rotten craft who preferred to risk their lives rather than fall into Russian hands. They feared retribution for their rebellion against the tsar, and with justification. The crossing was made more dangerous by the Kalmucks and enemy Cossacks swarming on the shore.

A near-victim of Kalmuck depredation was Johann Christian Schmidt, a 16-year-old from Saxony, attached to the baggage-train. At only 14 he had joined the Swedish army, more or less voluntarily, at Leipzig. This was less in a spirit of adventure than as a result of a minor accident. Sent by his parents to work in a Leipzig wine-shop, he had found mine host a very harsh master. One day, having broken a jug of wine, he ran away and hid in the household of Captain Wilhelm Bennet, a Swedish officer of Scots descent, born in Åbo, and a patron of the house. It was soon apparent that the enraged landlord was not going to forgive Johann Christian his clumsiness. The boy donned Swedish clothing and followed the captain as his servant when the army left Saxony in 1707.

The sights of sickness, starvation, torture, privation and mass slaughter he had seen in the two years since then had put him off the soldier's trade. When he saw the quantities of provisions so recently swallowed up in flames, he wished the Saxon peasants forced to contribute these bulky supplies had been able to watch the pitiful spectacle.

His regiment, Meijerfelt's Dragoons, were prepared to fight. They, and Johann Christian with them, were getting ready for the break through the Russian lines. He rode back to where they had camped the night, and where the abandoned, part-burned baggage-wagons were still smouldering. The boy was going through a couple of boxes, and throwing the supplies he found across his horse, when he saw a Kalmuck closing in. The man rode straight at him with a lowered lance, aiming to kill. Johann Christian leapt on his horse and rode through the jumble of carts in a frantic effort to get away. The Kalmuck was swifter, and the distance between them shrank.

With one wagon between him and his pursuer, Johann Christian knew he would be drilled through any moment. A shot rang out. Thinking the Kalmuck had emptied his pistol at him, the boy turned in the saddle, only to see his assailant lying lifeless on the ground, and a riderless horse galloping away towards a group of Kalmucks in the distance. A Swedish dragoon, a complete stranger to him, was standing with a smoking carbine behind a cart. The boy stared for a couple of moments at the dead man, and then at the man who had saved his life. The dragoon leapt on the corpse and rifled it. With a word of thanks, Johann Christian spurred his horse back to his regiment and the break-out he was expecting.

But there were not many on the Swedish general staff still talking about breaking out. Again the officers collected round Lewenhaupt. The result of the poll among the men was still unclear. The commanding officer of the Uppland Dragoons, Wennerstedt, asserted that his lads would fight but, unfortunately, they had no powder or ball. The commanders of the Mounted Life regiment, Åbo cavalry and the Life Dragoons reported that 'their men wanted to fight'. Meijerfelt's Dragoons and the Småland cavalry also seem to have been inclined to smash their way through the surrounding Russians. All the infantry colonels, with Posse in the lead, said their men favoured coming to terms, since they were so few. One colonel claimed only about 700 foot soldiers were drawn up for battle. The figure is almost certainly a misrepresentation, but there is little doubt the badly shaken, crippled infantry regiments were difficult to muster. Many of the cavalry commanders too, including the cursing Carl Gustaf Dücker, were very pessimistic.

Another messenger arrived from the Russians, insisting on a prompt decision. The pressure was increasing. Lewenhaupt requested yet more time to confer, which was granted. A decision had to be reached.

He ordered the commanders to ride off to one side, where they ranged themselves in a circle around him. In effect, the matter had already been decided. They were now no more than faceless executors of their own authority. The voting began. Each was to voice his opinion. The youngest spoke first. The arguments for and against were already known to all. What seems to have counted most was the judgement that wilting Swedish morale would lead to a total disaster. They also seem to have been attracted by the terms of surrender, the promise that the officers would be allowed to keep their baggage, and that they might be allowed home to Sweden on parole. These favours only applied to the officers, naturally. The votes were cast and weighed. Many wanted to fight; but fewer than those who wanted to surrender. The opponents were voted down.

Backed by this ballot, Lewenhaupt could take the decision he had so clearly been inclining towards for so long, and had so strongly shied away from. The fighting would end. The whole Swedish army were to ground arms and surrender. Capitulation.

It was about 11 o'clock. Announcement of the surrender was sent to Menshikov. After a time the Swedish command received the terms confirmed in writing, undersigned by Menshikov. The treaty was written in German and contained six clauses, the last inserted as an addendum at the end: an indication of the haste in which it had been drawn up.

The first clause stated that all troops under Lewenhaupt's command, and all others with them, were His Great Tsarist Majesty's prisoners. The second clause required all ranks to surrender all weapons and become prisoners of war, with prospects of buying their release, or being exchanged. They would be allowed to keep their goods, apart from horses, weapons and ammunition. The officers would be allowed to keep their horses. The third clause decreed that all Swedish officers could keep their baggage. When peace was concluded they would be released without ransom or exchange. The officers were promised 'honnête' treatment and the opportunity of travelling home on parole.

Clause four stipulated that all artillery, munitions, battle-standards, musical instruments and treasure-chests should pass to the tsar. Under clause five the Swedes committed themselves to handing over all Zaporozhians to the Russians. The sixth and last clause, tacked on as an addendum, allowed all commissioned officers to keep their servants. All senior civilians attached to the army – commissioners, judge-advocates, secretaries and field chaplains – could also keep their baggage and servants.

The haste of negotiation is further indicated by Creutz' forgetful oversight to pay the men a month's wages from the money-chests, and his attempts to be allowed to do this after the treaty was concluded.

The news of the capitulation went out to the Swedish army. The details were sketchy. No one, on pain of punishment, was to venture to fire a weapon. They were prisoners of war, to be freed when peace came. The officers were to keep their baggage.

The news seems to have been greeted with relief among many of the rank and file. They drew back from the river, emerged from hiding-places and returned to their units. The groups under the standards, recently so sparse, began to thicken. In other quarters, capitulation meant the death-knell of the last shreds of discipline. In a fuddled state of burning frustration, dejection and terminal defeat Swedish soldiers began to rifle and harry their own baggage-train. Bizarre scenes were acted out. A group of troopers from Taube's Dragoons threw themselves over the Life regiment's treasure-wagon in an attempt to pillage the 400 riksdaler it contained. A major intervened and managed to stop them.

The Russian troops advanced down the plateau sandhills towards the waiting Swedes. The soldiers now saw how tired their opponents really were. As Bauer's regiment of dragoons rode down the steep sandy tracks, young Gustaf Abraham Piper noticed up to twenty horses per squadron stumble and drop with fatigue.

The hasty accord caused numerous problems for the Swedish command. Unwilling to let secret army and regimental records fall into Russian hands, they ordered their wholesale destruction. The orders, plans, recommendations and accounts contained in the war-chest wagons were in extreme disorder. Much had already disappeared, but whatever remained was gathered up and set ablaze. Even the field secretariat was destroyed. Wagon-loads of chancellery documents went up in flames.

The money-chests, according to the terms of the treaty, were to be handed over to the Russians. But there was a desire to distribute these funds throughout the army. They would be needed. It was very rare for victorious powers to spend sums of any note on their prisoners of war. Time for this work could easily have been found earlier in the day. It now became a minor hazard, clearly in breach of the concluded treaty.

In the greatest haste, regimental commanders and other senior officials now began drawing out large sums of money, to share among the officers and men. Secretary Abraham Cederholm most discreetly began disgorging funds to appointed officers. He carried on with this work as the day unfolded, managing to parcel out more than 30,000 riksdaler, a vertiginous sum for the times, before a Swedish officer tipped the Russians off to what was going on. One of the tsar's aides, Paul Wendelbom, a Dane in his twenties, in Russian service, approached Cederholm and ordered him to hand over the coffers. Before long, the Dane initiated confidential discussions and offered, for a 'certain consideration', to secure the Swede his freedom. Cederholm swallowed the bait and offered 100 ducats, but the deal fell through.

Nicolaus Ingewald Hoffman, in his forties, from Filipstad, and regimental paymaster of the Skaraborg regiment of foot, was also involved in hectic distribution of funds to all sides. Earlier on, Creutz had stopped him doing this, since he thought it unfitting 'in sight of the enemy'. This still applied, in the highest degree, but it was no longer a matter of choice: the money had to be shared out. Major-General Carl Gustaf Kruse, commanding officer of the Uppland Tremänning of horse, and one of the most insistent advocates of surrender, went to Hoffman as he stood next to his coffers and sanctioned the withdrawal of funds for certain units.

Hoffman took the opportunity to ask if he could draw 2,000 riksdaler on behalf of the Skaraborg men, and this was granted. The Skaraborg chest, however, had been double-locked. Hoffman had one key, and the regimental commanding officer, Carl Gustaf Ulfsparre, had the other. The mortal remains of Carl Gustaf Ulfsparre lay decomposing 120 kilometres to the north, and his key lay with them. Hoffman urgently sent the regimental oboist, Gustaf Blidström, to look for Captain Wibbling. The captain arrived and the two men broke open the coffer. The 2,000 riksdaler were secured at the eleventh hour, for the wagons then rolled away.

Meanwhile an atrocious scene was being enacted before the eyes of the Swedish army. The fifth clause of the capitulation treaty can be regarded, with certainty, as a blot of infamy. The Swedes had promised that 'the Zaporozhian Cossacks and other rebels, who are found to be here with the Swedish troops, shall immediately be delivered up to His Tsarist Majesty'. These allies and comrades-in-arms, encouraged to rebel against the tsar and whose protection the king had guaranteed, were now shamelessly abandoned. The retribution exacted by the Russians was horrific.

Those Cossacks captured at Poltava had already been executed in the most brutal manner. Their bodies were now strung up round the battlefield, fastened to a variety of monstrous contraptions. Some dangled from gallows, others were threaded on poles. A number had been broken on wheels, their arms and legs cut off while still alive, and killed 'in many such ways as rebels are executed'. At the same time, the Russian victors made short work of captured deserters. Swedish prisoners were forced to watch the renegade Brigadier Mühlenfels being spitted. This was considered the grimmest possible method of execution. A long, sharpened pole was driven into the condemned man's rectum, and then raised up. His death-throes could last for more than twenty-four hours.

Down by the Dnieper the Russians began to round up the Cossack rebels. Men, and the women and children who had travelled with the baggage-train, were herded 'as if they were cattle'. Delivered up by their allies, abandoned by their leaders, all they were left with was death. The Russians cut them down on the spot. A number made a last doomed, desperate stand. Others drowned themselves in the Dnieper.

Count Adam Ludvig Lewenhaupt, General of Foot, the man who had delivered them, was sitting at table meanwhile with their executioner, Prince Alexander Danilovitch Menshikov, General of Horse. They were dining in the Russian's mess-tent, which had been erected on a high knoll, giving them a fine view of the Russian array of troops.

An army vanished. Almost exactly 20,000 men entered captivity this hot day in July; including 983 officers: one general, two major-generals, 11 colonels, 16 lieutenant-colonels, 23 majors, one field ordnance commander, 256 cavalry and infantry captains, one lieutenant-captain, 304 lieutenants, 323 cornets and ensigns, 18 regimental quarter-masters, two aides-de-camp and 25 adjutants. Non-commissioned officers and other ranks totalled 12,575: 9,152 cavalrymen, 3,286 infantrymen and 137 gunners.

There were a total of 1,401 non-combatants: including a head stable-master, 19 artillery sergeants, 40 chaplains, 10 commissioners, 80 field surgeons and medical orderlies, five judge-advocates, two notaries, 55 secretaries, 13 kettle-drummers, 145 drummers and pipers, 73 trumpeters and oboists, 13 provost-marshals and 945 artisans, draymen and baggage-servants. Large numbers of the royal household had followed the king across the river but some remained, and 33 of them fell into Russian hands: a field physician, a master cook, four trumpeters, a field apothecary, a clerk and 25 flunkeys and coachmen.

Then there were the civilian labourers, servants and other minions: all in all 3,402 souls. Finally, there were the families and female servants: 1,657 women and children of all ages. Add these 20,000 to the roughly 2,800 taken prisoner during the battle, and a grand total of about 23,000 Swedes went into captivity in the course of four hot, dusty summer days.

Forty-nine corps and regiments were eradicated. The host which had numbered fully 49,500 soldiers the previous summer had been reduced to 1,300: the handful who had crossed the Dnieper with the king. Many of those were sick and wounded. The rest were dead or captured. It was the greatest military disaster in Sweden's long history, and still is.

The Russians won rich plunder in material terms. All the remaining Swedish artillery, 31 pieces of ordnance, became Tsar Peter's property: 21 cannon, two howitzers and eight mortar. With these came tons of ammunition, hundreds of boxes of cartridges, tens of thousands of swords, carbines, muskets, cartridge-cases, bayonets, valises, shoulder-pouches, saddle-bags, fully harnessed horses with saddles, bits and pistols, and quantities of trumpets, kettle-drums and oboes. A total of 142 banners and standards were taken. Last but not least were the coffers which fell into the hands of the victors: the army's great treasure-chest with 2,000,000 coins of various values and denominations, the regimental coffers totalling about 400,000 coins, and Mazeppa's money-chests containing somewhat over 300,000 coins.

This was the official tally. Then there was the plunder the Russian troops extracted from Swedish baggage and Swedish soldiers. It soon became apparent the terms of the treaty would not be adhered to in a pedantic or over-punctilious manner. The clauses afforded little protection to the Swedish officers' baggage-wagons. Ornaments, costly carpets, services of gold and silver, tapestries in gold and silver thread, sable furs and leather goods all rapidly disappeared.

Countless carts and wagons acquired new owners. Their loads were shared among the Russian soldiers. The war-booty the Swedes had pirated by 'their own sweat and battle-blooded durance' on their long campaigns was lost. The robbers now were robbed.

The soldiers were subjected to somewhat mixed treatment. Some units ended up with most of their goods intact. Some were not even disarmed until a couple of days later. Others were cleaned out. Many were stripped of everything they owned, including the clothes they stood up in. Completely naked, they were tied together and 'hunted and driven like the devil' in large flocks.

As the afternoon drew on, the Swedish army began to surrender their weapons. The regiments marched up to the Russian camp. The foot were required to lay their arms before the Russian Guard. The Swedish Life Guards led the procession. The guardsmen presented arms and placed their muskets on the sandy soil. Then they struggled out of their cartridge-cases and sword harnesses. Pike Corporal Erik Smepust, serving with Oxenstierna's company, later noted sadly in his journal: 'with what heart this befell can be well conceived by one and all'.

The Swedish cavalry rode up to the place appointed. One blue-coated troop after another passed before a motionless line of Bauer's Dragoons. As they went, they threw down their swords and carbines, their guidons, and their kettle-drums. The young ensign Piper called it 'a piteous spectacle to see, and not without tears'. The clattering pile of weapons, instruments and battle-standards rose to mountainous proportions. Weaponless, the soldiers rode away in the afternoon sun. Some wept.

Down on the banks of the river Dnieper, deeds and documents from the campaign archives were being burnt. Two clerks, Granberg and Thun, set fire to voluminous stacks of paper and watched them dissolve to soot and ashes in the flames. Baltzar Thun noted that several swatches on the pyre had been drafted by the king's minister of propaganda, Olof Hermelin. In the warm air thin wreaths of smoke drifted from the piles of pamphlets and dispatches telling of Sweden's glory and power.

# EPILOGUE

What, then, do we retain of the days that are sped?
Grey memories, a dream, a shadow too soon fled,
    And a foreboding that the times of future date
    Will also speed behind us at as swift a rate.
Where are they now, whose lives on battlefields would blaze,
And they, for whom the world would quake in former days?

GEORG HENRIK VON BORNEMAN,
Swedish cavalryman captured at Perovolochna

# 'A Fist Filled with Soil'

Doubt and bitterness burgeoned among the survivors. Lieutenant Georg Henrik von Borneman was one of the many for whom the years ebbed away in captivity. He had served with the North Skåne cavalry, fought in the battle and fell into Russian hands when the regiment surrendered at Perovolochna. Early in 1711 he wrote a poem expressing his longing for home in Sweden, his desire for peace and his doubts about the war. It contains a forceful indictment of those in power:

> For what, O Kings, do ye wage wars so great,
> Waste men and realms and many lands despoil,
> Spill so much blood, and murders perpetrate?
> A hand full of dust, a fist filled with soil.

Georg Henrik never came home. At the age of 25, in the same year the poem was written, he was killed when attempting to escape.

Not many returned. Of the 23,000 made prisoner at Poltava and Perovolochna perhaps only about 4,000 saw their homes again. In some cases only a few tens came back from regiments which had departed for the field a thousand strong. As late as 1729, eight years after the end of the war and 20 after the battle, Swedish prisoners were still wending their way home. One of the very last was Guardsman Hans Appelman, who returned in 1745, after 36 years in captivity.

The few who came back found an altered Sweden. The land they had left long before had been a great power, one of the mightiest in Europe. The land they returned to was crippled and defeated, and had reverted to the secondary rank it once had held.

The battle of Poltava, and the ensuing surrender, marked an irrevocable turning-point in the war. When the long-delayed peace was finally concluded it signalled the end of the Swedish imperium. At the same time – more importantly – it confirmed the birth of a new great European power: Russia. This realm was to grow ever greater and more mighty; an empire in the lee of whose long dark shadow the Swedes would have to learn to live. In terms of world history, the people of an entire nation had left the stage and taken their seat among the spectators.

It all might well seem nothing but an evil dream, were it not still possible, excavating the fields at Poltava, to stumble on some forgotten grave, teeming with lacerated human bones. The slender fingers of the grass slacken their hold on a skull incised with sabre-cuts and grape-shot, cuneiform marks inscribed on bone, a barely decipherable legacy from another world.

# Sources and Literature

This is an historical work with a minimal academic apparatus. My justification is that I have not set out to write an account in the traditional format of academic history. An essential component of academic history is what, *pace* Nils Ahnlund, is sometimes called scaffolding; ie textual insertions of a technical, methodological, historiographic nature; causal reasoning, explanations of the grounds for certain views, statements etc. I have cleared away all this 'scaffolding', in order solely to present my conclusions and views. I am offering a structure, without explaining how I constructed it.

The original titles of Swedish works have been translated into English.

## Abbreviations

FHT    Finland's Historical Review
HH    Historical Documents concerning Scandinavian History
HT    Historical Review (Swedish)
KFÅ    Carolinian Association Year Book
KKD    Carolinian Soldiers' Journals
PHT    Biographical Review
VSLÅ    Academic Association of Lund: Year Book

## Sources

### UNPUBLISHED SOURCES

Uppsala University Library: Vol F 141.
Uppsala County Archives: Uppsala Town Archives Vol AI:25.
War Archives: Great Northern War: Dept 18; translations Vol no 6.

### PUBLISHED SOURCES

Adlerfelt, G: Journal ('Charles XII's Campaigns 1700–1716') pub S Bring. Stockholm 1919.
Agrell, S: Diary 1707–13. KKD V.
Ahlefelt, J: Service record. HH 18:3.
Ausführliche relation von der Den 27. Jun. . . . ohnweit Pultowa vorgefallenen glorieusen Bataille . . . Dresden 1709.
Bardilli, J W: Des Weyland Durchl. Printzens Maximilian Emanuels . . . Reisen und Campagnen. Stuttgart 1730.

Bielke, T G: Memoirs (Ture Gabriel Bielke's 'Reminiscences of Charles XII'). Pub C Hallendorff. Uppsala 1901.

Björck, E: Account. KKD III.

Bonde, N: Account (in Ennes, B A: 'Biographical memoirs of King Charles XII's Soldiers . . .' Vol II). Stockholm 1819.

von Borneman, G H: Poems (in 'Belles-lettres of Swedish authors from Stjernhjelm to Dalin'. Vol XI. Pub P Hanselli). Uppsala 1868.

Cederhielm, J: Letters. KKD VI.

Cederholm von Schmalensee, A: Recollections. KFÅ 1957.

Creutz, C G: Account. HH 34:2.

Dahlberg, A M: Memoirs ('The life story of a Carolinian composed by his own pen during his own lifetime') Pub R Antoni. Stockholm 1911.

Dahlberg, E: Diary. Pub A Åberg. Stockholm 1962.

von Dahlheim, C B: Service Record. PHT 1905.

De la Chapelle, J R: Een Militarisch Exercitiae Book/Or Mirror of a Regiment of an Infantry . . . Stockholm 1669.

De Laval, C M: Service record. KKD XII.

Dumky, H: Account (in Ennes, B A: 'Biographical memoirs of King Charles XII's Soldiers . . .' Vol I). Stockholm 1819.

Endliche Confirmation Der Königl. Schwedischen erlittenen grossen Niederlage . . . U.o. 1709.

von Fabrice, F E: Memoirs ('Die Memoiren des Kammerherren Friederich Ernst von Fabrice'). Pub R Grieser. Hildesheim 1956.

Floderus, G: Transactions concerning the history of King Charles XII. Stockholm 1819– 1826.

Frisk, N: Service record. HT 1891.

Förordning: Regulations and Ordinances for the Infantry . . . Reval 1701.

Gyllenkrok, A: Accounts ('Axel Gyllenkrok's accounts of the wars of Charles XII'). Pub N Sjöberg. Stockholm 1913.

Gyllenkrok, A: Account. HH 34:2.

Gyllenstierna, N: Account. KKD VIII.

Hager, F: Service record. HH 18:3.

Hierta, J: Service record. HT 1898.

Hoffman, N I: Account, KFÅ 1922.

Hultman, J D: Memoirs (in Floderus, G: 'Transactions concerning the history of King Charles XII'. Vol I). Stockholm 1819.

Hård, B: Service record. HH 18:3.

Jefferys, J: Letters. HH 35:1.

Journal de Pierre depuis L'anné 1698, jusqu'à la conclusion de la paix de Neustadt. Berlin 1773.

Kagg, L: Diary 1698–1722. HH 24.

Karl XII: Letters ('Autograph letters of King Charles XII'). Pub E Carlson. Stockholm 1893.

Karl XII: Letter ('Charles XII's communication to the Commission of Defence concerning the battle at Pultava'). HT 1888.

von Kochen, J H: Diary. KKD IV.

Krigs-Articlar: The Articles of War . . . renewed and enacted in the year 1683. Stockholm 1744.

Lambert, J: Account (in 'The History of Sweden's Apothecaries from the time of King Gustaf I to the present day' Vol I. Pub A Levertin, and others). Stockholm 1910–18.

Lewenhaupt, A L: Account. HH 34:2.

Lillienwald, L G: Account. PHT 1902.

Lyth, J M: Diary 1703–1722. KKD III.

Meijerfelt, J A: Account (in Villius, H: 'Charles XII's Russian campaign. Source studies'). Pub H Villius. Lund 1951.

Norsberg, J M: Diary 1707–1710. KKD III.

Oxe, H: Poems (in 'Belles-lettres of Swedish authors from Stjernhjelm to Dalin'. Vol XI. Pub P Hanselli). Uppsala 1868.

Petré, R: Diary 1702–1709. KKD I.

Pihlström, A: Diary 1708–1723. HH 18:4.

Piper, C: Diary 1709–1714. HH 21:1.

Piper, G A: Memoirs ('County Governor Gustaf Abraham Piper's recollections of his imprisonment in Russia and Charles XII's Russian campaign'). Pub K G Westman. Stockholm 1902.

Poniatowski, S C: Memoirs ('Stanislaus Poniatowski's account of his fortunes with Charles XII'). HT 1890.

Posse, C M: Diary 1707–1709. KKD I.

Posse, C M: Letters ('From the correspondence of Baron Carl Magnus Posse'). HT 1882.

Ramsvärd, A: Account. HH 34:2.

von Roland, C: Memoirs ('Recollections of captivity in Russia and the wars of Charles XII'). Pub S Bring. Stockholm 1914.

Roos, C G: Account. HH 34:2.

Schmidt, J C: Der Russische Robinson eine wahre Geschichte. Erster Theil. Greiz 1781.

Schultz, J: Diary. KFÅ 1948.

Schönström, P: Account ('Charles XII in the Ukraine. The account of a Carolinian'). Pub C Hallendorff. Stockholm 1915.

von Siltmann, D N: Letters ('Some documents from David Natanael von Siltman's hand touching the Swedish army's operations 1708–1709'). KFÅ 1937.

von Siltman, D N: Diary 1708–1709. KKD III.

Siöman, J O: Diary (in 'Miscellany in honour of Theodor Hjelmqvist'). Lund 1926.

Smepust, E L: Diary. KKD III.

Sparre, C: Memoirs (in 'The New Swedish Library'. Vol I. Pub Gjörwell, CC). Stockholm 1762.

Sperling, C H P: Diary 1700–1710. KKD III.

Spåre, H: Diary. KKD VII.

Stenbock, M (& Stenbock E): An exchange of correspondence. Vols I–II. Pub C M Stenbock. Stockholm 1913–1914.

Stiernhielm, G: Poems. Stockholm 1981.

Taube, W L: Service record. HH 34:1.

Tiesensten, L M: Account. HH 18:3.

Trudy Imperatorskago Russkago Voenno-Istoritjeskago obsjtjestva. Vol III. St Petersburg 1909.

Umständlicher, glaubwürdiger und ausführlicher Bericht, Der unglücklichen Schwedischen Niederlage bey Pultawa . . . Breslau (?) 1710.

Wallberg, J: Account. KKD 7.

von Weihe, F C: Diary. HH 19:1.

Westerman, A: Memoirs. KKD VII.

Vollständige Nachricht von dem Siegreichen Treffen . . . zwischen Poltawa und Potruka . . . Dresden 1709.

Öller, G: Account. HH 34:2.

The source situation with respect to the Russian campaign is somewhat singular. As the Swedish field chancellery disappeared at the time of the capitulation, official Swedish material and certain kinds of record are almost wholly lacking. By and large, all that remains are a number of narratives written by various participants in the war: the authors range from baggage-lads and corporals to generals. They are of very disparate value and character. Following Hans Villius

(*The Russian Campaign of Charles XII. Source Studies*; Lund 1951), they can be split into different groups.

First we have a variety of contemporaneous sources: letters, diaries and bulletins. This category presents a number of different problems. The bulletins are as a rule highly propagandistic and thus unreliable. The diaries are in part interdependent and often marred by pro-Swedish bias. The danger of interception caused some degree of censorship in the letters.

A second group comprises all those journals which were edited and worked over afterwards. In these too, considerable consanguinity can be detected – which naturally makes it very difficult to let one journal unreservedly confirm the assertions of another. Villius is of the opinion that this interdependence derives mainly from the authors' access to official material, which they incorporated in their journals. Gunnar T Westin (*Journals as Sources for Charles XII's Russian Campaign*; KFÅ 1953) maintains that in the final analysis the interrelationships can be traced to orders of the day which he assumes were posted in the field chancellery during the campaign. Eric Tengberg (*Charles XII in the Ukraine. Studies Concerning the Final Phase of the Russian Campaign*; Stockholm 1958) has strongly queried if it is really possible to detect such widespread interrelationship between journals as is conjectured, and finds it difficult to believe that there were any orders of the day at all (no such document has been preserved, or is even mentioned in the sources). My personal judgement is that the problem of interrelationship (which in this case I find somewhat over-emphasized – precisely these dependency criteria are otherwise one of the favourite hobby-horses of the strict source criticism of the Weibull school) is less acute in the case of the battle than in the campaign as a whole. Only minor parts of the interrelationships have arisen during later re-working and they mainly derive from the influence of official material – perhaps orders of the day – as the campaign progressed. It is very improbable however, not to say impossible to imagine, that there was time during the few tumultuous days after the conflict to produce any 'official material' at all, which could later be used in subsequent re-workings. In the latter case writers would surely as a rule have had to have recourse to their personal recollections.

A third important group comprises all the various accounts, memoirs and service records. Their detail, compass and value varies considerably. They are frequently tendentious; they incline to self-exculpation – members of the high command seek to dissociate themselves from all responsibility for the disaster – or self-glorification. (Biased material need not however be completely worthless. In certain cases where the bias is obvious and easy to expose it can be exploited: eg it can be inverted in order to guess what uncomfortable truths the author is attempting to conceal.) It has to be added that in order to extract from this unusually unmanageable midden of sources (more or less contemporaneous, more or less biased, more or less interdependent), 'wie es eigentlich gewesen ist', in the phrase used by old Leopold von Ranke, something more than pure source-criticism is required. What is needed is fact-criticism, a term coined by the German historian Hans Delbrück. The sources have to be subjected to various kinds of logical and factual criticism in order to ascertain whether their contents are possible or probable, and to obtain further guidance when weighing various assertions against each other.

## Literature

### MISCELLANEOUS GENERAL SURVEYS

Carlson, E: History of Sweden under the Kings of the House of Palatine. Vol VIII. History of Sweden under the rule of Charles XII. Part Three. Stockholm 1910.

The History of Sweden. Vol VIII. Charles XII, the fall of the imperium. Arvid Horn, general of peace. Stockholm 1980.

The General Staff: Charles XII on the battlefield. Carolinian field leadership in the context of the evolution of battle tactics from earliest times. Vols II–IV. Stockholm 1918–19.

Hatton, R M: Charles XII of Sweden. (In Swedish translation.) Köping 1985.

Rosén, J: Swedish history. Vol I. Lund 1978.

Rosén 1978 and *The History of Sweden* can be looked on as basic surveys. Carlson 1910 is rather antiquated but nevertheless stands up surprisingly well. *Charles XII on the Battlefield* is a monumental work, difficult not to be impressed by, but thoroughly criticized for its bias and its often contorted construction (those interested in the tactics of the time, the campaign or the battle will nevertheless find it an opus impossible to ignore or dispense with). Hatton's book could justifiably be classified as a biography but its greatest value is probably as a detailed and thorough synthesis of modern research on the epoch. (It is worth mentioning that my own categorization of a work under a particular heading reflects my personal use of it, and should not be regarded as a general classification – many works could be categorized under several different headings. Nor is this index a bibliography in the true sense of the word, but includes only the works I have had recourse to.)

### THE IMPERIUM AND THE GREAT NORTHERN WAR

Anderson, P: The evolution of the absolute state. Malmö 1978.

Attman, A: The Russian market in 16th century Baltic politics 1558–1595. Lund 1944.

Bring, S (Ed): Charles XII. On the 200th anniversary of his death. Stockholm 1918.

Cavallie, J: From peace to war. Financial problems at the outbreak of war in 1700. Uppsala 1975.

Delbrück, H: Eintritt Russlands in den westeuropäischen Kulturkreis und der Nordische Krieg. KFÅ 1927.

Elmroth, I: For king and country. Studies in the demography and civil function of the Swedish aristocracy 1600–1900. Lund 1981.

Englund, P: The Carolinian mentality. Ideology, attitude and myth in the Swedish officer corps 1700–1721. Unpublished thesis. Historical institute. Uppsala 1982.

Heckscher, E F: Swedish life and work. From the middle ages to the present. Stockholm 1971.

Hildebrand, K-G: Economic aims of Swedish expansionary policies 1700–1709 (in 'History surrounding Charles XII'. Ed G Jonasson). Stockholm 1964.

Jonasson, G: Charles XII and his advisors. The struggle for power in Swedish foreign policy 1697–1702. Stockholm 1968.

Kan, A: History of Scandinavia. Moscow 1981.

Konopczynski, W: Charles XII and Poland. KFÅ 1924.

Lindgren, J: The Swedish military state 1560–1720 (in 'Magtstaten i Norden i 1600-tallet og de sociale konsekvenser. Rapporter til den XIX nordiske historikerkongres Odense 1984.' Bd I). Odense, Denmark 1984.

Lindroth, S: Swedish educational history. The age of greatness. Stockholm 1975.

Lövgren B: Origins of the class war. A contribution to domestic Swedish political history under Queen Christina. Uppsala 1915.

Munthe, S A: Charles XII and Russian sea power. Vols I–II. Stockholm 1924–25.

Porfiriev, I E: Peter I. Founder of the art of war of the Russian regular army and fleet. Stockholm 1958.

Roberts, M: The Swedish Imperial Experience 1560–1718. (In Swedish translation.) Stockholm 1980.

Roberts, M: Sweden and Europe. Studies in Swedish history. Stockholm 1969.

Rosén, J: The history of Swedish foreign policy. Vol 2:I. 1697–1721. Lund 1952.

Schück, H (& Warburg, K): Illustrated Swedish literary history. Second part. The age of reformation and greatness. Stockholm 1927.

Sjögren, O: The war of defence in Livonia 1701 and 1702. Stockholm 1883.

Strindberg, A: Peasant distress and dreams of greatness. Helsinki 1971.

Sweden's Age of Greatness 1632–1718. (Ed M Roberts). London 1973.

Valentin, H: The house of nobility in the age of freedom. Commentary on its character. Stockholm 1915.

Wikander, J G: Survey of Swedish wars during the 18th century. Stockholm 1922.

Wittrock, G: State Treasurer Gustaf Bonde's political programme 1661. HT 1913.

Åberg, A: The Swedish Army, from Lützen to Narva (in 'Sweden's Age of Greatness 1632–1718'. Ed M Roberts). London 1973.

Åberg, A: The Carolinians and the Orient. Stockholm 1967.

A broad introduction to the various schools of thought and other literature dealing with the Swedish imperium is given in Roberts 1980. The anthology, *Sweden's Age of Greatness 1632–1718* contains several inspired essays by modern researchers on central problems of the history of this era. Attman was in its time a pioneering work which stresses the trade and politico-economic themes in the policies pursued. Anderson and Strindberg are very different in spirit, but both excellent instances of ways of looking at historical material – and also well exemplify the breadth of attitudes. (A picture of the Age of Greatness drawn from more modern Swedish historical material can be found in Lindgren's writing – modest in compass but intelligent.) The reader looking for a work which, in a more than excellent manner, sums up many of the points of view expressed in the re-evaluation of Charles XII, ought to turn to Bring's great anthology. In Munthe's exciting and for its time iconoclastic multi-volume work there are many interesting digressive analyses – *inter alia* his rapid sketch of Charles XII's personality, which seems to me almost unsurpassed in equivalent format. Konopczynski and Porfiriev offer an opportunity of seeing events through non-Swedish eyes; the latter's work was unfortunately written in the Soviet Union under Stalin and therefore contains a great deal of rubbish.

## THE RUSSIAN CAMPAIGN

Artéus, G: Theory of war and historical interpretation. I. Concerning Charles XII's Russian campaign. Uppsala 1970.

Hallendorff, C: Charles XII and Lewenhaupt 1708. Uppsala 1902.

Hildebrand, K G: Concerning the history of public perception of Charles XII. HT 1954–1955.

Jackson, W G F: Seven Roads to Moscow. London 1957.

Kostomarov, N: Mazeppa and Charles XII. HT 1883.

Kuylenstierna, O: Concerning Charles XII. Carolinian studies. Stockholm 1918.
Nilsson, S A: Turko-Swedish connections before Poltava. Scandia Vol XXII 1953–1954.
Stille, A: The campaign plans of Charles XII 1707–1709. Lund 1908.
Tarle, E: Charles XII and Poltava. Stockholm 1951.
Tarle, E: La guerre du Nord et l'invasion suédoise en Russie. Vol II. Moscow 1966.
Wernstedt, F: Contributions to knowledge of the strength of the Swedish main army during the campaign against Russia 1707–1709. KFÅ 1931.
Villius, H: Charles XII's Russian campaign. Source studies. Lund 1951.

Principally because of the source material problems mentioned above, but also because of changing external evaluations of Charles XII and his policies, this decisive phase of the war has been assessed very differently by different researchers. Many theories and schools have come and gone during the course of the years (for a survey of the historiography of the campaign see Hildebrand 1954–1955 and Artéus 1970). Hallendorff 1902 and especially Stille 1908 were in their time pioneering works, which vigorously broke with the critical attitudes of the 'old school' towards Charles XII, and called attention to the genius of his generalship (the line of this 'new school' later came to culmination in the General Staff opus). Good accounts of the campaign can be found in many of the general reviews mentioned; perhaps Hatton's can be singled out among these, since it contains a couple of important new items, and what amounts to a summing up of modern viewpoints.

## THE BATTLE, THE RETREAT AND THE CAPITULATION

Carlsson, E: Charles XII and the capitulation at Perovolochna. KFÅ 1940.
Carlsson, E: The planning of the battle of Poltava by Swedish headquarters. A comparison of literature and sources. KFÅ 1947.
Carlson, F F: The battle of Poltava and its military-historical pre-conditions according to contemporary sources (in 'Historical studies'. A miscellany in honour of Carl Gustaf Malmström). Stockholm 1897.
Creasy, E S: The Fifteen Decisive Battles of the Western World. London 1962.
Fuller, J F C: The Decisive Battles of the Western World. Vol II. London 1955.
Gejvall, N G: Skeletal finds at Poltava (Bulletin XVIII from the Royal Army Museum). Stockholm 1957.
Granberg, W: The redoubts at the battle of Poltava according to Russian sources and Russian academic military literature. KFÅ 1961.
Hedberg, J (& Medvedjev, G): The artillery – a decisive factor at the battle of Poltava. KFÅ 1961.
Jensen, A: The battle of Poltava described in a contemporary verse chronicle. HT 1907.
Johansson, U: A 'horse theft' at Poltava – and the judicial consequences. KFÅ 1979–80.
Kleen, W: The strategic context of the battle of Poltava. Some comments. KFÅ 1949.
Pavlovskij, I: Bitva pod Poltavoj. Poltava 1909.
Petrelli, T J: A few pages from a Russian diary of 1709. KFÅ 1910.
Petri, G: Revised judgement. KFÅ 1951.
Petri, G: The battle of Poltava. KFÅ 1958.
Tengberg, E: Charles XII in the Ukraine. Studies relating to the last phase of the Russian campaign. (Historical archive 7). Stockholm 1958.
Tengberg, E: Charles XII in the Ukraine in the spring of 1709. KFÅ 1948.
Villius, H: Before Poltava. VSLÅ 1951.
Villius, H: Peter the Great's decision to cross the Vorskla. KFÅ 1948.

The battle and the retreat have also been assessed very differently by different researchers. The two classic accounts of the battle of Poltava are Carlson 1897 and the General Staff opus, vol III. A couple of modern accounts are Tengberg 1958 and Petri the same year. Of these two works Petri's is the more important, even if he, like many others, tends to overvalue the importance of the king. Tengberg is slightly superficial in connection with the battle and only becomes really interesting when dealing with the capitulation – even if he then fails to make the actions of the participants plausible. Carlsson 1940 is a praiseworthy account of the retreat which killed off many myths in its time but which unfortunately does not handle the capitulation *per se*. Villius 1948 and 1951 – which take against Carlson 1947 and Tengberg 1946 – and Kleen clarify a great deal concerning the strategic situation in an excellent style. Hedberg and Granberg are two laudable detailed studies, which to a great extent fall back on more recent Russian research. (For a very good survey of the historiography surrounding this much-discussed battle see the afore-mentioned Artéus 1970.) Two easily accessible Russian accounts are Porfiriev and Tarle 1966 (both are unfortunately fairly dependent on the unreliable Russian Poltava diary, so-called, which was edited by Petrelli 1910).

## TACTICS, WEAPONS AND BATTLEFIELD CONDITIONS

Alm, J: Hand guns. Vol I. Stockholm 1933.

Artéus, G: Carolinian and European battle tactics 1700–1712. (War theory and historical explication II). Lidköping 1972.

Canetti, E: Crowds and Power. Harmondsworth 1981. (Swedish translation: Helsingborg 1985.)

Catton, B: Mr Lincoln's Army. New York 1951.

Cederlöf, O: A survey of weapons from ancient times to the end of the 19th century. Stockholm 1965.

von Clausewitz, C: On War. Harmondsworth 1974.

The Danish General Staff: Contributions to the history of the great Northern war. Vol I. Copenhagen 1900.

Delbrück, H: Geschichte der Kriegskunst im Rahmen der politischen Geschichte. Vierter Teil. Neuzeit, Berlin 1920.

Ericson, L (& Sandstedt, F): Men of the flag. The soldiers of the Swedish army during the first half of the 17th century. Stockholm 1982.

Griffith, P: Forward into Battle. Fighting Tactics from Waterloo to Vietnam. Strettington 1981.

Hemingway, E: The biology of the dead (in 'Satire. II. From Byron to Dagerman'. Pub B Holmqvist). Stockholm 1966.

Holmes, R: Firing Line. London 1987.

Hornborg, E: The war. Presented in accounts from more recent times. Helsinki 1921.

Hornborg, E: The Carolinian Armfelt and the struggle for Finland during the Great Northern War. Helsinki 1952.

Howard, M: War in European History. Oxford 1979.

Keegan, J: The Face of Battle. Harmondsworth 1983.

Lewis, L: Shiloh, Bloody Shiloh (in 'Men at War', Ed E. Hemingway). New York 1958.

*Lärobok*: Instructions in care of the sick for the armed services. Södertälje 1976.

Marshall, S L A: Soldiers in war. Stockholm 1952.

Meinander, K K: Swedish standards captured at Ljesna and Poltava. FHT 1921.

Montgomery, B L: History of the art of war. (In Swedish translation). Lund 1969.

Nordensvan, C O: The Swedish army in the years 1700–1709. KFÅ 1916.
Nordensvan, C O: On the road to Sweden's age of greatness. A chronicle of the times of Charles XI. Stockholm 1924.
Tingsten, L: Fundamentals of the art of war in the middle ages and new and more recent times. Stockholm 1928.
Törnquist, L: From banners to signals of command. A survey of Finnish and Swedish banners and standards through the ages, in Bulletin XXXVIII of the Army museum 1977–78.
Wernstedt, F: Linear tactics and Carolinian tactics. Reflections arising from the presentation in 'Charles XII on the Battlefield'. KFÅ 1957.
Åberg, A (& Göransson, G): The Carolinians. Höganäs. 1976.

With regard to formal tactics, Artéus 1972 has to be singled out as especially valuable for its detailed comparison of different armies of the period. It is also – with Wernstedt 1957 – an important corrective to many of the theses of the Swedish General Staff opus on these matters. (The General Staff opus nevertheless contains much nutritious information on tactics, organization and weapons.) There are intelligent and perspicacious analyses of contemporary modes of fighting and the mysterious psychology of battle in Hornborg's two works. Keegan contains an exciting discussion of the problems attendant on the writing of war history and also offers a new analysis model which has its points but which probably cannot be applied as universally as the author would like to think. Griffith's book contains many useful insights, but unfortunately he often tends to over-interpret his instances. (Both Keegan and Griffith stress the role of morale in battle in a very helpful way.) Canetti's fascinating work contains many observations which help to a better understanding of certain events during the battle and the retreat.

## BIOGRAPHICALLY ORIENTED WORKS

Bengtsson, F G: The life of Charles XII. Vols I–II. Malmö 1980.
Ennes, B A: Biographical memoirs of King Charles XII's soldiers . . . Vols I–II. Stockholm 1819.
Jarring, G: Brigitta Scherzenfeldt and her captivity among the Kalmucks. KFÅ 1983.
Kentrschynskyj, B: Mazepa. Stockholm 1962.
Lewenhaupt, A: The Carolinian Edvard Gyldenstolpe. Stockholm 1941.
Lewenhaupt, A: Charles XII's officers. Biographical notes. Vols I–II. Stockholm 1920–1921.
Massie, R K: Peter the Great. His life and world. (In Swedish translation) Stockholm 1986.
Modin, E (& Söderberg, E N): Register of northerners studying at Uppsala 1595–1889. Stockholm 1890.
Nordberg, J: History of King Charles XII. Stockholm 1740.
P-G, W: The Carolinian Georg Planting-Gyllenboga. PHT 1904.
Sandklef, A (et al): The death of Charles XII. Stockholm 1942–1945.
Swedish men and women. Biographical dictionary. Stockholm 1942–1945.
Swedish biographical dictionary. Stockholm 1918–.
Troyat, P: Peter the Great. Stockholm 1981.
Uddgren, H E: The Carolinian Adam Ludvig Lewenhaupt. Vols I–II. Stockholm & Uddevalla 1919–1950.
Uddgren, H E: The Carolinian Hugo Johan Hamilton. A biography. (Publications of the Hamilton family association II.) Stockholm 1916.

Waller, S M: Was Olof Hermelin captured at Poltava ? Russian accounts in a critical light. KFÅ 1955.
VD, N: Two Carolinians. PHT 1900.
de Voltaire, F M A: Charles XII. Stockholm 1961.

Lewenhaupt's two-volume work of 1920–1921 is yet another of those remarkable catalogue-type creations, which astound the reader that anyone had the energy to compile, but which are nevertheless relied on avidly and thereby fill their users with quiet gratitude towards all the world's calendar addicts and accumulators of useless information. Ennes can be thought of as his elder precursor: a very idiosyncratic work which contains numerous bits of information and references but which is unreliable. The Swedish *Dictionary of Biography* and *Swedish Men and Women* contain many excellent biographical sketches. Uddgren's account of Lewenhaupt has its merits, but often degenerates into a banal apologia – the most common failing of biographers. The author also misses much of the interesting complexity in Lewenhaupt's composite personality. The greatest value of Kentrschynskyj's book is not in the biographical area, but in its compassionate account of the role of the Cossacks in the drama. Bengtsson's justifiably well-known work is perhaps the most brilliant biography ever written in the Swedish language, but the shadow of the General Staff opus at times lies heavily over a presentation which has certain lacunae when looked on as pure history (the account of the battle nevertheless belongs to the more unimpeachable sections.) Massie's blockbuster is an ambitious project which has not completely reached fulfilment: he can be both careless and remarkably uncritical. His book can, like Bengtsson's, be read as a competent overview. Old Nordberg's history contains certain interesting points of detail.

## REGIMENTAL HISTORIES

Bensow, E: History of the Royal Skaraborg regiment. Vol II. Göteborg 1944.
Braunerhjelm, C A G: History of the Royal Mounted Life regiment. Vol III. Uppsala 1914.
Sparre, S A: History of the Royal Västmanland regiment. Vol IV. Stockholm 1930.
Tidander, L G T: Notes concerning the history of the Royal Kronoberg regiment. Karlshamn 1897.
Tidander, L G T: Notes concerning the history of the Royal Jönköping regiment. 2nd ed. Västerås 1916.
Zeeh, E: History of the Royal Värmland regiment, later edition 1617–1950. Karlstad 1951.

There are an incredible number of regimental histories and similar works and this is just a small selection. They vary as a rule from very mediocre, such as Tidander's two works, to solid, as Bensow for example – which is sometimes ponderously sentimental, however. Braunerhjelm is detailed and contains a good deal of technical information. Perhaps the greatest merit of both Sparre and Zeeh lies in the biographical details they provide.

# Biographical Appendix

*(Translator's compilation)*

The following brief biographies may help to answer readers' questions on the careers and final destinies of most, if not all, of the persons mentioned in *The Battle of Poltava*. The list is not representative of the up to 19,000 Swedes, mainly rank and file, who never returned from Russia. The great majority died from privation in forced labour, or ended their lives as serfs. The more resilient or better educated of the officers scraped a living as teachers, founded schools, or turned their hands to carpentry or tailoring. A very small number entered the service of the Tsar and one or two came to prominence.

The details given are drawn almost entirely from *Karl XII:s Officerare*, by Adam Lewenhaupt, (1920–21), and *Svenska Män och Kvinnor*, a Swedish dictionary of biography. A vignette of the fate of the more fortunate of the Swedish officers in captivity can be found in the fragmentary last chapter of Pushkin's unfinished novel *The Negro of Peter the Great* (included in *The Queen of Spades and other stories*, Penguin Classics).

**Adlerfelt:** Gustaf, 1671–1709, Student at Uppsala university 1684, travelled in Europe 1696–1700, at Halle university 1700, appointed historiographer to Charles XII 1701, accompanied king on subsequent campaigns, author of work published and translated several times during C18th. Amplified edition by his son, Carl Adlerfelt, published 1740: *Histoire militaire de Charles XII, roi de Suède*.

**Agrell:** Sven, 1685–1713, student at Lund university 1702, joined Swedish army on campaign in 1707, ordained 1709, battalion chaplain with the Kronoberg regiment, accompanied king to Bender, 2nd legation chaplain at the embassy in Constantinople, died and buried in Adrianopolis. His diary 1707–1713.

**Ahlefeldt:** Johan, d.1732, Standard-Bearer with Mentzer's Battalion 1678, Ensign with Modée's regiment 1683, Dutch service with Prince of Orange's Guard 1683–1686, Gamekeeper in Sweden 1688, Ensign with Närke-Värmland regiment 1695, Lieutenant 1699, Captain 1703, captured at Poltava but released, Major 1711, Lieutenant-Colonel Värmland militia 1714, Colonel 1717.

**d'Albedyhl:** Christer Henrik, 1679–1750, Second-Lieutenant in Polish service 1699, Drabant 1700, Marshal at the Warsaw embassy 1703, Lance-Corporal with the Drabants 1705, Corporal 1708, followed Charles to Bender, Major-General of Cavalry 1717, Baron 1720, Colonel of the Jönköping regiment 1725, Provincial Governor of Östergötland 1736, retired 1747.

**Appelbom:** Mårten, d.1709, Volunteer with Life Guard 1692, Standard-Bearer with Uppland infantry 1693, Sergeant 1696, Sergeant-Major 1698, Ensign 1700, Quartermaster 1702, Captain 1703, fell at Poltava.

**Appelgren:** Anders, 1670–1716, Lieutenant of Fortifications 1693, Ensign with Life Guard

1694, Lieutenant 1696, Captain 1700, Major 1706, Colonel of Östgöta regiment 1709, captured at Perovolochna, died in Moscow.

**Appelman:** Hans, Guardsman, last Swedish soldier to return to Sweden from Russian captivity, in 1745.

**Apraxin:** Count Fyodor, 1671–1728, creator of Russian Navy and favourite of Peter the Great, charged with embezzlement 1714 and 1718 and fined, but too useful to the Tsar to be dispensed with.

**(Frederick) Augustus II 'the Strong':** 1670–1733, King of Poland, Elector of Saxony, attacked Riga 1700, forced to abdicate by Charles XII in 1706, reclaimed the Polish throne in 1709.

**Bauer:** Adolf Rudolf (Rodion) Fredrik, 1667–1718, Holsteiner in Russian service, General of Cavalry, participated in the Ukrainian campaign, secured Livonia, died as commander of the Ukraine.

**von Baumgarten:** Nils-Christer, 1674–1727, Musketeer with Wellingk's regiment 1687, Corporal 1689, Sergeant with Dutch Blue Guard 1698, Drabant in Sweden same year, Lance-Corporal with Drabants 1708, followed Charles to Bender 1709, ennobled 1712, Colonel of Swedish Adelsfana 1717, fought in 18 battles, wounded 5 times, gave Charles XII his horse at battle of Stresow 1715.

**Behr (Bähr):** Johan, 1673–1742, Volunteer with Erskin's Swedish Regiment in Holland 1689, Ensign with Swedish troops in Dutch service 1692, Ensign Närke-Värmland Regiment 1695, Lieutenant & Captain 1700, Major 1706, captured at Poltava, returned 1722, Lieutenant-Colonel 1737, Commandant of Elfsborg 1740.

**Belau (Below):** Jacob Fredrik, 1669–1716, born into medical family of German origin, Student at Uppsala university 1680, Utrecht university 1691, Professor of Medicine Dorpat Academy 1695, Rector of Dorpat 1696–97, Professor at Lund university 1697, appointed Royal Physician to Charles XII 1706, captured at Poltava, subsequently practised medicine in Moscow.

**Bennet:** Wilhelm, 1677–1740, born in Åbo, Finland, of Scottish father, volunteer in Riga 1693, Cornet with Albedyhl's Regiment 1700, Grenadier Captain 1704, Major with Kronoberg Regiment 1709, accompanied king to Bender, sent to Sweden with despatches 1709, Lieutenant-Colonel Mounted Uppland Femmänning 1709, Major-General of Cavalry 1717, Baron 1719, Commandant of Malmö 1737.

**Bernow:** Mats, d.1703, Standard-Bearer with Life Guard 1699, married Brigitta Scherzenfeldt, fell at siege of Thorn.

**Bielke:** Count Thure Gabriel, 1684–1763, Volunteer with Mounted Life regiment 1704, Second Cornet 1705, Lieutenant 1706, wounded at Poltava, followed king to Bender, Colonel of Bohuslän Dragoons 1716, Major-General of Cavalry 1719, Minister in Vienna 1719, Parliamentary Councillor 1727; married 1715 daughter of First Minister Carl Piper.

**Blum:** Johan, b.1674 in Livonia, d. after 1727, Volunteer with Saxon troops of the Emperor 1695, Cornet in Polish service 1697, Ensign with Tiesenhausen's regiment in Sweden 1700, Lieutenant of Mounted Life regiment 1701, Captain 1704, captured at Perovolochna 1709, escaped and returned to Stockholm 1714, Major 1715, Lieutenant-Colonel's rank with Jämtland's Cavalry company 1719, retired 1727.

**Blyberg:** Jonas, 1669–1709, joined artillery 1687, Ensign with Närke-Värmland Infantry 1702, Ensign with Field Artillery 1704, fell at Poltava.

**Bonde:** Count Gustaf, 1620–1667, President of the Judicial Board for Public Lands and Funds 1660, State Treasurer, advocated peace and financial restraint, regarded foreign wars as wasteful of resources and a cause of state financial difficulties.

**Bonde:** Count Nils, 1685–1760, Student at Åbo University 1695, Student at Tübingen 1702, Lieutenant with Bremisch infantry 1703, Lieutenant-Captain 1705, Captain with Life Dragoons 1708, captured at Perovolochna, returned home 1723, retired 1723, County Governor in Södermanland 1730.

**von Borneman:** Georg Henrik, 1685–1711, Cornet with North Skåne Cavalry 1706, Second-Lieutenant 1706, captured at Perovolochna, sent to prison colony in Simbirsk, Siberia, escaped with four comrades while being transported 1711, all believed killed by band of peasants.

**von Buchwaldt:** Baron Georg, 166?–1709, Ensign with the Queen's German Life regiment 1687, Captain 1692, Adjutant-General 1702, Colonel of Riga Garrison regiment 1706, Colonel Jönköping regiment 1706, fell at Poltava.

**von Bünow:** Rudolf, 1651–1709, Musketeer with Life Guard 1671, Ensign Haren's regiment 1673, Lieutenant 1675, Lieutenant-Captain with Wulffen's regiment 1677, Captain with Count Carlsson's Artillery in Viborg 1680, Major of Artillery in Stettin 1694, Colonel 1706, captured at Perovolochna, died 4 days later on march to Moscow.

**Cederhielm:** Josias, 1673–1729, Student at Uppsala university, Steward at Peace of Ryswick 1697, Registrar of Field Chancellery 1700, present at Narva 1700, Secretary of Chancellery 1708, captured at Poltava, sent to Sweden on parole with Tsar's peace terms, returned to Moscow and remained in captivity until 1722.

**Cederholm von Schmalensee:** Abraham, 1680–1756, personal secretary to Carl Gustaf Creutz 1704, regimental Commissary to the Mounted Life regiment, captured at Perovolochna, returned home 1712, Chief Accountant at the War College.

**Charles X Gustav:** 1622–1660, 'King of Sweden, Count of the Palatinate, outstanding general, secured the present southern Swedish provinces of Skåne and Bohuslän.' (A. Åberg)

**Charles XI:** 1655–1693, 'King of Sweden, victor at battle of Lund 1676, peaceful defender of Sweden's borders, re-organized the kingdom's finances, created the Carolinian army.' (A. Åberg)

**Charles XII:** 1682–1718, 'King of Sweden, spent half his life on campaign in defence of the Swedish imperium, stubborn and fatalistic field commander, heroic figure, out of step with his era.' (A. Åberg)

**Clerckberg:** Hans, dates unknown, travelled in youth to Holland, France, Spain and England, Mate with Swedish Fleet, with Naval Ordnance at Narva 1700, Captain with Artillery 1705.

**Creutz:** Baron Carl Gustaf, 1660–1728, Page to King Charles XI 1675, Lieutenant-Captain with Mellin's Karelian cavalry regiment 1677, Captain 1679, Lieutenant with Mounted Life regiment 1682, Captain 1691, Major 1701, Lieutenant-Colonel 1703, Colonel 1704, Major-General of Cavalry 1706, captured at Perovolochna, returned 1722, General of Cavalry 1722. Fought in 16 battles.

**Creutz:** Baron Lorentz, 1687–1733, Sergeant with Life Guard, Second Cornet with Mounted Life regiment 1705, Drabant 1708, followed Charles XII to Bender, retired from Drabants 1715, (sentenced for accidental manslaughter), Captain with Mounted Life regiment 1725, Corporal with Drabants 1728, retired with Lieutenant-Colonel's rank 1731.

**Cronman:** Johan, 1662–1737, Lieutenant with Narva Garrison 1683, Second-Captain with Närke-Värmland regiment 1687, Captain with Zurlauben's regiment in French service 1694, Captain in Spanish service 1695–97, Major with Närke-Värmland regiment 1699, Lieutenant-Colonel 1701, Colonel of Kronoberg regiment 1706, captured at Perovolochna, returned 1722, Lieutenant-General of Infantry 1722, Baron 1727, County Governor of Malmöhus and Commandant of Skåne Province 1727. Fought in 13 battles, never wounded. Spoke 8 languages: Swedish, Latin, German, Estonian, Polish, Russian, French and Dutch.

**Dahlberg:** Alexander Magnus, 1685–1772, Volunteer with Närke-Värmland Tremänning infantry 1704, Dragoon with Skåne Dragoons 1705, Standard-bearer with Västerbotten regiment 1707, Sergeant 1708, Second Ensign 1709, captured at Perovolochna, escaped

1711 and served Prince Michael Ivanovich Volkonsky pretending to be German, returned to Sweden 1713, Lieutenant 1714, Second-Captain 1718, Captain 1719, Militia Major in Malmö 1742, Captain with Queen's Life regiment in Pomerania 1750, retired 1750. His memoirs: *The Life of a Carolinian.*

**von Dahldorf (Daldorff):** Johan Valentin, 1665–1715, born in Holstein, began career as trooper, said to have seen Spanish service as cavalry Lieutenant, also resided in Italy, Cornet with Bremisch cavalry 1692, retired 1697, Adjutant to Duke of Holstein 1700, Chamberlain to Charles XII 1702, Colonel of Uppland infantry 1703, Colonel of Småland cavalry 1706, Major-General of Cavalry 1709, followed king to Bender, Lieutenant-General of Cavalry 1710, General of Cavalry 1713, fell at battle of Stresow.

**von Dahlheim (Thalheim):** Carl Balthasar, 1669–1756, Volunteer in Imperial service 1683, Ensign with Hastfehr's regiment in Swedish service 1689, Lieutenant 1695, Lieutenant of Fortifications at Bremen and Verden 1702, Captain of Fortifications 1708, followed king to Bender, ennobled 1711, General Quartermaster-Lieutenant 1711, Colonel's rank 1715, captured at Stralsund 1715, returned 1718, General Quartermaster with Bohuslän army 1718, retired 1722.

**De la Gardie:** Magnus Gabriel, 1622–1686, born in Reval, Student at Uppsala university 1635, studied at Leiden, Amsterdam and in France, favourite of Queen Christina, brother-in-law to King Charles X Gustav, patron of the arts, Chancellor of the Realm, stripped of wealth and power by King Charles XI.

**De Laval:** Carl Magnus, 1680–1749, Dragoon with Bremisch Dragoons 1699, Musketeer with Kronoberg regiment 1700, Sergeant 1701, Sergeant with Life Guard 1702, Ensign 1704, Captain with Taube's Dragoons 1706, captured at Poltava, escaped and returned to Sweden 1710, Major in service of King Stanislaus of Poland 1711, Lieutenant-Colonel 1713, Lieutenant-Colonel of Västgöta cavalry 1713, Colonel of Uppland infantry regiment 1741, Colonel of Skaraborg regiment 1748.

**von Dittmar (Dittmer):** Joachim, 1681–1755, born in Narva, appointed to army Chancellery 1701, captured at Poltava, worked as Piper's secretary on behalf of Swedish prisoners in Moscow, sent to Siberia 1712, released 1722, diplomatic agent in Moscow 1724, ennobled 1727, Chancellery Councillor 1729, Envoy to Russia until 1739, Provincial Governor of Nyslott in Finland 1738–1741.

**Douglas:** Count Wilhelm, 1683–1763, Cadet in French service 1696, Ensign with Royal Allemand regiment in France 1699, Lieutenant 1701, Captain with Erik Sparre's regiment in France 1702, Lieutenant with Skaraborg regiment 1704, Lieutenant with Skåne Dragoons 1704, Captain 1705, Adjutant-General to Rehnsköld 1708, captured at Poltava, returned 1722, Captain with North Skåne cavalry 1722, Captain with South Skåne cavalry 1724, retired with Colonel's rank 1725, Major-General in Holstein-Gottorp service 1738.

**Drake:** Fredrik, 1660–1709, Pikeman with the Life Guard, Ensign with Kronoberg's regiment 1684, Lieutenant 1689, Captain with German Life regiment of foot 1698, Captain with the Life Guard 1701, Lieutenant-Colonel, fell at Poltava.

**von Düben:** Gustaf, 1659–1726, attendant to Charles XII when Crown Prince 1682, sinecure appointments as court musician from 1685, actual duties entailed acting as prince's companion, Court Steward 1698, ennobled 1698, accompanied king on all campaigns, Chamberlain 1712, Baron 1718.

**Dücker:** Carl Gustaf, 1663–1732, Cadet in French service 1688, Ensign 1689, finally Major, entered Swedish service as Adjutant-General 1700, Colonel of Dragoon regiment 1703, apparently released shortly after surrender at Perovolochna, Major-General of Cavalry 1710, Colonel of Västgöta cavalry 1710, Lieutenant-General 1711, Baron 1711, General of Cavalry 1713, Councillor of the Realm 1718, Count 1719, Governor-General of Livonia 1719, Field-Marshal 1719, President of Staff College 1720.

**Duwall:** Baron Jakob, d.1713, Musketeer with the Life Guard, Staff Sergeant 1695, Drabant 1700, Drabant Corporal 1708, Adjutant-General 1708, followed king to Bender, Colonel of South Skåne cavalry 1712, died in Bender. Of Scottish descent (Dougall).

**Eggertz:** Paul, 1687–1768, Volunteer with Kronoberg regiment 1704, Sergeant-Major 1705, Ensign 1705, Second-Lieutenant 1708, captured at Poltava, returned 1722, Captain 1722, ennobled 1731, retired as Drabant 1747.

**Ehrenklo:** Jonas, 1672–1709, Cornet North Skåne cavalry 1700, Lieutenant 1702, Second-Captain 1704, Lieutenant-Captain 1708, Captain 1709, captured at Poltava, died of his wounds a month later at Kriega.

**Ehrenskiöld:** Jan (Johan), 167?–1718, Ensign with Lewenhaupt's Swedish regiment in Holland 1688, Lieutenant Västerbotten regiment 1702, Drabant 1702, Drabant Lance-Corporal 1709, accompanied king to Bender, killed in Amsterdam on returning home 1718.

**Fehman:** Nils, 1669–1746, Sergeant-Major with Aminoff's German regiment 1689, Ensign Viborg regiment 1689, Lieutenant Uppland regiment 1700, Second-Captain 1701, captured in Poland 1704, returned 1705, Captain 1705, captured at Poltava, escaped and returned 1721, Major 1721, Lieutenant-Colonel 1722, Commandant of Dalarö 1722, retired 1731.

**Ferber:** Scottish-born officer in Russian service, Commandant at defence of Veprik 1708.

**Fock:** Gideon, 1668–1723, Private with Savolax regiment 1684, Ensign 1687, participated in Dutch war 1689–1690, Captain Närke-Värmland regiment 1694, Major 1701, Lieutenant-Colonel Västerbotten regiment 1702, Commandant in Posen 1706, Colonel Helsinge regiment 1708, captured at Poltava, returned 1722, Lieutenant-General 1722.

**Forbes af Lund:** Anders, d.1753, Ensign with Uppland regiment, Lieutenant Uppland Tremänning regiment 1700, captured at Poltava, returned to Sweden, lost both feet and three fingers of his left hand.

**Forsman:** Lars, c1662–1736, Private with Life Guard 1682, Corporal, Sergeant-Major Uppland regiment 1699, Ensign 1701, Lieutenant 1704, captured and stripped naked at Poltava, returned 1722, retired as Captain 1722.

**Frisk:** Nils, Guardsman 1709, captured at Poltava, exchanged 1710, returned to Sweden, Sergeant with Life Guard, carried king's bier at burial 1718.

**Funck:** Thomas, 1672–1713, Lieutenant-Colonel with Dücker's Dragoons 1703, followed king to Bender, Colonel of Södermanland regiment 1710, Envoy to Ottoman Porte 1711, died in Constantinople.

**Gadde:** Gustaf, 1680–1738, Pikeman with the Life Guard 1696, Ensign 1701, Lieutenant 1702, ennobled 1706, Captain 1707, captured at Poltava, exchanged shortly afterwards, Lieutenant-Colonel Närke-Värmland regiment, Commandant of Ny-Elfsborg 1716, Colonel Skaraborg regiment 1729, Colonel of Närke-Värmland regiment 1737.

**Galle i Finland:** Johan, 1664–1709, Student at Åbo University 1684, Musketeer with Life Guard 1691, Standard-Bearer 1692, Sergeant 1694, Cornet with Mounted Life regiment 1694, Lieutenant 1700, Corporal with Drabants 1704, Lieutenant-Colonel North Skåne cavalry 1707, fell at Poltava.

**von Gertten:** Arendt Johan, 1670–1709, Ensign Närke-Värmland regiment 1689, Quartermaster with Karelian cavalry 1700, Captain Helsinge regiment 1700, Major 1707, Lieutenant-Colonel 1708, fell at Poltava.

**Greek:** Nils (Johan Jakob), d.1709, foreign service, Second-Captain with Uppland Infantry regiment 1707, Captain 1708, fell at Poltava.

**Grissbach:** Georg Zacharias, d.1709, Staff Sergeant with Uppland infantry 1687, Ensign 1697, Lieutenant 1700, Captain 1701, fell at Poltava.

**Gyldenklou:** Anders Gideon, 1675–1735, Volunteer with Life Guard 1694, Drabant 1695, Cornet with Mounted Life regiment 1697, Lieutenant with Life Dragoons 1700, Captain 1702, Adjutant-General 1708, followed king to Bender, captured at Czernowitz 23/9/1709, returned 1722, Adjutant-General to King Fredrik I 1722, retired as Major-General 1734.

**Gyllenbögel:** Johan, 1678–1743, Volunteer Åbo cavalry 1700, Musketeer Life Guards 1701, Corporal 1702, Standard-Bearer 1703, Second-Lieutenant Nyland cavalry 1705, Lieutenant 1709, captured at Poltava, returned 1722, Captain 1729.

**Gyllenkrok:** Axel, 1665–1730, Private with Life Guard 1683, Sergeant 1685, Ensign 1688, Lieutenant 1693, Captain 1696, Major 1701, Lieutenant-Colonel of Life Guard 1706, Quartermaster-General 1706, accompanied king to Bender, captured at Czernowitz in Moldavia three weeks after Poltava, suffered intermittently from insanity during imprisonment in Moscow, later transported to Siberia, returned 1722, County Governor in Göteborg and Bohuslän 1723, Baron 1727. Fought in 16 battles, wounded 3 times.

**Gyllenpamp:** Johan Gabriel, 1687–1752, Volunteer with Uppland Dragoons 1703, Sergeant 1703, Aide-de-Camp 1704, Cornet 1705, Lieutenant 1707, captured at Perovolochna, returned 1722, Captain with Småland cavalry 1722, retired 1746.

**Gyllenstierna af Björkesund:** Count Nils, 1670–1731, Volunteer with Swedish troops in Holland and in French service 1690, Captain with Bohl's regiment in France 1691, Captain with North Skåne cavalry 1694, Major with Bremisch Dragoons 1698, Lieutenant-Colonel with North Skåne cavalry 1701, Colonel of own Dragoon regiment (formerly Görtz' Dragoons) 1707, captured at Perovolochna, Major-General of Cavalry 1720, Colonel of Life Dragoons 1721, Lieutenant-General and returned 1722, County Governor in Södermanland 1723, State Councillor 1727.

**Gyllenstierna af Ulaborg:** Baron Erik, 1678–1709, Ensign with Life Guard 1697, Lieutenant 1700, Captain 1702, Major 1708, fell at Poltava.

**Gynterfelt:** Karl Gustav, 1672–1738, Chamberlain, Royal Stablemaster on campaign.

**Hager:** Frans, 1681–after 1737, Volunteer with Småland cavalry 1706, Second-Corporal 1706, Quartermaster 1708, captured at Perovolochna, escaped 1715, Lieutenant with Småland cavalry 1716, Captain 1718, retired 1719, returned to army and still in service 1737.

**von Hallart:** Baron Ludvig Nikolaus, of Saxon birth, Lieutenant-General in Russian service.

**Hamilton af Hageby:** Baron Hugo Johan: 166?–1748, Ensign Elfsborg regiment 1683, Ensign Life Guard 1691, Lieutenant 1692, Captain 1695, Lieutenant-Colonel Life Dragoons 1700, Colonel of Östgöta cavalry and Major-General of Cavalry 1708, captured at Poltava, Lieutenant-General of Cavalry from 1720, returned 1722, Field-Marshal 1734, retired 1746.

**Hanck:** Fredrik, dates unknown, Corporal with Uppland infantry, Staff Sergeant 1701, Sergeant 1702, Adjutant 1703, Ensign 1706, Second-Lieutenant 1709, Captured at Poltava, died in captivity in Saranski.

**Hård:** Carl Gustaf, 1674–1744, student at Lund university 1684, Ensign with Life Guard 1696, entered French service, Drabant Corporal 1700, Cavalry Adjutant-General 1703, Colonel of Västgöta Dragoons 1706, Lieutenant of Drabants 1706, escaped with king to Bender 1709, Major-General of Cavalry and Lieutenant-Captain (ie the senior rank) of Drabants 1710, Baron 1710, Lieutenant-General 1713, General of Cavalry 1717, Governor-General of Skåne, Governor of Malmöhus 1719, Councillor of the Realm 1727, Count 1731.

**Hård af Segerstad:** Jesper Abraham, 1682–1733, entered army 1698, Standard-Bearer with Life Guard, Ensign with German Life regiment 1703, Second-Lieutenant Södermanland regiment 1704, Lieutenant 1706, Quartermaster 1708, Second-Captain 1708, captured at Poltava, returned 1722, Captain Skaraborg regiment, retired 1731.

**Hermelin:** Olof Nilsson Skragge, 1658–1709, Professor of Rhetoric and Poetry at Dorpat Academy 1689, Professor of Roman and Swedish Law 1699, his reply to the manifesto of Tsar Peter the Great and King Augustus of Poland against Sweden at outbreak of war in 1700 attracted attention of Charles XII, appointed State Secretary and historiographer 1701, called to army headquarters 1702, ennobled 1705, according to tradition killed by the Tsar after capture at Poltava.

**Hielm:** Nils, 1667–1726, Volunteer with Life Guard 1687, Sergeant-Major with Lewenhaupt's regiment in Holland 1688, Ensign 1695, retired 1697, Drabant 1700, Drabant Corporal 1701, cavalry Adjutant-General, Colonel of (formerly Stenbock's) Dragoons 1706, ennobled 1706, captured at Perovolochna, returned 1722, Lieutenant-Colonel of Västmanland regiment and Major-General's rank 1722.

**Hierta (Gierta):** Adam, 1674–1739, born in Ingria, Volunteer with von Funcken's regiment in Narva 1689, Volunteer with Life Guard 1694, Drabant 1697, Drabant Lance-Corporal 1708, accompanied king to Bender, ennobled 1710, Drabant Corporal 1711, Lieutenant-Colonel with Karelian Dragoons 1714, Court Chamberlain 1714, Colonel 1721, Colonel of Kymmenegård's battalion 1721, Colonel of Kalmar regiment 1739.

**Hierta (Gierta):** Christian, 1671–1746, born in Narva, Musketeer with von Funcken's regiment 1688, NCO 1688, Drabant 1694, Lance-Corporal 1706, Corporal 1708, accompanied king to Bender, ennobled 1710, Lieutenant-Colonel with Skåne Dragoons 1714, Second Colonel 1720, Colonel of Björneborg regiment 1722, retired as Major-General 1741.

**Hierta (Gierta):** Johan, 1666–1740, Musketeer with von Funcken's regiment in Narva 1679, Drabant 1687, French service 1695, Drabant Corporal 1700. Colonel's rank and Lieutenant with Drabants 1708, accompanied king to Bender, ennobled 1710, Major-General of Cavalry 1713, captured at Stralsund 1715, returned 1717, Baron 1719, Lieutenant-General 1717, President of War College 1732.

**von Holden:** Erik Johan, d.1722, born in Livonia, Staff Sergeant with Tavastehus infantry 1677, Standard-Bearer, Corporal with Pahlen's Livonian Cavalry 1677, Cornet 1678, Lieutenant 1679, Lieutenant with Queen's Mounted Life regiment 1681, Captain with Björneborg Dragoons 1695, Captain with Åbo and Björneborg cavalry 1698, Major 1707, captured at Perovolochna, returned 1721 to Åbo.

**Holstein-Gottorp:** Duke Fredrik IV of, 1671–1702, married Princess Hedvig Sophia of Sweden (Charles XII's sister) 1698, Generalissimus of Swedish troops in Germany, fell at battle of Klissow.

**Horn af Åminne:** Baron Svante, 1675–1756, Volunteer with Småland cavalry 1693, Corporal with Jönköping regiment 1697, Sergeant with Liewen's regiment in Wismar 1699, Ensign 1700, Lieutenant with Skåne Dragoons 1702, Lieutenant-Captain 1703, Captain 1704, captured at Perovolochna, returned 1722, Lieutenant-Colonel's rank with Bohuslän Dragoons, with Jönköping regiment 1725, retired 1743.

**Horn af Marienborg:** Baron Gustaf, 1670–1728, Trooper with Bielke's regiment 1686, Cornet 1687, Ensign with Bielke's Pomeranian infantry 1688, Ensign with Life Guard 1693, Lieutenant 1693, Drabant Corporal 1700, Drabant Quartermaster 1700, Colonel of North Skåne cavalry 1704, captured at Perovolochna, exchanged 1715, Major-General of Cavalry 1720, Lieutenant-General of Cavalry and again Colonel of North Skåne cavalry 1722, retired 1727.

**Horn af Rantzien:** Carl Johan, d.1709, in Dutch service, Lieutenant with Östgöta infantry 1700, Second-Captain 1703, Captain 1707, fell at Poltava.

**Hultman:** Johan, c1666-1735, in royal service 1680, lackey to Charles XII when Crown Prince 1694, steward 1711 in Bender. His memoirs dictated c1734, published 1819.

**Jeffreys:** James, c1690–1739, born in Stockholm, son of an Irish officer in Charles XI's army, British envoy with the Swedish army during the Russian campaign and with Charles XII in Bender, Minister in St Petersburg 1718–1719, Resident in Danzig 1719–1725, Governor in Cork, Ireland. Lived in Blarney Castle near Cork, which still contains a portrait of Charles XII. His reports 1707–1709.

**Kålbom:** Erik, d.1713, Corporal with Kruse's cavalry 1677, Quartermaster 1678, Standard-Bearer with Uppland infantry 1680, Sergeant-Major 1689, Ensign 1692, Lieutenant 1700, Second-Captain 1701, Premier Captain 1707, captured at Poltava, died in Tumen.

**Kelen:** Alexei Stepanovitch, Colonel, Russian Commandant at siege of Poltava, subsequently Governor.

**Kihlman:** Georg, 1675–1744, Sergeant with Småland Tremänning infantry 1700, Sergeant-Major, Ensign 1705, fought at Lesnaya, captured at Perovolochna, returned 1722, retired same year, severe wound in knee still unhealed 1729.

**Klinckowström,** Otto Wilhelm, 1683–1731, served with Chancellery 1705, Commission Secretary at Polish Court 1708, sent with military despatches to Charles XII disguised as a Pole 1709, arrived shortly before Poltava, accompanied king to Bender, on return mission from Bender was apprehended by Poles and delivered over to Russians, escaped to Pomerania, returned to Bender 1712, Envoy to Poland again, Mission Secretary to Germans 1715, Envoy at Prussian Court 1726.

**Kling:** Sven, d.1709, Staff Sergeant with Skaraborg regiment 1702, Ensign 1709, fell at Poltava.

**Koltza:** Sandul, b.1678, born in Wallachia, in Swedish service 1703, Colonel of the Vallack regiment 1709, captured at Perovolochna, married in Tobolsk (Siberia) 1717, returned 1722, retired same year (on double pay provided he remained in Sweden).

**von Krassow:** Ernst Detlov, c1660–1714, Pomeranian, Ensign with the Life Guard 1677, Major-General of Cavalry 1706, Baron 1707, supported King Stanislaus in Poland, retired as Vice-Governor in Wismar 1712.

**Kruse af Kajbala:** Carl Gustaf, d.1732, Cornet with Mounted Life regiment 1676, entered foreign service, finally Lieutenant-Colonel in Hungarian service, returned to Sweden and Colonel of Uppland Tremänning cavalry regiment 1700, Major-General of Cavalry 1706, captured at Poltava, returned 1722, Colonel of Västgöta cavalry regiment, General of Cavalry 1722, retired 1731.

**Lagerberg:** Sven, 1672–1746, Sergeant with Skaraborg regiment 1690, Ensign 1695, Lieutenant 1700, Quartermaster 1701, Grenadier Captain 1702, Major 1709, saved by Sven Agrell at Perovolochna, escaped to Bender, Lieutenant-Colonel 1710, Colonel of Kronoberg regiment 1714, Major-General of Infantry and Colonel of Skaraborg regiment 1717, Baron 1719, Parliamentary Land-Marshal 1723, Councillor of the Realm 1723, Count 1731.

**Lagercrona:** Anders, d.1739, Ensign with Västerbotten regiment 1675, Lieutenant-Captain 1676, Quartermaster 1678, Major 1694, Lieutenant-Colonel 1696, Adjutant-General 1700, Colonel of Västerbotten regiment 1702, Major-General of Infantry 1704, Baron 1705, escaped with Charles XII to Bender, returned to Sweden 1711 and retired same year.

**Leijonhielm:** Anders, 1655–1727, Student at Lund university, Volunteer with Life Guard 1673, Ensign with Kalmar regiment 1674, Lieutenant 1677, Captain 1683, Major 1701, Lieutenant-Colonel 1709, escaped to Bender, Colonel of Jönköping regiment 1710, captured at the 'kalabalik' in Bender 1713, returned to Sweden 1714, Major-General and County Governor in Jönköping 1718, Baron 1719.

**Leszczynski:** see Stanislaus, King of Poland.

**Lewenhaupt:** Count Adam Ludvig, 1659–1719, Student at Lund university 1671, Student Uppsala university 1675, Student Rostock university 1680. Volunteer under Elector of Bavaria against the Turks 1685, Cornet with Bielke's Bavarian cavalry regiment, Captain 1686, Major with Nieroth's Swedish regiment in Dutch service 1688, Lieutenant-Colonel of Oxenstierna's Swedish regiment in Dutch service 1691, Colonel of Brahe's regiment 1697, left Dutch service 1698, Colonel of Uppland's Tremänning regiment 1700, Major-General of Infantry and Governor of Courland, Pilten and Samogitia 1703, Lieutenant-General of Infantry 1705, General of Infantry 1706, Governor of Riga and General-in-Chief of the standing army in Livonia, Courland and Lithuania 1706, captured at Perovolochna, died in Moscow. His monumental apologia for events at Poltava. 'Leijonhufvud' is Swedish version of name.

**Lewenhaupt:** Count Carl, 1676–1712, Ensign with G. M. Lewenhaupt's Swedish regiment in Dutch service 1690, Lieutenant with Bielke's Swedish regiment in Dutch service 1693, Captain with C. W. Sparre's regiment and retired from Dutch service 1698, Captain Södermanland regiment 1700, Drabant 1700, Corporal of Drabants 1703, Lieutenant-Colonel with Stenbock's (subsequently Hielm's) Dragoons 1704, captured at Poltava, died in Moscow.

**Lindberg:** Samuel, 1682–1731, Corporal Småland cavalry, Quartermaster 1706, Second-Cornet with Meijerfelt's Dragoons 1707, Premier Cornet with Småland cavalry 1708, captured at Poltava, returned 1723, retired as Lieutenant 1723.

**Lyth:** Joakim Mathiae, 1679–1746, born in Gotland, Student at Uppsala university 1698, Volunteer 1703, Lieutenant with the Skåne Dragoons 1709, captured at Perovolochna, sent to Siberia, returned 1722, retired from army, died in Visby, Gotland. His memoirs 1703–1721.

**Mannersvärd (Kock):** Hans, d.1709, volunteer with Life Guard 1688, Standard-Bearer 1689, Sergeant 1692, Ensign 1700, Lieutenant 1700, Quartermaster 1702, Captain 1704, ennobled 1706, fell at Poltava.

**Mazeppa:** Ivan Stepanovich, c1629–1709, born in the Ukraine when part of Poland, brought up at Polish Court, fled back to the Ukraine, then under Russia, allegedly as result of a romantic escapade, elected Hetman of the Cossacks 1688, gained confidence of Tsar but worked secretly to liberate the Ukraine from Russia, joined Charles XII in the autumn 1708, escaped from Perovolochna, but died soon afterwards.

**Meijerfelt:** Johan August, 1664–1749, Volunteer with Pahlen's Livonian cavalry regiment 1684, Cornet 1686, Lieutenant 1688, Captain with Hastfehr's Swedish infantry in Holland 1693. Major with Krassow's regiment in Holland 1697, Lieutenant-Colonel Åbo cavalry regiment 1701, Colonel 1702, raised own regiment of dragoons 1703, Major-General of Cavalry 1704, Baron 1705, captured at Poltava, exchanged shortly after battle, Lieutenant-General at battle of Hälsingborg 1710, Commandant in Stettin 1710, Vice-Governor of Stettin 1711, revisited king in Bender 1711, General of Infantry 1711, Governor-General of Swedish Pomerania and Royal Councillor 1713, Count 1714, Chancellor of Greifswald university 1715, Swedish State Councillor 1719.

**Menshikov:** Prince Alexander Danilovitch, c1673–1729, son of a stableman, Tsar Peter's favourite, Field-Marshal, overthrown by old Russians after the Tsar's death, died in disgrace in Siberia.

**Muhl:** Robert, 1683–1760, Volunteer with Life Guard 1698, Sergeant with Life Dragoons 1700, Cornet 1702, Lieutenant 1704, Captain 1706, followed king to Bender, captured at Czernowitz 1709, escaped from Russia 1720, Lieutenant-Colonel with Life Dragoons 1721, Colonel 1740, Major-General 1751.

**Mühlenfels:** d.1709, German Colonel in Russian service, went over to the Swedes 1708, tortured and killed at Perovolochna.

**Neumann:** Melchior, 1670–1741, born in Prussia, came to Sweden 1692, qualified as military surgeon 1699, with Mounted Life regiment, Royal Surgeon to Charles XII 1703, treated king's broken leg after Cracow, treatment of king's foot at Poltava prevented amputation, accompanied king to Bender, returned to Sweden 1715, General Staff Surgeon 1716, embalmed king's corpse in 1718.

**Nordberg:** Jöran Andersson, 1677–1744, Student at Uppsala university 1693, Ph.D 1703, Chaplain with Artillery, Field Chaplain in Poland, Premier Chaplain to Drabant corps 1707, captured at Poltava, transported to Moscow, ransomed 1715, Confessor to Charles XII 1716, attended Parliaments of 1719, 1723, 1731, published *History of Charles XII* 1740, translated into German and French.

**Norin (Nordensvärd):** Niklas (Nils), 1684–1762, Sergeant with Västmanland regiment 1701, Ensign 1704, Lieutenant-Captain 1707, captured at Poltava, returned 1722, Major 1723, ennobled 1727 (as Nordensvärd), retired Lieutenant-Colonel 1728.

**Norsbergh**: Magnus, Clerk to Drabant Corporal Johan Ehrenskiöld, escaped to Bender, returned 1710. His memoirs.

**von Öller**: Göran, 1680–1732, Pikeman with Life Guard 1697, Sergeant 1698, Ensign 1700, Lieutenant 1701, Captain 1708, captured at Perovolochna, returned 1722, retired, Lieutenant-Colonel's rank 1723. Wounded 5 times at Poltava, was blind when returned to Sweden.

**Örnestedt**: Philip, 1674–1739, Lieutenant with Gyllenstierna's Swedish infantry regiment in Holland 1697, Captain with Life Dragoons 1700, Major 1704, Lieutenant-Colonel 1709, captured at Perovolochna, returned 1722, Colonel 1723, Baron and Major-General of Cavalry 1727, fought in 10 battles.

**von der Osten-Sacken**: Johan Gustaf, 1667–1717, Lieutenant-Colonel with the Ösel Dragoon squadron 1701, captured at Perovolochna, exchanged 1710, retired 1711.

**Oxe**: Harald, d.1723, Private with German Life regiment of foot 1687, Ensign 1696, Ensign Södermanland regiment 1697, Lieutenant 1700, Second-Captain Jönköping regiment 1700, Captain 1703, Major 1708, captured at Poltava 1709, returned 1722, Colonel.

**Oxenstierna af Croneborg**: Count Axel Gabriel, 1679–1755, Volunteer Officer 1700, Captain Life Guards 1703, Major 1709, captured at Perovolochna, returned 1722, rank of Colonel from 1721, retired as Major-General 1723.

**Palmfelt**: Carl, 1686–1753, Volunteer 1700, Lieutenant Hälsinge Tremänning battalion 1703, Captain 1704, captured at Perovolochna, returned 1722, placed with Närke-Värmland regiment with rank of Lieutenant-Colonel 1723, retired as Colonel 1751.

**Peter I 'The Great'**: Alexeivitch; Tsar of Russia, 1672–1726, practical genius, reformed Russia by adopting European values.

**Petré**: Robert, 1681–1725, Västmanlander of Scottish descent, Ensign with the Hälsinge regiment 1706, wounded at Poltava, captured at Perovolochna, returned 1722, Colonel. His diary.

**Pihlström**: Anders, d.1730, recruiting officer with Dalecarlia regiment 1700, Ensign 1707, captured at Poltava, returned 1723, Lieutenant.

**Pinello**: Giovanni Batista, 1682–1775, born in Genoa, entered Swedish service at siege of Thorn 1703, Volunteer with Mounted Life regiment 1704, Ensign with Västmanland Regiment 1707, captured at Poltava, returned via Archangel 1715, Second Captain Bohuslän Dragoons 1716, retired 1748, naturalized Swedish nobleman 1751, rank of Lieutenant-Colonel 1759.

**Piper**: Carl, 1647–1716, Student at Uppsala 1660, with Chancellery 1668, accompanied Oxenstierna's embassy to Russia 1673, Field Chancellery Registrar in Charles XI's Skåne war 1677, gained trust of Charles XI, ennobled 1679, State Secretary and Royal Councillor on accession of Charles XII 1697, Baron and Count 1698, First Minister, only member of Council to accompany Charles XII on campaign, officiated at peace treaties with Poland 1705 and Saxony 1706, captured at Poltava, headed Tsar's triumphal procession of Swedish prisoners in Moscow, administered central organization for Swedes in Moscow, died in captivity in Nöteborg, remains buried in Stockholm 1718.

**Piper**: Gustaf Abraham, 1692–1761, volunteer 1706, Ensign with Helsinge Femmänning battalion 1706, Ensign Östgöta infantry regiment 1708, Ensign with Life Guard 1708, captured at Perovolochna, returned 1715, Captain 1716, War Councillor 1743, member of commission for economic aid to Finland 1744, County Governor of Österbotten 1746, rank of Major-General 1753.

**Pistol**: Gustaf, d.1709, Musketeer with Erskin's Swedish regiment in Holland 1688, Sergeant Östgöta regiment 1699, Ensign 1700, Second-Captain 1705, Major with Kronoborg's regiment 1705, fell at Poltava.

**Pistolsköld**: Gustaf Reinhold, 1687–1731, Corporal with Mounted Life regiment 1704, Quartermaster 1706, Cornet 1709, captured at Perovolochna, returned 1722, Lieutenant 1723.

**Planting-Gyllenbåga:** Claes, 1677–1712, Second-Lieutenant Mounted Life regiment 1701, Captain 1709, captured at Perovolochna, died in Tobolsk, Siberia.

**Planting-Gyllenbåga:** Georg, 1682–1747, page to Count Fabian Wrede, Ensign Uppland infantry regiment 1701, Quartermaster 1707, Second-Captain 1709, wounded and captured at Poltava, returned 1722, Lieutenant-Colonel 1723, retired 1732.

**Pommerijn:** Olof, 1678–1744, joined army 1696, Sergeant with Dalecarlia regiment 1704, Second-Ensign 1705, Ensign 1708, Lieutenant 1708, captured at Poltava, returned 1722, retired as Captain 1722, entered Vadstena soldiers' home.

**Poniatowski:** Count Stanislaus, 1676–1762, born in Cracow, volunteer in Imperial service in Hungary, Captain, entered Swedish service 1702, Castellan of Cracow, loyal servant of Charles XII in Bender, General of Artillery in Polish service, Governor-General in Zweibrücken and Colonel of Zweibrücken infantry regiment 1718, retired 1719, father of last king of Poland, Stanislaus Augustus. His *Remarques d'un Seigneur polonais* published 1741.

**Posse af Säby:** Baron Carl Magnus, 166?–1715, Sergeant in the Life Guard 1676, Ensign with Västmanland regiment 1678, Ensign with Life Guard 1682, Lieutenant 1684, Captain 1695, Major 1701, Lieutenant-Colonel 1702, Colonel 1706, led the Guard's last stand at Poltava, captured at Perovolochna, died in Moscow.

**von Post:** Arendt Fredrik, 1673–1709, Volunteer with Life Guard 1692, Ensign with Uppland Infantry 1692, Lieutenant 1698, Quartermaster 1700, Captain 1700, Major 1707, Lieutenant-Colonel 1709, fell at Poltava.

**Rålamb:** Baron Bror, 1668–1734, Student at Greifswald university and at Uppsala, Volunteer with Life Guard 1692, Ensign 1693, Lieutenant 1699, Drabant 1700, Corporal of Drabants 1705, captured at Perovolochna, imprisoned in Tobolsk, Siberia, returned 1722, Lieutenant-Colonel Västgötadal regiment 1722, Colonel of Adelsfana regiment in Sweden and Finland 1727, retired 1732, Governor in Österbotten province 1733.

**Ramsvärd:** Anders, d.1727, Musketeer with Life Guard 1684, NCO 1685, Cornet with Mounted Life regiment 1688, Lieutenant 1693, Drabant Corporal 1700, Adjutant 1700, Colonel of Västgöta Dragoons 1706, Colonel of Swedish Adelsfana 1708, captured at Perovolochna, returned 1722, Lieutenant-General, retired 1727.

**Ranck:** Gustaf, d.1709, Ensign with Elfsborg regiment 1671, Lieutenant 1676, Lieutenant-Captain 1677, Captain 1680, Major 1692, Brabant campaign 1693–94, Lieutenant-Colonel with Kalmar regiment 1700, Commandant in Libau 1701–1702, Colonel of Kalmar regiment 1701, fell at Poltava.

**von Rango:** Carl, 1682–d.after 1739, born in Pomerania, Sergeant-Major with Kronoberg regiment 1701, Ensign 1702, Lieutenant 1703, Second-Captain 1705, captured at Poltava, returned 1722, Captain 1727, retired as Lieutenant-Colonel 1733.

**Rappe:** Niklas, 1668–1727, accompanied Nils Bielke to Imperial army in Hungary 1684, Constable with Artillery 1687, Warrant Officer with army in Rhen 1690, Master of Pyrotechnics in Dutch service 1690, returned to Sweden 1696, Quartermaster of Artillery 1696, Captain of Pyrotechnics 1698, Major of Artillery Ordnance 1701, Lieutenant-Colonel of Artillery in Göteborg 1706, Lieutenant-Colonel of Artillery on campaign 1708, captured at Perovolochna, returned 1721, Lieutenant-Colonel of Göteborg garrison 1721, Major-General's rank 1723.

**von Redeken:** Carl Fredrik, d.1709, Musketeer with Taube's battalion in Dorpat 1683, Standard-Bearer with the Garrison regiment in Stade 1687, Sergeant-Major with Tiesenhausen's regiment in Holland 1688, Adjutant with Wangenheim's Swedish regiment in Holland 1695, Lieutenant 1696, left Dutch service 1698, Quartermaster with Meijerfelt's regiment 1700, Captain with Uppland infantry 1701, fell at Poltava.

**Rehbinder,** Baron Henrik Johan, 1672–1734, Ensign with Närke-Värmland regiment 1688, Lieutenant 1691, Lieutenant-Captain with Jönköping regiment 1694, Captain with

Närke-Värmland regiment 1697, Major 1703, Lieutenant-Colonel 1706, captured at Poltava, returned 1722, Colonel and Commandant of Bohus fortress 1722.

**Rehnsköld:** Carl Gustav, 1651–1722, born Stralsund, Pomerania; Student at Lund University, Ensign Närke-Värmland regiment 1673, Lieutenant Uppland infantry 1675, Lieutenant with Life Guard 1676, Captain Queen's Mounted Life regiment 1676, Lieutenant-Colonel 1677, Colonel German Life regiment 1689, Colonel North Skåne cavalry 1693, Major-General of Cavalry 1699, Governor-General of Skåne and created Baron 1698, General of Cavalry 1703, King's Councillor 1705, Field-Marshal and Count 1706, captured at Poltava, returned 1718, Supreme Commander of Skåne 1719.

**Repnin:** Nikita, Russian General, court-martialled at Holowczin and temporarily relieved of command by Tsar 1708.

**Ridderborg (De Maré):** Jacob, 1655–1709, Warrant Officer with Östgöta cavalry 1674, Standard-Bearer with Seton's German Dragoons 1675, Sergeant 1675, Lieutenant with Småland Dragoons 1676, Lieutenant with Östgöta cavalry 1677, Lieutenant-Captain 1678, Captain with Uppland Tremänning cavalry 1700, ennobled 1704, Drabant 1704, fell at Poltava.

**Ridderhielm:** d.1709, Hans Isak, Volunteer with Life Guard 1674, Ensign 1675, Lieutenant 1677, Captain with Mounted Life regiment 1678, Major with Bielke's Dragoons 1679, Lieutenant-Colonel 1680, Commandant of Ny-Elfsborg 1680, Lieutenant-Colonel with Governor's regiment in Riga 1693, Colonel and Commandant in Stralsund 1697, Colonel of North Skåne Dragoons 1698, Major-General of Cavalry 1700, Lieutenant-General and Governor of Wismar 1704, Baron 1704, Colonel of Garrison regiment in Wismar 1704, died in Wismar.

**Ridderschantz:** Ebbe, 1686–1767, Cornet South Skåne Cavalry 1702, Drabant 1705, followed king to Bender, Lance-Corporal with the Drabants 1714, Colonel of an Imperial Cavalry regiment, Adjutant-General to Prince Eugene of Savoy, left Imperial service 1737, left Swedish service 1752, Major-General 1755.

**von Roland:** Carl, 1684–1761, Trooper with Hielm's (formerly Stenbock's) Dragoons 1703, NCO 1704, Cornet 1707, Second-Lieutenant 1709, captured at Perovolochna, escaped across Archangel 1715, Captain with Bender Dragoons 1715, captured at Rügen 1715, returned 1716, ennobled 1720, Major and Commandant of Skenäs and Säter forts 1721. His exciting and colourful memoirs.

**Roos:** Carl Gustaf, 1655–1722, Volunteer and Ensign in Imperial service 1674, Second-Lieutenant with Queen Dowager's Mounted Life regiment 1677, Lieutenant with Life Guard 1678, Major with Skaraborg infantry 1686, Lieutenant-Colonel with Governor's regiment in Riga 1696, Colonel of Närke-Värmland regiment 1701, Baron 1705, Major-General 1706, captured at Perovolochna, died on return to Åbo 1722. In an appendix to Lewenhaupt's account he defends his conduct at the redoubts at Poltava without noticeably enlightening the reader.

**Rosenkamp(ff):** Johan Henrik, d.1723, NCO with Karelian Dragoons; Ensign, Ensign with Åbo infantry, Lieutenant, Captain with Schlippenbach's Dragoons 1700, Major 1702, captured at Perovolochna, returned 1722.

**Rosensköld:** Per, d.1709, Trooper with Jämtland Dragoons 1685, Warrant Officer 1686, Sergeant 1689, Sergeant-Major 1690, Ensign 1693, Lieutenant 1698, Lieutenant with Uppland regiment 1702, Quartermaster 1703, Captain 1704, fell at Poltava.

**Rosenstierna:** Baron Libert, 1679–1732, Student at Uppsala university 1697, Pikeman with Life Guard 1697, Standard-Bearer 1698, Sergeant-Major 1699, Ensign and Lieutenant 1700, Captain 1704, captured at Poltava, returned 1715, Colonel and Flank Adjutant-General 1716, Commandant of Malmö 1716, Colonel of Västgötadal regiment 1716, Baron 1720, Major-General of Infantry 1722.

**Rühl:** Johannes Fredrik, 1675–1740, Aide with Pahlen's Livonian cavalry 1690, Cornet 1693, Drabant 1700, Lance-Corporal 1707, Corporal 1708, captured at Poltava, returned 1722, Captain with Adelsfana regiment 1722, ennobled 1723, Lieutenant-Colonel with Adelsfana 1732.

**Sa(h)lstéen:** Bengt, 1678–1735, Volunteer with Östgöta cavalry 1705, Corporal 1706, Quartermaster 1708, Ensign with Västmanland infantry 1708, captured at Perovolochna, returned 1722, retired 1722 with Lieutenant's rank dating from 1709, re-joined regiment 1728.

**von Sass:** Johan Christoffer, 1671–1745, entered service abroad 1686, Captain with Östgöta Tremänning infantry regiment 1700, Major with Närke-Värmland Tremänning regiment 1701, Lieutenant-Colonel with De la Gardie's Livonian regiment 1709, captured at Poltava, returned 1722, retired 1722 as Colonel, returned to Livonia.

**Scherzenfeldt:** Brigitta Christine, 1684–1736, married Standard-Bearer Mats Bernow 1699 (d.1703), married Sergeant-Major Jonas Lindström 1705, captured at Perovolochna, transported to Moscow, Lindström d.1711, married Lieutenant Michael Sims 1712 who, not a Swedish subject, entered Russian service, with Sims accompanied Colonel Buckholtz to the borders of the Kalmuck steppe. Attacked on arrival, Sims was killed and Scherzenfeldt captured by Kalmucks. After initial ill-treatment she was donated by the local Khan to his wife as a slave, and gained influence. Married Johan Gustaf Renat c1714, a Swedish Warrant Officer captured at Perovolochna, also a prisoner of the Kalmucks. Left captivity 1733, returned with husband to Stockholm via St Petersburg 1734. Renat (1682–1744) was son of Moses Renat, from Vienna, one of a number of Jews baptized en masse in Stockholm 1681.

**von Schlippenbach:** Wolmar Anton, 1658–1739, Major with garrison regiment in Riga 1678, Lieutenant-Colonel 1688, Lieutenant-Colonel of Savolax & Nyslott's regiment 1693, Colonel of a Livonian Dragoon regiment 1700, Major-General of Cavalry 1701, captured at Poltava, furlough to Livonia 1713, entered Russian service, Lieutenant-General in Russian army, died in Moscow.

**Schönström:** Peter, 1682–1746, Captain with De la Gardie's Livonian infantry 1703, Second-Captain with Swedish Adelsfana 1705, Captain 1709, captured at Perovolochna, returned 1722, Lieutenant-Colonel's rank, retired 1726.

**Schultz (von Schultzenheim):** Johan Jakob, 1684–1751, born in Stettin, Sergeant with Taube's Dragoons 1703, Warrant Officer 1705, Adjutant 1707, Cornet 1708, captured at Poltava, returned 1711, Quartermaster with Östgöta cavalry 1711, Captain 1715, ennobled 1717, retired as Major 1747.

**Seréen (Reenstråle):** Johan Henrik, 1682–1731, born in Finland, Volunteer with Uppland Tremänning infantry 1703, Sergeant with Taube's Dragoons 1703, Sergeant-Major 1707, captured at Poltava, returned 1710, Lieutenant with Uppland Femmänning cavalry 1710, Second-Captain 1711, Captain 1717, ennobled 1719, retired as Major 1721. His widow married Captain Frans Hager.

**von Siegruth:** Gustaf Henrik, d.1709, Volunteer in French service 1688, Captain 1694, Lieutenant with Swedish Life Guard 1695, Captain 1700, Lieutenant-Colonel with Dalecarlia regiment 1702, Colonel 1706, fell at Poltava. Fought in 14 battles.

**Silfverhielm:** Göran, 1681–1737, Volunteer with Life Guard 1696, Staff Sergeant 1698, Drabant 1700, Captain with South Skåne cavalry 1704, Major 1704, Lieutenant-Colonel 1706, accompanied king to Bender. Second-Colonel 1712, captured at Stralsund 1715, Colonel of Småland cavalry 1716, Major-General of Cavalry 1717, Baron 1719, Lieutenant-General 1720, Colonel of Mounted Life regiment 1728, General of Cavalry 1728, Field-Marshal 1734.

**Silfverlåås:** Carl Gustaf, 1673–1733, Volunteer with Life Guard 1691, Ensign with Uppland infantry 1697, Lieutenant 1700, Second-Captain 1701, Captain 1707, wounded and captured at Poltava, returned 1722, retired as Colonel 1733. Wounded 9 times.

**Silfversparre:** Per, 1679–1750, Volunteer with Buddenbrock's Swedish regiment in Holland 1694, Pikeman with Life Guard 1696, Ensign with Governor's regiment in Riga 1697, Lieutenant 1700, Drabant 1701, Major with Södermanland regiment 1708, captured at Czernowitz 24/9/1709, escaped from Russia 1720, Colonel's rank 1721, Lieutenant-Colonel's appointment with Västmanland regiment 1723, Lieutenant-Colonel with Östgöta infantry 1728, Colonel of Jönköping regiment 1739, retired as

Major-General 1747. There were 20 officers named Silfversparre in Charles XII's army; 10 fought at Poltava: 2 escaped, 5 were captured and 3 killed.

**Sinclair:** Carl Anders, 1674–1753, Volunteer with Artillery 1694, Pyrotechnician 1695, Sergeant with Helsinge regiment 1696, Ensign 1697, Lieutenant 1701, Captain 1703, Adjutant-General 1705, Lieutenant-Colonel Åbo infantry 1705, captured at Perovolochna, returned 1722, Colonel 1734, Colonel of Östgöta infantry 1743, retired as Major-General.

**Sinclair:** Malcolm, 1691–1739, Ensign with Life Guard 1708, captured at Perovolochna, returned 1722, Lieutenant 1722, in Holland 1724 and 1726, Major with Uppland regiment 1737, member of Council's secret mission to Turkey 1738, on returning murdered in Grünberg in Silesia by Russian agents.

**Smepust:** Erik Larsson, 1681–1741, son of a smallholder, farm labourer, recruited to Lewenhaupt's regiment in Livonia 1701, Pike Corporal, captured at Perovolochna, escaped from Russia 1714, Sergeant-Major with the Dalecarlia Regiment, Lieutenant, fell at battle of Villmanstrand.

**Sneckenberg:** Jakob, 1683–1709, Sergeant-Major with Uppland regiment 1704, Ensign 1706, Second-Lieutenant 1709, captured at Poltava, died of his wounds 6 weeks after battle.

**Spåre:** Henrik, 1664–1747, Musketeer with Life Guard 1683, Sergeant with Björneborg infantry 1687, Standard-Bearer 1691, Warrant Officer 1694, Staff Sergeant 1700, Ensign 1702, Lieutenant 1705, Lieutenant-Captain 1708, Captain 1709, captured at Poltava, returned 1722, Lieutenant-Colonel's rank 1730, retired 1741.

**Sparre:** Axel, 1652–1728, Student Uppsala university 1662, Volunteer with Life Guard 1671, Ensign with Stooheim's German regiment in Holland 1672, Lieutenant 1673, Captain 1674, Captain with Field Marshal Horn's German regiment in Swedish service 1675, Captain Life Guard 1676, Lieutenant-Colonel Närke-Värmland regiment 1677, Colonel of Västmanland regiment 1699, Major-General of Infantry 1705, escaped to Bender 1709, Lieutenant-General 1710, General of Infantry 1713, Envoy to Count Carl of Hessen-Cassel 1716, recalled 1719, Count 1720, Field Marshal 1721.

**Sparre:** Bengt, 1686–1748, Ensign with Närke-Värmland regiment 1708, captured at Poltava, returned 1722, Captain's rank 1725, retired as Major 1732.

**Sparre:** Baron Conrad, 1680–1744, Student at Uppsala university, Page at Court 1697, Cadet with E. Sparre's regiment in French service 1698, Ensign 1700, Lieutenant 1702, Captain 1705, left French service 1706, Volunteer with Swedish army in Saxony 1707, Lieutenant with Life Dragoons 1708, Captain with Närke-Värmland regiment 1709, accompanied king to Bender, Captain with Life Guard 1711, Captain with King Stanislaus' Guard, captured at Stralsund 1715, returned 1717, Lieutenant-Colonel with Halland regiment 1717, retired as Colonel 1719. Fought at Ramillies.

**Stackelberg:** Berndt Otto, 1662–1734, entered army service 1685, Dutch service 1688–90, visited France, Adjutant-General with infantry 1700, Colonel of Björneborg infantry regiment 1702, Major-General of Infantry 1706, captured at Poltava, returned 1721, General of Infantry, Commander of Finnish army and Colonel of Åbo infantry regiment 1722, Baron and Field Marshal 1727.

**Stanislaus Leszczynski:** 1677–1766, King of Poland 1705, later Duke of Lorraine, whose daughter became Queen of France, wife to Louis XV. Political thinker, wrote political and social treatises: *La voix libre du citoyen, ou Observations sur le Gouvernement de Pologne*, 1749.

**Stenbock:** Count Magnus, 1664–1717, Student at Uppsala university, Ensign with Count Carlsson's regiment in Dutch service 1685, Ensign Prince of Orange's Guard 1687, Major in Bielke's Swedish regiment in Holland 1688, Colonel in Imperial service 1693, Colonel of Kalmar regiment 1699, Colonel of Dalecarlia regiment 1700, Major-General of Infantry 1700, Commandant of Cracow 1702, Governor of Thorn 1703, Governor-General of Skåne 1705, Field Marshal 1710, captured at Tönningen 1713, died incarcerated in Fredrikshamn castle, Denmark.

von Sternbach: Didrik Celestin, 1679–1733, born in Stettin, joined army 1696, Ensign with Pomeranian infantry 1700, Lieutenant 1703, Second-Captain with Taube's Dragoons 1704, Captain 1706, captured at Perovolochna, returned 1722, appointed Lieutenant-Colonel with Queen's Life regiment 1722.

Stiernhielm (Lillie): Georg, 1598–1672, universal genius, after cultivating philology, mathematics and Scandinavian antiquity, in 1638 decided that 'the Muses must learn to sing in Swedish'. Founder of Swedish poetry, published *Hercules* 1658.

Stiernhöök: Gustaf, 1671–1709, Ensign with Life Guard 1694, Lieutenant 1697, Quartermaster 1700, Captain 1701, Major 1706, Lieutenant-Colonel with Uppland infantry 1709, Colonel 1709, fell at Poltava.

Strokirch: Carl (Anders Johan), 1683–1761, Student with Uppsala university, Volunteer with Fortification corps 1701, Lieutenant with Uppland Femmänning infantry 1703, Captain with Helsinge Femmänning battalion 1706, Lieutenant with Life Dragoons 1708, captured at Perovolochna, returned 1722, Lieutenant-Captain 1724, Quartermaster 1734, Captain 1736, Major 1743, Lieutenant-Colonel 1750, Baron 1756, Colonel 1757, retired 1761.

Strömsköld: Anders, 1674–1722, Corporal with South Skåne cavalry 1695, Cornet with Life Dragoons 1700, Lieutenant 1702, Second-Captain 1704, Captain 1706, Major 1709, captured at Poltava, died in Moscow.

Taube af Odenkat: Baron Wilhelm Ludvig, 1690–1750, Page to Queen Dowager 1704, Grenadier with Life Guard 1706, Second-Ensign 1707, Lieutenant with Östgöta cavalry 1707, captured at Poltava, escaped from Wolodga in a small boat over Archangel to Amsterdam 1715, Captain with Life Guard 1716, Lieutenant-Colonel with Entergaste regiment 1717, Lieutenant-Colonel with Västerbotten regiment 1719, retired 1720, Colonel in Holstein service 1721, Lieutenant-Colonel with Uppland infantry 1730, Colonel 1737, Governor of Blekinge 1742, State Councillor 1746, Colonel-Marshal 1747.

Ti(e)sensten: Lars, 1671–1733, Volunteer with Life Guard 1688, Sergeant 1695, Warrant Officer 1695, Staff Sergeant 1700, ennobled 1700, Ensign 1700, Lieutenant 1701, Quartermaster 1704, Captain 1705, captured at Poltava, returned 1712, Lieutenant-Colonel 1712, retired 1725. Lost leg at Poltava.

Toll: Carl Fredrik, 1681–1741, Volunteer with Garrison regiment in Riga 1698, Sergeant with Uppland infantry 1700, Ensign with Uppland Tremänning infantry 1700, Second-Lieutenant with Östgöta infantry 1703. Lieutenant 1705, Captain 1707, captured at Perovolochna, returned 1722, Major 1722, ennobled 1723, retired 1724.

Torstensson: Count Anders, 1676–1709, Ensign with Saxon Life Guard 1694, Second-Lieutenant 1695, Lieutenant 1696, Captain 1697, Captain with Stralsund infantry 1698, Captain with Dalecarlia regiment 1700, Captain with Life Guard 1700, Adjutant-General 1703, Colonel of Viborg Fördubbling cavalry 1706, Colonel of Nyland and Tavastehus cavalry 1707, fell at Poltava.

von Trautwetter: Carl Gustaf, 1685–1722, born in Livonia, Cornet with Meijerfelt's Dragoons 1702, Lieutenant 1704, Captain with Hielm's Dragoons 1707, captured at Perovolochna, retired 1724, Major-General in Russian service.

Trautwetter: Johan Reinhold, 168?–1740, born in Livonia (brother of above), Ensign with Swedish troops in Holland, Captain with Albedyl's Dragoons 1700, Major 1701, Lieutenant-Colonel with Meijerfelt's Dragoons 1703, captured at Poltava, returned 1712, Colonel of Queen Dowager's Life regiment in Pomerania 1712, Major-General of Infantry 1715, captured at Stralsund 1715, returned 1718, Supreme Commandant of Stralsund and other Pomeranian fortresses 1719, Lieutenant-General of Cavalry 1719, Ambassador Extraordinary to Britain, Prussia and Poland 1719, Baron 1720, Colonel of Garrison regiment in Stralsund 1721, retired 1732.

Tungelfelt: Anders, 1681–1751, Volunteer with Life Guard 1700, Sergeant 1701, Cornet with Taube's Dragoons 1704, Lieutenant 1705, Captain 1707, Captain with Life Guard 1707, captured at Perovolochna, escaped same year in November, returned to Sweden

3 days before battle of Hälsingborg in which he served as Adjutant-General 1710, then travelled to Bender, accompanied Sven Lagerberg to Tartary, arrested for duelling in 1713, escaped from arrest to Constantinople, returned to Stockholm and gave himself up 1715, under arrest until 1718, Drabant 1718, Drabant Corporal 1719, Lieutenant-Colonel's rank 1723, Drabant Quartermaster 1734, Drabant Second-Lieutenant 1736, Colonel of Bohuslän Dragoons 1740, Governor of Jönköping 1746, Major-General's rank 1747. Wounded 20 times.

**Tungelfelt:** Marcus, 1682–1736, Volunteer with Life Guard 1702, Standard-Bearer 1702, Lieutenant with Taube's Dragoons 1704, Quartermaster 1706, Second-Captain 1707, Captain 1709, captured at Poltava, returned 1710, Major with Life Dragoons 1712, Lieutenant-Colonel 1722.

**Ulfsparre:** Carl Gustaf, d.1709, Dragoon with Jämtland regiment 1686, Cadet with Tiesenhausen's Swedish infantry in Holland 1692. Private with Greder's German regiment in French service 1693, Ensign with Life Guard 1694, Drabant 1700, Drabant Corporal 1700, Lieutenant-Colonel with Dalecarlia regiment 1706, Colonel of Skaraborg regiment 1709, fell at Poltava.

**Urbanovitch:** Christoffer Cyprianus, d.1731, of Polish birth, entered Swedish service 1702, Colonel of a Polish cavalry regiment 1709, Colonel of Niester Dragoons 1712, retired 1719, Minister for King Stanislaus at Swedish Court, entered Russian service and appointed General, drowned in river Philis.

**Wachslager:** Georg, 1648–1720, born in Pomerania, entered Swedish service for religious reasons, Secretary to Swedish Ambassador in Poland 1674, duped by Augustus II's war preparations, subsequent reports to Charles XII guided Swedish policies in Poland, Swedish State Secretary 1705, Swedish Minister to King Stanislaus in Poland 1708, continued active in Poland on return of Augustus, ennobled 1711, returned to Sweden 1715, Court Chancellor 1716, Baron 1719.

**Wachtmeister:** Baron Axel Gustaf, 1688–1751, Standard-bearer with Life Guard 1704, Ensign 1706, Quartermaster with Östgöta Cavalry 1708, Captain 1708, captured at Perovolochna, returned 1722, Major, retired as Lieutenant-Colonel 1741.

**Wallberg (Wahlberg):** Jonas, d.1759, Volunteer with Dalecarlia regiment 1706, Sergeant-Major, captured at Poltava, escaped and returned to Sweden 1714, Ensign with Södermanland regiment 1717, Lieutenant 1718, retired as Captain 1719.

**von Wangersheim:** Axel Conrad, dates unknown, Major with Königsmarck's regiment in French service, Colonel of Hastfehr's regiment in Dutch service 1695, Commandant in Riga 1700, registered but not confirmed as Colonel of Österbotten regiment, Lieutenant-General of Infantry 1721, retired same year.

**von Weidenhaijn:** Gabriel, d.1709, Page to Charles XI 1669, joined Helsinge regiment 1675, Ensign 1676, Lieutenant 1677, Quartermaster Södermanland regiment 1677, Captain 1680, Major 1697, Lieutenant-Colonel 1703, Colonel 1708, fell at Poltava.

**von Weihe:** Friderich Christoph, d.1713, of German birth, Sergeant-Major with Savolax regiment 1704, Lieutenant with Uppland Tremänning regiment 1708, fought at Lesna, captured at Perovolochna 1709, died Solvytschegodsk, Siberia. His diary.

**Wendel:** Christoffer Adolf, Captain, 1659–1709, born in Mark Brandenburg, Lieutenant with Fyen regiment in Danish service 1675, captured by Swedes at battle of Halmstad 1676, Lieutenant with Queen Dowager's Life regiment 1676, Lieutenant with Södermanland regiment 1678, Quartermaster 1688, ennobled 1690, Second-Captain 1700, Premier Captain 1702, shot at Poltava.

**Wennerstedt:** Anders, 1650–1712, Student at Uppsala University, Volunteer and Adjutant in Rehnsköld's Cavalry regiment 1676, Lieutenant 1677, Quartermaster 1677, Captain of a company of conscripts at Hisingen 1678, Second-Captain with Östgöta cavalry 1679, ennobled 1681, Premier Captain 1683, Lieutenant-Colonel Uppland Tremänning cavalry 1700, Colonel Uppland Dragoons 1703, captured at Perovolochna, returned 1722, Major-General of Cavalry.

**Westerman:** Andreas Svensson, 1672–1739, son of a Stockholm bourgeois, battalion chaplain with the Life Guard 1705, captured at Perovolochna, returned 1722, died as vicar in Gävle.

**Wibbling:** Magnus, 1672–1713, Ensign with Skaraborg regiment 1700, Second-Captain 1703, Captain 1709, captured at Poltava, escaped September 1713 and shot dead by his own servant same month.

**Wolffelt:** Magnus Johan, 168?–1709, in Saxon service before joining Swedish army 1700, Lieutenant-Captain with Östgöta infantry 1700, Captain 1702, Second Captain with North Skåne Cavalry 1703, Captain 1704, Major 1708, fell at Poltava.

**Wrangel af Adinal:** Baron Carl Henrik, 1681–1755, Trooper with Tiesenhausen's Livonian cavalry 1697, Sergeant with Life Guard 1700, Lieutenant 1701, Captain 1705, Lieutenant-Colonel Skåne Dragoons 1709, captured at Perovolochna, returned 1721, Colonel Tavastehus regiment 1727, Major-General 1732, Lieutenant-General 1743, retired 1748, Field-Marshal 1755.

**Wrangel:** Georg Johan, 1657–1709, Ensign 1674, Adjutant to Duke of Birkenfeld in French Service 1677, Dutch service with Prince of Orange 1678, Captain with Närke-Värmland regiment 1680, Colonel of Åbo, Björneborg and Nyland Tremänning regiment 1705, fell at Poltava.

**Württemberg:** Prince Maximilian Emanuel of, 1689–1709, son of Duke Fredrik Carl of Württemberg, joined army 1703, aged 14, Colonel of Skåne Dragoons 1709, captured at Poltava, released, died 3 months later at Dubno.

# Index